The Idea of the Castle in Medieval England

YORK MEDIEVAL PRESS

The Idea of the Castle in Medieval England

Abigail Wheatley

YORK MEDIEVAL PRESS

First published 2004

A York Medieval Press publication
in association with The Boydell Press
an imprint of Boydell & Brewer Ltd
PO Box 9   Woodbridge   Suffolk IP12 3DF   UK
and of Boydell & Brewer Inc.
668 Mt. Hope Avenue   Rochester   NY 14620   USA
website: www.boydellandbrewer.com
and with the
Centre for Medieval Studies, University of York

ISBN 1 903153 14 X

A CIP catalogue record for this book is available
from the British Library

Library of Congress Cataloging-in-Publication Data
Wheatley, Abigail, 1974–
    The idea of the castle in medieval England / Abigail Wheatley.
      p. cm.
Includes bibliographical references and index.
    ISBN 1–903153–14–X (alk. paper)
1. Castles – England. 2. England – Civilization – 1066–1485.
3. England – Social life and customs – 1066–1485. I. Title.
DA660.W525 2004
728.8′1′09420902 – dc22   2004004689

Printed in Great Britain by
Antony Rowe Ltd., Chippenham, Wiltshire

CONTENTS

ILLUSTRATIONS

Black and white plates

Colour plates

placed between pp. 72 and 73

ACKNOWLEDGEMENTS

This book represents the end product of a Ph.D. dissertation of the same name, undertaken at the Centre for Medieval Studies, University of York, and completed in 2001. Both the book and the thesis are about castles, but also about interdisciplinarity. This project could not have been undertaken without the rigorous commitment to interdisciplinary research of the Centre for Medieval Studies and its staff. I hope this study demonstrates that this approach can produce worthwhile results. I also hope it may encourage others to undertake, or to support, interdisciplinary projects in the future. I am most happy to be able to acknowledge, both below and in the footnotes, help and advice generously given by many colleagues, but any errors are entirely my own responsibility.

    This study would not have been possible without substantial support. I am indebted to the Arts and Humanities Research Board for funding my Ph.D., and to the British Archaeological Association for a generous Ochs Scholarship, which assisted materially in the completion of this thesis. I am also most grateful to the Society of Architectural Historians of Great Britain for a Dorothy Stroud Bursary which has contributed towards the cost of the colour illustrations in this book. Numerous colleagues and friends have also provided unstinting academic and personal support. I thank especially my Ph.D. supervisors Jane Grenville, Christopher Norton and Felicity Riddy, who have all in their different ways contributed greatly to the spirit and substance of this project. Jeremy Ashbee, Priscilla Bawcutt, Jim Binns, John Clark, Helen Fulton, John Goodall, Louise Harrison, Nicola McDonald, Linda Monckton, Mark Ormrod, Caroline Palmer, David Parsons, Robert Liddiard, James Simpson, David Stocker, Craig Taylor, Matthew Townend and Judith Weiss have all supplied crucial advice and encouragement, for which I thank them sincerely. Special thanks are also due to Laura Parker and John Russell for their generous help in preparing the illustrations. My family, friends and colleagues have provided unwavering encouragement in this project. I thank especially Helen Wheatley and Michael Smith, Bill Wheatley and Margaret Cole, Ben Wheatley and Victoria Wheatley and George Frankland, my tower of strength.

EDITORIAL NOTE

In order to make this work accessible to readers from a range of disciplines, the spelling of various words in both Latin and vernacular languages has been silently standardized. Translations and photographs are the author's own, unless otherwise acknowledged.

Introduction

The castle had a dominant presence in medieval society, both physically and ideologically. Controlled by elites, castles towered over medieval villages and towns and were sites of judgement and administrative control. However, castles were also depicted over and over again in the medieval arts as heraldic devices, as pastry or paper table decorations,[1] on seals (see Plates 1, 2 and 3) and as large-scale props in pageants.[2] They featured figuratively in sermons,[3] theological treatises[4] and religious lyrics[5] and in manuscript marginalia (see Plate X), as well as in the more familiar contexts of romance and chronicle. To the modern understanding, there is a wide gap between these ephemeral, miniature and symbolic castles and the imposing stone-and-mortar fortresses scattered over medieval Europe and beyond. This book sets out to show that medieval thinking on these matters was very different.

Numerous studies have demonstrated that medieval ecclesiastical architecture was fully integrated into the intellectual and aesthetic culture of its time. Deliberate resonances were created between the soaring spires of the Gothic cathedral and the miniature pinnacles represented on tombs and reliquaries and in paintings and sacred texts inside the church. Indeed, it is recognized that microarchitecture (as the diminutive, decorative form is known) was an important adjunct to ecclesiastical architecture, expressing its symbolic properties and associations in a particularly concise way.[6] It is precisely

---

[1] See 'Sir Gawain and the Green Knight', lines 1407–12, p. 168; 'Cleanness', line 802, p. 238; in *The Poems of the Pearl Manuscript: Pearl, Cleanness, Patience, Sir Gawain and the Green Knight*, ed. M. Andrew and R. Waldron (Exeter, 1987, repr. 1994); Geoffrey Chaucer, 'The Parson's Tale', in *The Riverside Chaucer*, ed. L. D. Benson, 3rd edn (Oxford, 1987, repr. 1992), line 443, p. 301; R. W. Ackerman, '"Pared out of Paper": *Gawain* 802 and *Purity* 1408', *Journal of English and Germanic Philology* 56 (1957), 410–17.

[2] A pageant castle is illustrated in Paris, Bibliothèque Nationale MS Français 2813, fol. 473v. This prop was used to enact the siege of Jerusalem at a banquet given in Paris by Charles V of France for Emperor Charles VI in 1378.

[3] G. R. Owst, *Literature and the Pulpit in Medieval England*, 2nd edn (Oxford, 1961), pp. 77–85.

[4] R. D. Cornelius, *The Figurative Castle: A Study in the Mediaeval Allegory of the Edifice with Especial Reference to Religious Writings: A Dissertation* (Bryn Mawr, 1930).

[5] See (?) William of Shoreham, 'A Song to Mary', in *Medieval English Lyrics: A Critical Anthology*, ed. R. T. Davies (London, 1966, repr. 1971), line 57, p. 105.

[6] See N. Coldstream, *Medieval Architecture* (Oxford, 2002), pp. 162–5.

this kind of relationship I am seeking to explore in the medieval castle and its artistic and literary representations. I set out to establish the medieval castle as a meaningful architecture, involved in a sophisticated series of ideological relationships with its cultural context. This necessarily demands a rethinking of traditional approaches to the castle in modern scholarship.

The castles of the medieval landscape are, by definition, defensive architectural forms. They are usually considered to have been built with military functions in mind. It is from this point of view that they have most often been approached in modern scholarship. Because defence is such a practical consideration, rooted in engineering, technology and military strategy, it has not often occurred to scholars to treat medieval castle architecture as ideological. By contrast, medieval ecclesiastical architecture has long been understood as a meaningful architecture, which operates at an ideological as well as a practical level. It is appreciated as the highest technological achievement of its period, but also as a vessel for the most important religious ideas and beliefs. Its characteristic architectural forms have become so closely associated with their context that a spire or a crocketed pinnacle immediately communicates the idea of religious architecture, even to a modern eye. In a similar way, architectural features such as arrow-loops mark out the castle from all other forms of architecture and are synonymous with ideas of defence and power. However, while historians of ecclesiastical architecture accepted long ago the most basic associations of their subject, and moved on to engage with the particular nuances of theological movements, stylistic expression and structural typologies, the ideological exploration of castle architecture has only recently reached this most basic stage.

It is therefore still worth noting that medieval castle architecture communicates ideas of defence, of power and lordship. It is also still worth emphasizing that these ideological functions can be separated off, to a certain extent, from the practical capabilities of the architecture. Small-scale, decorative depictions of castles can communicate these ideas just as effectively as their macroarchitectural counterparts. Pageant castles were constructed to enable the enactment of mock sieges, actively imitating martial functions, but constructed as flimsy theatrical props. Depictions of castles in the decorative arts reproduce architectural features, such as arrow-loops and crenellations, which could never be used for practical purposes, but which describe a military capability. The idea of defence these castles communicate is a fiction, but it is the same idea of architectural power communicated by the very practical defensive features in the stone-and-mortar castles of the medieval landscape.

It is necessary to accept the basic ideas of lordship and defence communicated by the castle's characteristic architectural features, as a first step in recognizing it as a meaningful architecture. However, the second step is to move beyond these basic meanings, to explore texts, images and ideas that reveal the castle's more complex symbolic and ideological connotations. Only then can the castle be appreciated as an architectural form as sophisticated in its own right as medieval ecclesiastical architecture, meaningful in a similar way and to a similar extent. Some studies of the castle have already been made with these intentions in mind. However, they have also served to highlight the bewildering array of methodological and critical approaches currently applied to the subject of defensive architecture.

One volume, *The Medieval Castle: Romance and Reality*, contains papers from an interdisciplinary conference of the same name, held in 1983.[7] An empirical study on the cost of castle building[8] jostles alongside more speculative architectural approaches, one comparing castle and church architecture around the time of the Conquest, another considering the castle-like qualities of fortified houses and monastic granges.[9] On the literary side, a comparison of castles in medieval French literature with French and English castle buildings contrasts with a study of Celtic otherworld motifs in the castles of Middle English Arthurian Romance.[10] Art History is brought into a discussion of castles in Gothic manuscript painting and an analysis of Malory's castles in text and illustration.[11] This impressive range of approaches gives some idea of the breadth of the field. It also shows how scholars from different disciplines have begun to compare materials and approaches. However, this kind of study does not set out to address the complexities of the relationship between architecture, text and image in the Middle Ages, nor does it ask, or answer, the fundamental questions about the castle's position as a culture-wide phenomenon of the Middle Ages.

Like medieval ecclesiastical architecture, castles seem to me to invite a more thoroughly interdisciplinary approach. This book aims to integrate architectural, visual and textual evidence, to explore the idea of the castle in medieval writing and thought, in art and in architectural practice. My methodology is drawn mainly from literature, art history and archaeology, and it should be of interest to, and comprehensible by, anyone with an interest in these areas of medieval history. Unfortunately it is inevitable, within an academic system that studies different aspects of the same period entirely

---

7 *The Medieval Castle: Romance and Reality*, ed. K. Reyerson and F. Powe (Dubuque, 1984).
8 B. S. Bachrach, 'The Cost of Castle Building: The Case of the Tower at Langeais, 992–994', in *The Medieval Castle*, ed. Reyerson and Powe, pp. 47–62.
9 S. Bonde, 'Castle and Church Building at the Time of the Norman Conquest'; M. A. Dean, 'Early Fortified Houses: Defenses and Castle Imagery between 1275 and 1350 with Evidence from the Southeast Midlands'; both in *The Medieval Castle*, ed. Reyerson and Powe, pp. 79–96, 147–74.
10 W. van Emden, 'The Castle in Some Works of Medieval French Literature'; M. A. Whitaker, 'Otherworld Castles in Middle English Arthurian Romance'; both in *The Medieval Castle*, ed. Reyerson and Powe, pp. 1–26, 27–46.
11 A. D. McKenzie, 'French Medieval Castles in Gothic Manuscript Painting'; B. Gaines, 'Malory's Castles in Text and Illustration'; both in *The Medieval Castle*, ed. Reyerson and Powe, pp. 199–214, 215–28.

separately, that various methodological quirks have developed which threaten to make these disciplines mutually incomprehensible. I believe it is helpful to identify and discuss these contradictions and inconsistencies, in order to clarify their causes and ramifications. Analysis of past methods is also very helpful in pointing the way to new ones. Some readers will therefore find that certain sections of this book repeat familiar arguments in tedious detail; others may have similar thoughts about completely different passages, depending on their training. However, I hope this groundwork is justified by the results of an integrated approach.

It is only because of recent developments in medieval scholarship that I have been able to apply an interdisciplinary approach to castles and their symbolism in medieval England. Castles have for a long time been excluded both from the mainstream of medieval architectural studies and from any ideological or symbolic significance. Ecclesiastical and military architecture have traditionally been treated quite separately, both in terms of their architecture and their functions. The obvious differences between a cathedral and a castle have resulted in the one being studied largely as an exercise in spirituality and aesthetics, the other as a piece of purely practical military engineering. It is to this divide, and the reasons for it, that attention now turns. What follows is a summary of recent developments in the study of medieval English castles, by architectural and art historians, archaeologists and literature scholars. With this context in place, the plan of this book is then set out and the main topics and themes outlined.

The nineteenth-century scholar Thomas Rickman developed a vocabulary for dating and describing medieval architecture (Decorated, Perpendicular and so on) exclusively for the study of ecclesiastical buildings.[12] This taxonomy has remained the basis of medieval architectural scholarship. Rickman's typology promotes comparison of architectural forms and details as a means of establishing chronological and stylistic patterns. Stylistic analysis of decorative features such as moulding forms, or of iconographic schemes of sculpture or painting, are all a part of this approach. Formal analysis of the structure, materials and form of a building may also be included. Historical documents that help to illuminate dating, construction details or patronage have always played an important part in this kind of typological analysis.[13]

Interest in building processes and materials resulted more recently in the development of an archaeological approach to medieval architecture,

---

[12] See T. Rickman, *An Attempt to Discriminate the Styles of Architecture in England from the Conquest to the Reformation* (London, 1819).

[13] For a summary of developments in ecclesiastical architectural history, see E. C. Fernie, 'Contrasts in Methodology and Interpretation of Medieval Ecclesiastical Architecture', *The Archaeological Journal* 145 (1988), 344–64.

epitomized by the work of Warwick Rodwell.[14] In this form of investigation the building is analysed and stripped back according to the 'value free' systems employed in archaeological digs, whereby every feature is deemed to have equal value and is recorded with equal care.[15] The social and intellectual implications of medieval architecture have also been added to this list of approaches. Peter Kidson was instrumental in introducing this development and its results can be seen clearly in the work of subsequent scholars such as Richard Gem, Paul Crossley and Christopher Wilson.[16] Perhaps the most impressive synthesis by one individual of all these techniques of architectural analysis is demonstrated by Paul Binski.[17] In the work of all these scholars, architecture is seen as an art form responsive to, and inspiring, other modes of creative expression, religious thought, social movements and intellectual trends.[18]

Castles, however, have remained at the fringes of such developments until relatively recently. As military buildings were excluded from the typology of medieval architecture, they did not obviously fit into the mainstream of formal and typological discussion. Separate typologies and chronologies had to be devised for castle architecture by specialist castle scholars. The circumstantial lack in extant castles of surviving decoration and iconographic schemes has often discouraged the inclusion of castles in important architectural studies, although exceptions have sometimes been made for features such as mouldings, doors and windows and chapels, which are deemed to fit into ecclesiastical patterns. It has also been hard to include castles in ideological and textual

---

[14] See, for example, W. Rodwell, *The Archaeology of the English Church: The Study of Historic Churches and Churchyards* (London, 1981); W. Rodwell, *English Heritage Book of Church Archaeology* (London, 1989); W. Rodwell, 'Church Archaeology in Retrospect and Prospect', in *Church Archaeology: Directions for the Future*, ed. J. Blair and C. Pyrah, Council for British Archaeology Research Report 104 (1996), pp. 197–202.

[15] Fernie, 'Contrasts in Methodology and Interpretation', p. 345.

[16] Ibid., p. 357; *A History of English Architecture*, ed. P. Kidson, P. Murray and P. R. Thompson (Harmondsworth, 1965); *Medieval Architecture and its Intellectual Context: Essays in Honour of Peter Kidson*, ed. P. Kidson, E. C. Fernie and P. Crossley (London, 1990); C. Wilson, *The Gothic Cathedral: The Architecture of the Great Church, 1130–1530* (London, 1990); R. Gem, 'Towards an Iconography of Anglo-Saxon Architecture', *Journal of the Warburg and Courtauld Institutes* 46 (1983), 1–18; R. Gem, 'Lincoln Minster: *Ecclesia Pulchra, Ecclesia Fortis*', in *Medieval Art and Architecture at Lincoln Cathedral*, ed. T. A. Heslop and V. A. Sekules, British Archaeological Association Conference Transactions 8 (1986), pp. 9–28.

[17] His most impressive volume is P. Binski, *Westminster Abbey and the Plantagenets: Kingship and the Representation of Power, 1200–1400* (New Haven, 1995).

[18] For a more detailed analysis of the methodological development of ecclesiastical architecture, see R. Krautheimer, 'Introduction to an Iconography of Medieval Architecture', in *Studies in Early Christian, Medieval and Renaissance Art* (1969), 115–50; E. Fernie, 'Archaeology and Iconography: Recent Developments in the Study of English Medieval Architecture', *Architectural History* 32 (1989), 18–29; Fernie, 'Contrasts in Methodology and Interpretation'.

debates. The theological texts cited in relation to church architecture have seemed irrelevant to defensive structures and castle architecture has also been deemed to lack aesthetic and intellectual content. Through their exclusion from the mainstream architectural typology, castles have also been excluded from notice as important medieval architectural achievements.

It is fair to say that ecclesiastical architectural historians have consistently been at the forefront of new thinking on medieval architecture, because they have worked on the symbolic and iconographic elements that castles have appeared to lack. Partly as a result of this, there are few scholars who work both on medieval defensive and ecclesiastical buildings. Such trends have been perpetuated by the dominant attitudes within castle studies. The military concerns that first prompted academic interest in castles have been a persistent force. For obvious reasons they have only increased the division which architectural historians originally made between ecclesiastical and defensive architecture.

George T. Clark might be classed as the Thomas Rickman of medieval castle architecture. His book of 1884, entitled *Mediaeval Military Architecture in England*,[19] classified castles within a typological system. Rickman's architectural periods represent successively more complex and daring feats of architectural engineering, but they are also identified and discussed in aesthetic terms, as changes of style. Clark identified changes of form in his castle typology, but technological developments were identified as their sole motivation. His typology represents what he took to be successive stages in the evolution of military engineering. Changes were, for him, due to advances in defensive strategy or changing military conditions, rather than stylistic or aesthetic considerations. By these solely military criteria, the more lightly defended residences of the later Middle Ages could only be viewed as a sad falling-off from the technological achievements of previous years.

Ella Armitage was an early voice opposing Clark's views, and was responsible for introducing an element of social and political analysis into the discussion of castle types. In her book of 1912, *The Early Norman Castles of the British Isles*, Armitage employed a wide variety of evidence, including charters and other documents, visual depictions and arguments drawn from linguistics and sociology. Her most prominent contribution was to demonstrate that the motte-and-bailey was a form associated exclusively with the Normans[20] (Clark had thought it an Anglo-Saxon form of defence). Armitage argued that the social and administrative changes at the Conquest were given material expression in the motte-and-bailey castle. She therefore saw castles

---

[19] G. T. Clark, *Mediaeval Military Architecture in England* (London, 1884).
[20] E. S. Armitage, *The Early Norman Castles of the British Isles* (London, 1912); modern studies have confirmed this argument: see R. Eales, 'Royal Power and Castles in Norman England', *The Ideals and Practice of Medieval Knighthood* 3 (1990), 49–78 (pp. 50–1).

as a private fortifications for the protection of the ruling feudal elite, in opposition to Anglo-Saxon *burhs* which, she argued, were built as communal defences for the people.[21] For her, the introduction of the new word *castel* to England (and English) from the French at the Conquest expressed this complete social change. She used this term exclusively to describe fortresses built from the time of the Conquest onwards.

Alexander Hamilton Thompson's work, *Military Architecture in England during the Middle Ages*, was published in the same year as Armitage's book. Thompson was thoroughly convinced by her arguments, and worked her observations into his survey of defences in England from the Roman conquest onwards. His approach can be summed up by two phrases from his preface, where he refers to military architecture as a 'branch of science', and states his intention to give an account of its 'evolution'.[22] The pattern of development Thompson outlines, starting with earth and timber castles and ending with the move away from castles with the development of gunpowder, echoes Clark, though, following Armitage, he makes room for cultural and linguistic punctuation to his sequence.

The patterns set by Thompson and Armitage were accepted enthusiastically by subsequent castle scholars. B. H. St J. O'Neil declared in 1953, in support of Armitage, that 'it is now clear that the term [castle] should not properly be applied to any structure in the British Isles, whether of earth or stone, erected before the Conquest'.[23] R. Allen Brown repeated the same sentiment in various ways between 1969 and 1992, and was happy to acknowledge his debt to Armitage in his phrasing:

> The castle . . . was a residential fortress, the fortified residence of a lord, and in that sense was private as opposed to communal or public . . . Castles . . . are the perfect architectural expression of feudal lordship of which they were the conscious symbol as well as much of the substance.[24]

Brown himself replaced Thompson's survey volume with his own, *English Medieval Castles*, published in 1954.[25] In it, Brown brought in important evidence of social conditions and relations, to reconstruct the changing role of the castle in medieval life. This is reminiscent of Armitage's work on the Conquest period. However, Thompson's emphasis can also be seen in Brown's typology of castle forms. He begins with the Norman motte-and-bailey earthwork topped by its

---

[21]   Armitage, *Early Norman Castles*, p. 24.

[22]   A. H. Thompson, *Military Architecture in England during the Middle Ages* (London, 1912), Preface, p. vii.

[23]   The handful of castles built before the Conquest by Duke William's close allies are excepted, as being early Norman imports. B. St J. O'Neil, *Castles: An Introduction to the Castles of England and Wales* (London, 1953), p. 1.

[24]   R. A. Brown, M. Prestwich and C. Coulson, *Castles: A History and Guide* (Poole, 1980), pp. 13–14; see also Brown, 'An Historian's Approach', pp. 13–14, 136 and *passim*.

[25]   R. A. Brown, *English Medieval Castles* (London, 1954).

timber tower, and describes the gradual replacement of these elements with a stone tower and bailey walls. Shell keeps, he suggests, were a variant, making use of a larger surface area of the restricted motte. As construction in stone became more feasible, tower keeps without mottes took over, combined with stone gatehouses and walls. Brown's 'perfected castle' followed from around 1250 to 1350, with defensive developments such as flanking towers, impregnable gatehouses, concentric defences and machicolations – all seen, for example, in Edward I's Welsh castles. After this perfection 'the remaining architectural history of the castle is one of rather saddening anti-climax'.[26] A period of decline completes Brown's typology, with the construction of elegant but increasingly residential castles such as Bodiam and Nunney.[27]

While this sequence summarizes many careful architectural and historical observations, it is flawed in many respects. Clark, Thompson and Brown all tied their typologies to chronological development, arguing, for example, that stone walls necessarily replaced wooden ones, and that round towers followed square ones, because the new forms were militarily more effective. Detailed dating of many castles has in fact revealed that there is no simple relationship between particular forms and chronologies: different architectural forms and features came and went for a number of reasons, including symbolic ones.[28] However, Brown's work shows how persistent the military agenda is, especially in studies that describe castles chronologically.

More recent work has questioned the emphasis placed on military considerations. Battles continue to be fought over Bodiam Castle in debates as to the extent, or lack, of its military provisions. Scholars cannot agree whether it is a small but well-defended castle, or a miniature pastiche of a castle with minimal defensive capabilities.[29] But castles were from the earliest days of the Norman Conquest residences, centres of local administration and architectural markers of prestige and power. Pure military engineering could not

---

[26] Ibid., p. 89.

[27] Ibid., pp. 93–6.

[28] For detailed comment on this subject, see Eales, 'Royal Power and Castles in Norman England'; D. Stocker, 'The Shadow of the General's Armchair', *The Archaeological Journal* 149 (1992), 415–20; C. Coulson, 'The State of Research: Cultural Realities and Reappraisals in English Castle-Study', *Journal of Medieval History* 22 (1996), 171–208.

[29] See, for example, C. Taylor, P. Everson and W. R. Wilson-North, 'Bodiam Castle, Sussex', *Medieval Archaeology* 5 (1961), 169–175; D. J. Turner, 'Bodiam Castle, Sussex: True Castle or Old Soldier's Dream House?', in *England in the Fourteenth Century*, ed. W. M. Ormrod, Proceedings of the 1985 Harlaxton Symposium (1986), pp. 267–77; C. Coulson, 'Bodiam Castle: Truth and Tradition', *Fortress* 10 (August 1991), 13–15; C. Coulson, 'Some Analysis of the Castle of Bodiam, East Sussex', *Medieval Knighthood* 4 (1992), 51–107; C. Whittick, 'Dallingridge's Bay and Bodiam Castle's Millpond – Elements of a Medieval Landscape', *Sussex Archaeological Collections* 131 (1993), 119–23; P. Everson, 'Bodiam Castle, East Sussex: Castle and its Designed Landscape', *Château Gaillard* 17 (1994), 79–84.

begin to accommodate these important functions. Why should scholars then reject later and more residential buildings from the category of castles, when they merely emphasize features already present in earlier castles?

Armitage's depiction of the Conquest as a decisive event in castle history has also come into question. Brian Davison has been a key player in this debate, presenting new archaeological evidence to show that Anglo-Saxon *burhs* were not as different from castles as Armitage assumed.[30] Many of the fortresses of the Norman Conquest were in the form of rampart defences or ringworks, not mottes-and-baileys. These ringworks are notably similar to the ramparted defences of the Anglo-Saxons, which Armitage had been at pains to contrast with Norman works.[31] Davison also draws attention to the lack of mottes in Normandy before the Conquest, as well as transitional motte forms in English Conquest castles such as South Mimms and Eynsford. This evidence shows that the motte was developed during and as a response to the process of Conquest, rather than as a pre-designed form imposed as a mark of feudalism.[32] More recent work has supported these findings.[33] Studies on *burh* sites and documents have suggested that Anglo-Saxon *burhs* were not all communal defences or towns, as Armitage assumed; many were in fact private defended residences,[34] and may have had many similarities to the castles that came to replace them at the Conquest.[35] This is continuity is illustrated vividly by the castle at Goltho in Lincolnshire, where an Anglo-Saxon defended enclosure first built around 850 was succeeded in the eleventh century by a Norman motte-and-bailey which seems to have re-used part of the earlier defences.[36] Recent research on Anglo-Saxon *burh-geats* suggests they were probably substantial towers situated on the wall of *burh* enclosures, which may have influenced the design of the early Norman tower keeps and gatehouses.[37]

[30] B. K. Davison, 'The Origins of the Castle in England: The Institute's Research Project', *The Archaeological Journal* 124 (1967), 202–11. I examine Davison's arguments and other contributions to this debate in Chapter 1, p. 21.

[31] See D. J. C. King and L. Alcock, 'Ringworks of England and Wales', *Château Gaillard* 3 (1969), 90–127; Eales, 'Royal Power and Castles in Norman England', p. 51; B. English, 'Towns, Mottes and Ringworks of the Conquest', in *The Medieval Military Revolution*, ed. A. Ayton and J. E. Price (London, 1995), pp. 45–61.

[32] Davison, 'The Origins of the Castle in England', pp. 205, 207 and n. 10.

[33] For broad emphasis on the continuity of the pre- and post-Conquest defences, see English, 'Towns, Mottes and Ringworks of the Conquest', pp. 51–2; J. A. Green, *The Aristocracy of Norman England* (Cambridge, 1997), especially pp. 172–93.

[34] A. Williams, 'A Bell-house and a Burh-geat: Lordly Residences in England before the Norman Conquest', *Medieval Knighthood* 4 (1992), 221–40.

[35] Coulson, 'The State of Research', pp. 172–3.

[36] J. R. Kenyon, *Medieval Fortifications* (London, 1990), pp. 6, 17.

[37] Coulson, 'The State of Research', pp. 172–5; Davison, 'The Origins of the Castle in England', p. 207; D. Renn, 'Burhgeat and Gonfanon: Two Sidelights from the Bayeux Tapestry', *Anglo-Norman Studies* 16 (1994), 177–98 (pp. 177–86); Williams, 'A Bell-house and a Burh-geat', *passim*.

These findings cast serious doubt on the definition of the castle as essentially feudal and Norman, and undermine the social and formal analysis of castle architecture that followed from Armitage's ideas. Davison put the case succinctly in 1967:

> The question is, of course, to what extent can a private defended residence of this sort [i.e., a *burh*] be called a castle? Or, to phrase the question in archaeological terms, in what way did it differ from the private defended residence of a Norman Lord of equivalent status? This really is the crux of the whole problem: just what do we in fact mean by the term 'castle'?[38]

From the time of Armitage onwards it has been commonplace to restrict the meaning of the word *castle* to medieval defensive buildings of the post-Conquest period. If, however, the most fundamental reasons for making this cultural and chronological distinction disappear, then some other rationale must be found for defining the remit of the word. As Davison suggests, the modern usage of the word is a cause of possible ambiguity because of all the different interpretations and definitions of the castle given by different castle scholars.

A few studies have considered in some depth the meanings of specific documentary references to castles and other fortifications,[39] the most recent being Charles Coulson's book, *Castles in Medieval Society*. In it, Coulson consolidates his earlier work, showing that uses of the words *castle* and *castellum* in the medieval documentary record are much more various and nuanced than many previous studies have recognized. In particular, he underlines many Continental and British sources that use the words *castle* and *castellum* to refer to non-feudal, non-private structures. He also emphasizes uses encompassing the authority and status of the whole caput or castlery, a much wider concept than the defensive architecture alone.[40]

Coulson has also applied these observations to defensive architecture, carrying out groundbreaking work on the symbolic significance of crenellations. He advocates social and ideological interpretations of the crenellation motif in castles and other architectural forms, emphasizing the ubiquity of this symbolism in civic and ecclesiastical buildings as well as castle architecture.[41] This

---

[38] Davison, 'The Origins of the Castle in England', p. 204.

[39] J. H. Round, 'Tower and Castle', in *Geoffrey de Mandeville: A Study of the Anarchy* (London, 1892), pp. 328–46; J. F. Verbruggen, 'Note sur les sens des mots *castrum, castellum*, et quelques autres expressons qui désignent des fortifications', *Revue belge de philologie et d'histoire* 28.1 (1950), 147–55; discussed more fully in Chapter 1, pp. 26–7.

[40] C. Coulson, *Castles in Medieval Society: Fortresses in England, France, and Ireland in the Central Middle Ages* (Oxford, 2003), especially pp. 29–63.

[41] Ibid.; C. Coulson, 'Structural Symbolism in Medieval Castle Architecture', *Journal of the British Archaeological Association* 132 (1979), 73–90; C. Coulson, 'Hierarchism in Conventual Crenellation', *Medieval Archaeology* 26 (1982), 69–100; Coulson, 'The State of Research'.

approach has encouraged others to see the forms of defensive architecture in a similarly symbolic light. Philip Dixon, working with various collaborators, has examined the social and formal symbolism of other motifs of castle architecture, such as the great tower, and their expression of concepts of power and lordship.[42] The dramatic and processional potential of castle spaces is also important in his work, aligning his approach with work on the liturgical significance of ecclesiastical space.[43] T. A. Heslop and M. W. Thompson have made links between castles and literary texts, which I discuss in more detail in a moment. Sheila Bonde has worked specifically on the overlaps between defensive and ecclesiastical architecture.[44] All these studies have demonstrated the ideological potential of defensive forms, using methodologies that draw on the scholarship of ecclesiastical architecture.

These developments in specialist studies have gradually percolated through to the overview of medieval castles. While documentary material had always been important, N. J. G. Pounds' work, *The Medieval Castle in England and Wales*, collects and collates an impressive array of documentary references and examines in detail the administrative and socio-political role of the medieval castle.[45] Patronage and social and political symbolism are also important in the work of scholars such as Colin Platt.[46] M. W. Thompson's complementary pair of works, entitled respectively *The Rise of the Castle* and *The Decline of the Castle*,[47] deploy a wide range of material, but the titles demonstrate the persistence of the military agenda. The most recent survey volume by Tom NcNeill has broken free of this mould and features a chapter discussing the different methodologies that can be applied to castles – a refreshingly public forum for this important debate.[48]

While some of these methodologies have taken a long time to make their way from ecclesiastical architecture to castles, certain new approaches have been applied to both from the start. Analysis of the planning of

---

[42] P. Dixon and B. Lott, 'The Courtyard and the Tower: Contexts and Symbols in the Development of the Late Medieval Great House', *Journal of the British Archaeological Association* 146 (1993), 93–101; P. Dixon, 'The Donjon of Knaresborough: The Castle as Theatre', *Château Gaillard* 14 (1988), 121–40; P. Dixon and P. Marshall, 'The Great Keep at Hedingham Castle: A Reassessment', *Fortress* 18 (August 1993), 16–23; P. Dixon and P. Marshall, 'The Great Tower in the Twelfth Century: The Case of Norham Castle', *The Archaeological Journal* 150 (1993), 410–32.

[43] See especially Dixon, 'The Donjon of Knaresborough'.

[44] S. Bonde, *Fortress Churches of Languedoc: Architecture, Religion and Conflict in the High Middle Ages* (Cambridge, 1994); S. Bonde, 'Castle and Church Building'.

[45] N. J. G. Pounds, *The Medieval Castle in England and Wales: A Social and Political History* (Cambridge, 1990, repr. 1994).

[46] C. Platt, *The Castle in Medieval England and Wales* (London, 1982).

[47] M. W. Thompson, *The Decline of the Castle* (Cambridge, 1987); M. W. Thompson, *The Rise of the Castle* (Cambridge, 1991).

[48] T. McNeill, *English Heritage Book of Castles* (London, 1992).

medieval buildings has become an area of interest in both fields.[49] Access analysis and sociological/anthropological theories have also been applied to both kinds of medieval building to determine the status and probable functions of various rooms. Such techniques have been employed, notably by Roberta Gilchrist, to the architectural enclosure of medieval women, so introducing the important question of gender into architectural debates.[50] Bonde's work, as I mentioned, has made fundamental architectural and cultural connections between castles and churches in her study of the fortress churches of the Languedoc region. She has also produced a smaller-scale study of similar overlaps in medieval England after the Conquest.[51] Castle architecture has not yet, however, been integrated fully into the iconographic and intellectual methodologies that are applied to the great ecclesiastical architecture of the Middle Ages. The intellectual background to castle architecture has proved harder to find.

Nevertheless, there are isolated exceptions. Various attempts have been made to link medieval castles with contemporary texts. Paul Frankl, an architectural scholar, also made a survey of literary architecture, including castles, collected under the heading of 'Gothic'.[52] Frankl was well qualified to make stylistic connections between the buildings described in texts and medieval architectural forms, and his identification of architectural styles provides an interesting commentary on medieval works of literature. However, he did not look into the deeper workings of the relationship between these two media, or into the ideological role of architecture in mediating between them. Other attempts to link architecture and text also lack this dimension. Thompson has examined the architectural descriptions in the Middle English alliterative poem 'Sir Gawain and the Green Knight', and attempted an identification of

---

[49] P. A. Faulkner, 'Domestic Planning from the Twelfth to the Fourteenth Century', *The Archaeological Journal* 115 (1958), 150–84; P. A. Faulkner, 'Castle Planning in the Fourteenth Century', *The Archaeological Journal* 120 (1963), 215–35; B. Morley 'Aspects of Fourteenth-century Castle Design', in *Collectanea Historica: Essays in Memory of Stuart Rigold*, ed. A. Detsicas (Maidstone, 1981), pp. 104–13; E. Fernie, 'The Ground Plan of Norwich Cathedral and the Square Root of Two', *Journal of the British Archaeological Association* 129 (1976), 77–86; E. Fernie, 'Anglo-Saxon Lengths: The Northern System, the Perch and the Foot', *The Archaeological Journal* 142 (1985), 246–54.

[50] R. Gilchrist, *Gender and Material Culture: The Archaeology of Religious Women* (London, 1994); R. Gilchrist, 'Medieval Bodies in the Material World: Gender, Stigma and the Body', in *Framing Medieval Bodies*, ed. S. Kay and M. Rubin (Manchester, 1994), pp. 43–61; R. Gilchrist, 'The Contested Garden: Gender, Space and Metaphor in the Medieval English Castle', in R. Gilchrist, *Gender and Archaeology: Contesting the Past* (London, 1999), pp. 109–45; G. Fairclough, 'Meaningful Constructions: Spatial and Functional Analysis of Medieval Buildings', *Antiquity* 66 (1992), 348–66.

[51] Bonde, *Fortress Churches of Languedoc*; Bonde, 'Castle and Church Building'.

[52] P. Frankl, *The Gothic: Literary Sources and Interpretations through Eight Centuries* (Princeton, 1960).

the castle in the text.[53] Richard Morris has undertaken a more general view of Arthurian resonances in medieval castles.[54] Heslop has taken a more ideologically ambitious approach, and argued for references at Orford Castle to specific texts and ideas on an imperial theme.[55] These groundbreaking studies acknowledge the importance of literary representations in the medieval understanding of castle architecture, but they use literary texts without addressing fully the literary conventions by which they are governed. For example, Thompson matches the Gawain-poet's description, feature by feature, to Beeston Castle.[56] He does not acknowledge that these descriptive elements, and their arrangement, may be determined by literary convention rather than the desire to describe accurately any specific building. On the contrary, the castle is compared in the text to a paper table-decoration, which surely points readers towards miniature, ephemeral castle images, rather than to full-scale, practical architecture.[57]

Studies of the architectural imagery employed in literature and art, on the other hand, lack any comparison with the medieval architecture to which, at some level, they are related. Yet these more literary and art-historical studies do recognize the symbolic importance of architecture and the artistic conventions in which its depictions participate. Theological and literary castles have been compiled exhaustively and discussed briefly by Roberta Cornelius.[58] Jill Mann has provided a short survey of some of the literary uses of architectural devices, concentrating mainly on Middle English literature.[59] Discussions of particular architectural motifs, including castles, have been made for specific authors including St Theresa of Ávila and Chaucer.[60] Arthurian castles and

---

[53] M. Thompson, 'Castles', in *A Companion to the Gawain-poet*, ed. D. S. Brewer and J. Gibson (Cambridge, 1997), pp. 119–30.

[54] R. K. Morris, 'The Architecture of Arthurian Enthusiasm: Castle Symbolism in the Reigns of Edward I and his Successors', in *Armies, Chivalry and Warfare in Medieval Britain*, ed. M. Strickland, Proceedings of the 1995 Harlaxton Symposium (1998), pp. 63–81.

[55] T. A. Heslop, 'Orford Castle, Nostalgia and Sophisticated Living', *Architectural History* 34 (1991), 36–58. For more detailed information and bibliography on specific castles mentioned in this book, see D. J. C. King, *Castellarium Anglicanum: An Index and Bibliography of the Castles in England, Wales and the Islands*, 2 vols. (New York, 1983); J. R. Kenyon, *Castles, Town Defences, and Artillery Fortifications in Britain: A Bibliography*, 3 vols. (London, 1978–90).

[56] Thompson, 'Castles', pp. 123–5.

[57] 'Sir Gawain and the Green Knight', p. 238, line 802; Ackerman, 'Pared out of Paper', *passim*.

[58] Cornelius, *The Figurative Castle*.

[59] J. Mann, 'Allegorical Buildings in Mediaeval Literature', *Medium Aevum* 63 (1994), 191–210.

[60] J. Chorpenning, 'The Literary and Theological Method of the *Castillo Interior*', *Journal of Hispanic Philology* 3 (1979), 121–33; B. E. Kurtz, ' "The Small Castle of the Soul": Mysticism and Metaphor in the European Middle Ages', *Studia Mystica* 15.4 (1992), 19–39; D. Lloyd-Kimbrel, 'Architectonic Allusions: Gothic Perspectives

the Castle of Love motif have also been singled out for special attention.[61] Frances Yates and Mary Carruthers have both made important studies of the use of architectural structures as frameworks for rhetorical, mnemonic and devotional purposes.[62]

These discussions all agree on the huge variety of medieval architectural symbolism and the wide range of literary sources on which medieval authors drew, including Classical texts such as Ovid's *Metamorphoses* and its House of Fame, Biblical references to the Temple of Solomon and the Heavenly Jerusalem and many additional examples from medieval works. Literary and artistic studies are quick to recognize that, with such a diverse range of sources and traditions, sacred, secular and defensive architectures often overlap and cannot be discussed in isolation. Their approach is, however, generally typological. Examples that share similar features are compared and routes of transmission are discussed. This approach allows useful insights into complex patterns of influence and the creation of artistic conventions. However, it does not facilitate comparison with architecture in other contexts. It is, for example, hard to see how a typology of otherworld castle motifs in romances could be compared with the Clark-derived defensive sequence of developing castle architecture. There is no common concept of the castle through which the buildings can be compared to their mental and artistic representations.

This is the state of scholarship on English medieval castles and their cultural reception in the Middle Ages. It should now be clear why interdisciplinary examinations of these topics have been rare. However, things are changing, and more and more studies in recent years have moved towards viewing the castle as an ideological architecture. The following section contains an outline of this book, laying out its structure and showing how it sets out to bring together different methodologies and disciplines.

The definition of the castle has been a crucial factor in shaping critical attitudes towards medieval defensive architecture and its study. However, definitions have shifted several times over the last hundred years, when castle scholars had new ideas or found new evidence that did not fit the existing

---

and Perimeters as an Approach to Chaucer', *Mediaevistik* 1 (1988), 115–24; P. Brown, 'The Prison of Theseus and the Castle of Jalousie', *The Chaucer Review* 26.2 (1991), 147–72; M. Hallissy, 'Writing a Building: Chaucer's Knowledge of the Construction Industry and the Language of the *Knight's Tale*', *Chaucer Review* 32 (1997–8), 239–59.

61 C. Ross, *The Custom of the Castle from Malory to Macbeth* (Berkeley, 1997); Whitaker, 'Otherworld Castles'; Gaines, 'Malory's Castles'; R. S. Loomis, 'The Allegorical Siege in the Art of the Middle Ages', *American Journal of Archaeology* 23.3 (1919), 255–69.

62 F. A. Yates, *The Art of Memory* (London, 1966); M. J. Carruthers, *The Book of Memory: A Study of Memory in Medieval Culture* (Cambridge, 1990), p. 101 and *passim*.

definition. As the preceding summary showed, it has been difficult to compare architectural discussions of castles with scholarship on their literary and artistic representations, because the terms of reference have been so different. My approach to the medieval castle has the effect of reducing the gap between these two fields, because it takes evidence from both into account. This statement may seem obvious or redundant. However, it seems worth making, merely to emphasize the simplicity of the enterprise. The rethinking of the castle I propose differs from recent scholarly definitions in certain ways, but it flows directly from the evidence of the medieval sources themselves.

The most fundamental juxtaposition of the idea and the form of the castle occurs in the word itself. The first chapter of this book, 'The Idea of the Castle', re-examines the medieval evidence for the origins and early meanings of the word, broadening the range of examples away from the charters and other legal documents usually cited in other discussions. The castle was an innovative defensive form, developed as a tool of the feudal system of government, and it has often been assumed that the Middle English term *castel*, which was loaned from French around the same time as the arrival of the buildings, reflected these new and feudal origins. It is certainly possible to connect the term with these historical processes. However, certain contexts show plainly that the word in medieval usage often has quite different connotations. It reflects the use of the Latin term *castellum* in prominent Classical and Biblical texts and denotes a wider range of fortified enclosures than the Norman, feudal and private defences with which it is usually associated. In an example at the end of this chapter, I show how these wider meanings could be used and combined in an interplay of Biblical and Classical symbolism with communal connotations. These wider meanings for the term castle then become the focus for the remaining chapters.

In Chapter 2, 'The Urban Castle', I investigate ties between the castle and the wider community, in terms of symbolic and aesthetic as well as physical and political relationships. This challenges some assumptions arising from the habit of defining the castle in opposition to communal defences, and takes further recent studies emphasizing the important role of castles in the wider community. Civic seals, for example, deploy images of castles as badges of communal pride and prestige. This imagery represents symbolically the physical continuity between town and castle defences at many urban sites, some of which (like the planted towns and castles of Edward I's Welsh campaigns) were built and planned together to be mutually supportive in terms of trade and defence. This chapter also investigates examples of castles creating or participating in local legends. These castles have a reciprocal relationship with mythology, both generating and reflecting references to local narratives, and so are bound up with the identity and prestige of the wider community. These resonances demonstrate the complex ideology attached to the castle in its urban setting, but not encompassed by many traditional analyses.

Chapter 3, 'The Spiritual Castle', deals in a similar way with castles and their relationship to ecclesiastical architecture, in structural and stylistic, cultural and political terms. Castles were from the earliest period of Norman rule an essential part of the Church's administration in Britain, built alongside churches by and for the same patrons, often using the same craftsmen. This close relationship is reflected in intellectual culture, as the castle became a significant motif in medieval theology. The text of Luke 10. 38, 'ipse intravit in quoddam castellum . . .', for example, was often interpreted as a Biblical reference to a castle, understood to refer literally to a castle in which the sisters Mary and Martha lived, and allegorically to the castle of the Virgin's body, into which Christ entered at the Incarnation. Such images made their way throughout medieval English culture. The complexity and refinement of some of the relevant imagery confirms that castle architecture was intellectualized to a similar extent, and often in similar ways to ecclesiastical architecture.

The final chapter, 'The Imperial Castle', investigates the imagery and politics of empire associated with medieval English castles. I argue that Classical references containing the word *castellum*, like similar Biblical references, were understood to refer to castles of the medieval type. The famous example of Caernarfon's polychrome walls, which are thought to imitate the land walls of Constantinople, has been accepted as a reference to empire in one particular castle. However, material allusions to Roman construction techniques, architectural styles and extant remains can be detected at a wide variety of castle sites. I identify early examples including Chepstow and Colchester, as well as later work at Dover and the Tower of London. As with the Biblical examples, medieval castles are projected back through history into Classical contexts by legendary histories and foundation myths. I argue that polychrome motifs, which were used to decorate several important medieval castles, made connections with imperial architecture described in medieval literature and art, as well as with the extant Roman remains which were readily visible in medieval Britain. Such connotations were used to bolster the political pretensions of successive royal dynasties, and can be linked to imperial claims in national foundation legends. This final chapter demonstrates above all the full extent to which castles were involved in the ideological and mythographic life of the nation.

There are, of course, many approaches, themes and topics I have not tackled in this study. *The Idea of the Castle in Medieval England* examines in detail a number of contemporary medieval architectural symbolisms in carefully worked examples, comparing particular buildings, literary descriptions and visual representations. It does not attempt to cover the whole range of castle symbolism. However, the themes that have emerged in this project have proved very suggestive, and create resonances amongst many examples I have not discussed, as well as those I have. This is simply because they flow from the medieval evidence. I am sure another scholar covering the same range of material would have little difficulty recognizing the trends I have identified. It is only interdisciplinary difficulties that have hindered this kind of approach in the past. Much of the evidence speaks so clearly that I am only surprised these connections have not been made before.

CHAPTER ONE

The Idea of the Castle

Þa undernam Godwine eorl swyðe þæt on his eorldome sceolde
swilc geweorðan, ongan þa gadrian folc ofer eall his eorldom,
7 Swein eorl his sunu ofer his, 7 Harold his oðer sunu ofer his eorldom, 7 hi gegaderedan ealle on Gleawcesterscire æt Langatreo
mycel fyrd 7 unarimedlic, ealle gearwe to wige ongean þone cyng,
buton man ageafe Eustatsius 7 his men heom to hand sceofe, 7 eac
þa Frencyscan þe on þam castelle wæron.[1]

(Then Earl Godwine was very indignant that such things should
happen in his earldom, then began to gather people all over his
earldom, and Earl Swein, his son, over his, and Harold, his second
son, over his earldom; and they all gathered in Gloucestershire at
Longtree, a great and countless army all ready for war against the
king unless Eustace and his men were given into their hands – and
also the French who were in the castle.)[2]

A close correlation exists in British castle studies between theories about the
origins of the castle in England and the question of the proper meaning of the
term *castle*. No thorough linguistic study has yet been made of the meaning
and development of the word, despite its great significance for the understanding of the medieval castle. This chapter cannot provide an exhaustive
survey, but it sets out a summary of the word's origins and development in
English usage in order to clarify this point.

The passage quoted above, from the entry for 1052 in British Library MS
Cotton Tiberius B.iv, the Worcester manuscript of the Anglo-Saxon chronicle,
has been central to this debate, as it is identified as one of the first occurrences
of the word *castle* in English. However, none of the discussions of this text by
castle scholars has looked to recognized linguistic methodologies, or set out
to investigate work by historical linguists on the early meaning of the word
castle. This has led to several inconsistencies and circularities in a debate that
is crucial to the modern and medieval idea of the castle.

Brown, for example, thought the pre-Conquest date of this passage too
early to allow for a reference to a Norman castle: 'It is . . . extremely probable,

---

[1] *The Anglo-Saxon Chronicle: A Collaborative Edition 6. MS D: A Semi-diplomatic Edition*,
    ed. G. P. Cubbin (Cambridge, 1996), p. 70.
[2] *The Anglo-Saxon Chronicle*, ed. and transl. M. J. Swanton (London, 1996), p. 175, D.

in a period when feudal terminology had not yet hardened into its precise eventual meanings, least of all in England, that the "castle" referred to . . . was in fact an Anglo-Saxon *burh*.'[3] In Brown's eyes, then, the *castel* of the text is therefore not a proper castle at all – which is why he surrounds his term 'castle' with apostrophes. In this, Brown follows the argument, originating with Armitage, 'that the term "castle" should not properly be applied to any structure in the British Isles, whether of earth or stone, erected before the Conquest'.[4]

The same assumption is used differently by Ann Williams, arguing, conversely, that a similar reference, in the Anglo-Saxon chronicle for 1051, does refer to a Norman castle. She notes that 'there were several native words which the chronicler could have used to describe a fortification – *burh, geweorc, hereborg* . . . The chronicler chose none of them.' The fortress referred to must therefore have been a distinctively Norman defence: 'something new, to be described in the tongue of the . . . foreigners who built it'.[5] These scholars both rely absolutely on the definition of the word *castle* as an essentially Norman, private and feudal form. It is instructive that they come to opposite conclusions about its meaning in these instances. Such contradictory explanations can only strengthen the case for re-examining the meaning of the word *castle*, and the meaning of the medieval documents which have traditionally been interpreted according to one particular definition of the term.

The problem of historical terminology and its meaning is a very general one, not confined by any means to the two authors I have discussed above, or even to castle studies. Recent scholarship has pointed to similar contradictions in historians' understanding of the terminology of feudalism. Susan Reynolds, for example, observes that familiar terms and concepts, such as 'feudalism', tend to become normative in historical criticism.[6] Once a meaning is generally accepted amongst historians, this becomes the yardstick against which the historical record is measured, hindering the examination of each example for its own meaning and within its own context. Texts that seem to comply with the accepted meanings are regarded as typical, while those

---

3   R. A. Brown, 'An Historian's Approach to the Origins of the Castle in England', *The Archaeological Journal* 126 (1969), 131–48 (pp. 144–5).

4   B. H. St J. O'Neil, *Castles: An Introduction to the Castles of England and Wales* (London, 1953), p. 1.

5   A. Williams, 'A Bell-house and a Burh-geat: Lordly Residences in England before the Norman Conquest', *Medieval Knighthood* 4 (1992), pp. 221–40 (p. 221). Williams chooses the account of the incident described in the Peterborough manuscript of the Chronicle: Oxford, Bodleian Library MS Laud 636. Brown was convinced that this passage did not refer to the same incident he described: Brown, 'An Historian's Approach', p. 144. However, it seems likely that the two accounts describe the same incident. The editors of the latest comparative translation, for example, cross-reference the two accounts: *The Anglo-Saxon Chronicle*, ed. Swanton, p. 173, n. 15.

6   S. Reynolds, *Fiefs and Vassals: The Medieval Evidence Reinterpreted* (Oxford, 1994), chapter 1 and *passim*.

that use the terms in unexpected ways are dismissed as inaccurate. The way Reynolds defines these difficulties is linguistically very acute, and is worth quoting at some length for the light it sheds on the complex issue of defining meaning in historical contexts:

> If we start by discussing words we are liable to assume that [they] were used in the sense we expect unless the contrary is specified . . . To do this is to ignore how language works. Words used in real life, especially abstract nouns, do not have core meanings which are more central or more right than others. Dictionary makers deduce meaning from usage. They do not control usage. It varies from place to place, even from speaker to speaker, as well as from time to time.[7]

> Historians who define fiefs generally say that they are defining the 'concept of the fief', but they nearly always start by discussing the word and its etymology and origins, while what they are really concerned with is neither the word nor the concept or notion that people may have in their heads when they use the word, but the phenomena that the word and concept represent . . . The *concept* of the fief . . . is essentially post-medieval: it is a set of ideas or notions about the essential attributes of pieces of property that historians have defined as fiefs . . . But when the subject under investigation involves notions or attitudes held by people in the society concerned it is vital to distinguish whether a concept is ours or theirs . . . Much of the discussion of fiefs, as of vassalage, seems to me to assume the identity of words with concepts, our concepts with medieval concepts, and all three with the phenomena.[8]

As the preceding quotations showed, this lesson is particularly applicable to castle terminology. Scholars including Davison and Coulson have repeatedly questioned the rigid definition of the castle as an exclusively private, feudal fortress. They point to the marked similarities between early castles in Britain and indigenous defences, and to the ambiguities and contradictions in traditional interpretations of the documentary record.[9] Coulson comments acerbically on the 'linguistic burglary' of scholars who dismiss medieval documentary uses of terms such as *castel* or *castellum*, when these do not agree with modern concepts of the castle.[10] His book, *Castles in Medieval Society*, sets out convincing documentary evidence to argue for a wider meaning for the

---

[7] Ibid., p. 13.

[8] Ibid., pp. 9–10, 12–13.

[9] B. K. Davison, 'The Origins of the Castle in England: The Institute's Research Project', *The Archaeological Journal* 124 (1967), 202–11 (p. 204); C. Coulson, *Castles in Medival Society: Fortresses in England, France, and Ireland in the Central Middle Ages* (Oxford, 2003), especially pp. 29–63; discussed in the Introduction.

[10] C. Coulson, 'The State of Research: Cultural Realities and Reappraisals in English Castle-Study', *Journal of Medieval History* 22 (1996), 171–208 (p. 174); O'Neil, *Castles: An Introduction*, pp. 1–2.

term, less strictly tied to feudalism and private fortification. Just as importantly, it points out that 'castle' is just one of many terms used in medieval documents to indicate defences, and that the exclusive focus on this word is a modern preoccupation.[11] To tackle this problem, both Reynolds and Coulson turn to case studies.[12] Careful examination of a range of documentary evidence does not necessarily produce a consistent definition of the terms in question. However, it does provide an array of different contexts and connotations, which form a composite picture of the range and complexity of the term in contemporary use. This is the approach I intend to take in this chapter. However, while most historians, including Coulson, choose to concentrate on conventional historical documents, such as charters and grants, I have looked towards sources more often regarded as literary, and so not included in historical assessments. These alternative kinds of evidence are just as valid for linguistic analysis, and complement the arguments, already presented through historical texts, that the castle had a much broader range of meanings and a much wider cultural significance than its usual definition in modern use. My focus on the word *castle* is in some senses anachronistic, as it draws attention away from the full range of different words used to indicate defences in medieval usage. However, I feel this in-depth analysis is a necessary remedy for the exclusive appropriation of the word by modern castle scholarship.

Reynolds' distinction between word, concept and phenomenon is a helpful way of clarifying the complicated issues involved in such an undertaking. I have therefore used this triple distinction to structure this chapter. However, as Reynolds implies, the phenomenon – in this case, evidence for early castles in historical documents and archaeological sources – is the aspect on which historians usually concentrate. For this reason I will refer the reader back to the summary of the evidence for castle forms and origins given in the Introduction. The rest of this chapter will be divided into a section on the linguistic evidence for the introduction and meaning of medieval castle vocabulary, and a section discussing the wider implications of how both phenomena and words were understood and used in the Middle Ages. Obviously, discussion of the words and concepts will overlap, as will that of concepts and phenomena, so these general sections will be used as organising devices, rather than strict divisions between ideas.

In order to problematize the word, concept and phenomenon of the castle from the start, I will be very careful to specify which of these particular aspects I am referring to each time I use the word, and to indicate whether I am referring to a modern or a contemporary understanding. I will denote the medieval phenomenon by the phrase 'medieval castle', 'Norman castle', and so on. The phrase 'castle words' will be used as a collective term for

---

[11] Coulson, *Castles in Medieval Society*, p. 30.
[12] Ibid., p. 7.

medieval words for castles in all languages, or in any languages specified. *Castel* will stand for Middle English castle words, even when these are not spelled in this precise way in the sources. *Chastel* will act similarly for medieval French castle words and *castellum* for medieval Latin castle words. *Castle* (italicized) will be used to indicate a linguistic discussion of the term. I will identify the concept with phrases like 'medieval concept', 'modern concept'. The undifferentiated word castle will be used as an inclusive term for the overall subject and debate.

Armitage made a neat summary of her arguments for the novelty of the castle as a technology and as a concept when she suggested that 'the thing as well as the term was new'.[13] She was commenting on the borrowing of the word *castel* into English from Norman French around the time of the Conquest, and correlating this with the introduction of the motte-and-bailey castle by the Normans at around the same date. Recent work has weakened one side of Armitage's equation, by showing that Norman fortifications were not wholly the result of importation from France, but were influenced by existing British fortifications during the process of Conquest.[14] There is also reason to reassess Armitage's claims for the linguistic novelty of the word *castle*.

In an English context, the words *castellum* and *castel* were not entirely new at the time when Norman influences, linguistic and otherwise, were making themselves felt. While the experts agree that *castel* was re-borrowed into English from French around the time of the Conquest, there also existed an older loan of the word *castel*, from Latin into English, at some point before the year 1000.[15] Words loaned into Old English were relatively rare at this period.[16] The roughly 150 examples that were borrowed from Latin were absorbed in the context of scholarly research, as a result of Benedictine reforms and the growth of learned monastic communities. These loan words reflect the Classical Latin read in monasteries.[17] The word *castellum* had been around in Latin from Classical times,[18] and also occurs a number of

---

[13] E. S. Armitage, *The Early Norman Castles of the British Isles* (London, 1912), p. 24.

[14] Williams, 'A Bell-house and a Burh-geat'; B. English, 'Towns, Mottes and Ringworks of the Conquest', in *The Medieval Military Revolution*, ed. A. Ayton and J. L. Price (London, 1995), pp. 45–61 (pp. 51–2); J. A. Green, *The Aristocracy of Norman England* (Cambridge, 1997), especially pp. 172–93.

[15] *Dictionary of Old English*, ed. A. C. Amos, A. di Paulo Healey, J. Holland, D. McDougall, I. McDougall, N. Porter and P. Thompson (Toronto, 1988–), 2nd fascicle.

[16] D. Kastovsky, 'Semantics and Vocabulary', in *The Beginnings to 1066*, ed. R. M. Hogg, The Cambridge History of the English Language 1 (1992), pp. 290–408 (p. 294); see also B. M. H. Strang, *A History of Old English* (London, 1970, repr. 1974), p. 314.

[17] Kastovsky, 'Semantics and Vocabulary', p. 307.

[18] *Oxford Latin Dictionary*, ed. P. G. W. Glare (Oxford, 1982).

times within the Vulgate translation of the Bible. In these contexts it is usually translated as meaning a village or small town, as this accords with the ancient meaning of the words in these texts. The attested examples of *castel* and *castellum* at this period in English sources confirm a specialized use in Biblical study, associated closely with Biblical instances of the word *castellum*.[19] However, occasional contemporary uses of the Latin word *castellum* indicate that this word could also be used outside the context of Biblical commentary, to refer to the kinds of defences that Norman castles were later to replace.[20]

While the first loan of the word *castel* is attested by only a few examples, the second, from French at the time of the Conquest, was marked by a sudden and frequent usage, and was borrowed under very different circumstances. There are therefore some important distinctions between these two separate loans. Linguists have suggested that the sense of the earlier loan-word lived on well into the Middle Ages, reserved exclusively for dealing with Biblical, and sometimes Classical uses of *castellum*. However, the need to interpret and translate the Biblical word *castellum* in English usage did not end with the introduction of Norman terminology. If *castellum* could be used in an English context in the ninth century to describe a defended settlement,[21] and the Norman term could also be used in a similar way around the time of the Conquest, there was obviously some overlap between the meanings of the two loan-words. I will suggest later that this specialist Biblical usage need not necessarily be kept separate from the mainstream meaning adopted for the words *castel* and *castellum* under Norman influence, if the evidence for this period is examined without pre-formed expectations as to the military and feudal meaning of the words. The Conquest certainly did herald some profound changes in the content and use of the English language, but as with developments in defensive architecture, these shifts are not always attributable to abrupt switches of administration, technology or vocabulary.

Linguists characterize the relationship created between French and English at the Conquest by the term 'intimate borrowing'. This is often the linguistic result of a conquest, annexation or mass migration which juxtaposes one language against another. In these circumstances, the less dominant language group borrows words from the language of the dominant group, and these words often mark the nature of the social and political relationship between

---

[19] *Dictionary of Medieval Latin from British Sources*, ed. R. E. Latham and D. R. Howlett (Oxford, 1975–); *Dictionary of Old English*, ed. Amos *et al.*

[20] J. H. Round, 'Tower and Castle', in *Geoffrey de Mandeville: A Study of the Anarchy* (London, 1892), pp. 328–46 (p. 332); Coulson, *Castles in Medieval Society*, pp. 15–28.

[21] See for example Round, 'Tower and Castle', p. 332; M. Chibnall, 'Orderic Vitalis on Castles', in *Studies in Medieval History Presented to R. Allen Brown*, ed. C. Harper-Bill, C. J. Holdsworth and J. Nelson (Woodbridge, 1989), pp. 43–56.

the two groups.[22] Leading linguists Jeffers and Lehiste include the word *castle* in their examples of loans from Norman French into English, which occurred, by intimate borrowing, from the eleventh to the thirteenth centuries.[23] However, Jeffers and Lehiste note that 'intimate borrowing, unlike cultural borrowing, is not limited to cultural novelties'.[24] In other words, in intimate borrowing contexts, words are not borrowed only to describe those new phenomena for which a word did not exist in the recipient language. Words may also be loaned for social reasons, when the borrowers adopt terminology associated with the prestige of a powerful group.[25] Careful attention to the documentary evidence shows, to my satisfaction, that the word *castle* falls into this category: it is borrowed into English around the Conquest to reflect the terminology of the dominant social group, but not to mark a completely new form of defensive architecture.

Certain sources from around the time of the Norman Conquest are often quoted as illustration of the earliest evidence for castles, and for the word *castel*, in an English context.[26] One is the passage cited at the beginning of this chapter. The same source, the 'D' manuscript of the Anglo-Saxon chronicle, also mentions Duke William's policy of castle building, and its unfortunate effects on the English people, in the entry for the year 1066:

> Oda biscop 7 Wyllelm eorl belifen her æfter 7 worhton castelas wide geond þas þeode, 7 earm folc swencte, 7 a syððan hit yflade swiðe.[27]

> (Bishop Odo and Earl William were left behind here, and they built castles widely throughout this nation, and oppressed the wretched people; and afterwards it always grew very much worse.[28])

Similar sentiments are conveyed in Latin by Orderic Vitalis. He mentions in his *Historia ecclesiastica* (Ecclesiastical History) (1109–1113)[29] the effect the new fortifications had on the English, who were ill equipped to deal with them:

> Munitiones num quas castella Galli nuncupant Anglicis provinciis paucissime fuerant, et ob hoc Angli licet bellicosi fuerint et audaces ad resistendum tamen inimicis extiterant debiliores.

---

[22] R. L. Jeffers and I. Lehiste, *Principles and Methods for Historical Linguistics* (Cambridge, MA, 1982, repr. 1989), p. 150.
[23] Ibid.; see also A. M. S. McMahon, *Understanding Language Change* (Cambridge, 1994), p. 202.
[24] McMahon, *Understanding Language Change*, p. 202.
[25] Ibid., p. 201.
[26] N. J. G. Pounds, *The Medieval Castle in England and Wales: A Social and Political History* (Cambridge, 1990, repr. 1994), pp. 3, 7; M. W. Thompson, *The Rise of the Castle* (Cambridge, 1991), p. 48.
[27] *The Anglo-Saxon Chronicle*, ed. Cubbin, p. 81.
[28] *The Anglo-Saxon Chronicle*, ed. Swanton, p. 200.
[29] M. Chibnall, *The World of Orderic Vitalis* (Oxford, 1984), p. 176.

(For the fortifications called castles by the Normans were scarcely known in the English provinces, and so the English – in spite of their courage and love of fighting – could put up only a weak resistance to their enemies.)[30]

It is not surprising that these sources are often quoted in debates on the origins of English castles. They provide very succinct evidence of the Normans' use of fortifications before and during the Conquest, of the name – *castel, castelas, castella* – which the conquerors gave them, and also of the application of this name to these fortifications by English speakers, whether they were writing in Latin or in Anglo-Saxon.[31] Orderic's observation particularly seems to imply a perception of the Norman castle as a novel piece of technology, and the attachment of the word *castellum* to this novel concept. However, careful study of the context of Orderic's comments suggests that they may be directed specifically towards the novelty of the Norman defences in remote rural areas, where defences of any kind may have been lacking at the time of the Conquest.[32] Furthermore, Orderic's phrase, 'munitiones num quas castella Galli nuncupant', expresses explicitly the urge to preserve the correct Norman terminology, indicating, I suggest, a social motive for perpetuating Norman vocabulary, rather than a need to coin a new term.

A broader survey of Orderic Vitalis's work shows evidence of very diverse uses of Latin castle words.[33] Orderic uses *castellum* and *castrum* interchangeably with several other Latin words, such as *municipium, praesidum* and *oppidum*, to describe a range of defences from fortified towns to military defences and fortified houses.[34] This usage is echoed in other documents of the time.[35] It seems, therefore, that the words *castellum* and *castrum* in these sources covered a wide range of fortifications and were not confined specifically to Norman fortresses, even if they did often refer to the new defences.[36] The social motivation behind the use of the word *castel* may have promoted its increasing occurrence in England around and after the Conquest, but did not tie it to one specific kind of structure.

The small number of studies focused on the early use of castle vocabulary confirm this wider range of meanings for the Latin terms *castrum* and *castellum*, both before and after the Conquest. J. F. Verbruggen, writing in 1950 and using a variety of Continental and British Latin sources of the periods before and after the Conquest, came to some similar conclusions as to the

---

[30] Orderic Vitalis, *The Ecclesiastical History of Orderic Vitalis*, ed. M. Chibnall , 6 vols. (Oxford, 1990), II, Book 4, paragraph 184, pp. 218–19.

[31] Although Orderic spent his adult life at the Norman monastery of St Evroul, he was born and brought up in Shrewsbury: Chibnall, *The World of Orderic Vitalis*, pp. 3–4.

[32] Coulson, 'The State of Research', p. 172.

[33] Chibnall, 'Orderic Vitalis on Castles', pp. 53–4.

[34] Ibid., p. 53.

[35] Ibid., p. 53, n. 67.

[36] Ibid., p. 53.

wider meaning of the terms *castrum* and *castellum*.[37] His impressive collection of documentary examples includes many instances in which *castrum* and/or *castellum* is/are used to describe lordly fortresses, but also ecclesiastical and urban defences. Examples of these wider meanings start with the annals of the abbey of Saint-Vaast for the year 895 and end with Roger of Wendover writing in 1197.[38] Coulson has provided a similar range of references in pre-Conquest Continental sources to defended towns and the fortified precincts of abbeys as *castra* or *castella*, complementing Verbruggen's thesis very effectively.[39] Crucially, Coulson also notes that pre-Conquest work services of *burh-bot* were Latinized afterwards as *operatio castellorum*, providing further evidence of the linguistic equivalence of *burhs* and early castles.[40] There is, therefore, a substantial amount of documentary evidence already collected, from both before and after the Conquest and from English and Continental sources, to back up a wider range of meanings for the Latin words *castrum* and *castellum*. Any special relationship between the word *castle* and the new Norman fortresses would certainly be of a social nature, as the word did not imply any particular kind of fortification except by context. It would also be entirely possible for this range of meanings to encompass the earlier, Latin-derived loan-word: the small towns or villages of Biblical examples.

A thorough survey of the words *castel*, *castellum* and, indeed, *castrum* in early post-Conquest sources concerned with Britain is much needed. However, even this brief summary shows that the conventional definition of the castle needs to be rethought, as a few castle scholars have been arguing. The strength of this evidence has not previously been identified because, upon seeing castle words in the documentary record, most readers have assumed they could only refer to Norman private fortresses, and have interpreted the sources accordingly. Conversely, the use of alternative words to describe Norman defences has often been ignored, as readers have only been on the look-out for passages containing the word *castle*. The evidence has simply been written out of the record. However, even the most thorough linguistic survey would not be able to provide a complete picture of the range of meaning at one period, or of changes in meaning over time, and many of the examples it identified might at best be highly ambiguous. This is inevitable from the fragmentary nature of the record with which historical linguists have to deal.[41] What follows here is not an attempt to provide exhaustive coverage.

---

[37] J. F. Verbruggen, 'Note sur le sens des mots *castrum*, *castellum*, et quelques autres expressions qui désignent des fortifications', *Revue belge de philologie et d'histoire* 28.1 (1950), 147–55.

[38] Ibid., pp. 148, 152.

[39] Coulson, *Castles in Medieval Society*, p. 45.

[40] Coulson, 'The State of Research', p. 173.

[41] McMahon, *Understanding Language Change*, p. 185.

Instead, the discussion proceeds through a series of carefully selected examples, which provide particular insights into the range of meanings attached to castle words at particular points in the medieval period. Many of these sources have not been examined with the idea of the castle in mind, and illustrate some important aspects of the medieval castle which fall outside the range of definitions previously offered.

Bearing in mind the reductive and normative tendencies castle definitions have had in the past, I have avoided suggesting any alternative definition. Instead I have tried to argue for a broader, less specific understanding of the word for the early period after the introduction of the word to Britain at the Conquest. However, I have come across several medieval explanations of castle terminology, which read rather like definitions. A contemporary definition, like any other kind, may simplify a concept for concision, or apply only to certain contexts, and it may be particularly hard to interpret these nuances in a historical context with incomplete information. However, the following examples have the virtue of being remarkably specific, yet keeping open a number of possibilities. They treat the castle not as a social or political unit, but as a collection of architectural elements in relationship to one another. They are sufficiently broad yet sufficiently succinct to represent the range of possibilities medieval people might have had in mind when they thought about castles. I present them here not as the final word on the meaning of medieval castle words, but as a contemporary illustration of some of the ways in which these words could be understood.

The first example comes from a homily sometimes attributed to Anselm of Canterbury (1033–1109) and dated tentatively to twelfth century or earlier.[42] The work elaborates on the text of Luke 10. 38, and is headed with the Biblical text: 'ipse intravit in quoddam castellum'.[43] The Biblical passage describes Jesus's literal entry into the *castellum* of Bethany to visit Mary and Martha. However, in the Middle Ages, this was interpreted as a figurative description of Jesus's entry into the protective body of the Virgin Mary at the

---

[42] R. D. Cornelius, *The Figurative Castle: A Study in the Mediaeval Allegory of the Edifice with Especial Reference to Religious Writings: A Dissertation* (Bryn Mawr, 1930), p. 43.

[43] Luke 10. 38: 'Factum est autem dum irent, et ipse intravit in quoddam castellum; et mulier quaedam, Martha nomine, excepit illum in domum suam' ('Now it came to pass as they went, that he entered into a certain *town*: and a certain woman named Martha, received him into her house'). In all cases where Biblical passages are cited in the Vulgate, I quote from *Biblia Sacra Vulgatae Editionis* (1959). All translations are taken from *The Holy Bible Translated from the Latin Vulgate: The Old Testament first Published by the English College at Douay and The New Testament first published by the English College at Rheims* (London, Manchester and Glasgow, 1899). I italicize or replace the Douay-Rheims translation of the Vulgate term *castellum* throughout this book in order to problematize assumptions about translations of this word. The Douay-Rheims edition routinely translates this word as 'town' or 'village'.

Incarnation.[44] The author develops this text into an allegory of the Virgin as a *castellum*, using a description of the castle as a basis for his comparison:

> Castellum enim dicitur quaelibet turris, et murus in circuitu eius[45]
>
> (Any tower with a wall around it is called a castle)

Most architectural historians would recognize this arrangement as a castle, yet this description is elegantly succinct and open-ended. A tower surrounded by a wall might well be found in an Anglo-Saxon *burh*, or in a later fortified urban setting, as at Rouen, Le Mans or London, where Norman tower keeps were defended by city walls. It could also, depending on the nature of the tower, refer to an ecclesiastical arrangement. This medieval definition of a castle demonstrates how a broad range of meanings could be understood to come together in a certain combination of structures. It provides a concept of the castle that is both succinct and carries the possibility of application to a wide variety of structures with equal validity. There is nothing here to suggest that castles are necessarily feudal or private fortresses, or that the word can only be applied to particular types of structure. The use of the adjective *quaelibet* (meaning 'any' or 'whatever') is particularly notable, as it indicates the open nature of the definition, inviting readers to supply their own range of examples freely. It encapsulates the inclusiveness the author envisages for the term *castellum*.

The Biblical inspiration for this description makes a compelling case for reintegrating the whole range of excluded, Biblically inspired medieval castle words into the mainstream of the modern understanding of the castle. The open nature of this definition explains simply and effectively how medieval readers of the period could have reconciled their ideas of the castle with the *castella* mentioned in Classical and Biblical contexts. The symbolic comparison of the Virgin Mary to a castle further underlines the point that castles were in no way seen as being incongruous in a Biblical context. Yet this is not an isolated example.

Aelred, abbot of Rievaulx from 1147 to 1167,[46] chooses the same text and a similar interpretation for his sermon on the Assumption of the Virgin.[47] The

---

[44] This text seems to have been interpreted in connection with the Virgin since the seventh century, and interpreted as an image of the Virgin as a *castellum* from the ninth: Cornelius, *The Figurative Castle*, pp. 37–48.

[45] Anselm of Canterbury, 'Homilia IX', in *Patrologiae Latinae Cursus Completus*, ed. J. P. Migne (Paris, 1844–64), 158, col. 645.

[46] P. Fergusson and S. Harrison, *Rievaulx Abbey: Community, Architecture, Memory* (New Haven, 1999), p. 38; M. L. Dutton, 'The Conversion and Vocation of Aelred of Rievaulx: A Historical Hypothesis', in *England in the Twelfth Century*, ed. D. Williams, Proceedings of the 1988 Harlaxton Symposium (1990), pp. 31–49 (p. 33).

[47] Aelred of Rievaulx, 'Sermo XVII: In Assumptione beatae Mariae', in *Patrologiae Latinae*, ed. Migne, 195, cols. 303–5.

castle Aelred describes has three elements, a ditch (for humility), a wall on the ditch (chastity) and a tower (charity):

> In castello fiunt tria quaedam, ut forte sit, scilicet fossatum, murus et turris [48]
>
> (Three things make up a castle, so that it may be strong, and they are a ditch, a wall and a tower)

Again, the openness of this description is striking, especially in contrast to the definitions created by modern historians, cited in the Introduction. Still, there is no suggestion of social or political criteria to define this castle, and still the three elements are described in loose affinity. Perhaps it is no coincidence that Aelred, a monk, leaves open the possibilities for his definition of the castle to be applied to structures such as monasteries as well as to lordly fortresses.[49] There may also be a similar motivation behind the 'quaelibet' of the previous example, inviting readers or listeners to fit the castle scenario to their own surroundings. Once again, the evidence suggests that, far from being carefully segregated from the main contemporary meaning of medieval castle words, Biblical castles were integrated into a broader, less feudal definition of the concept.

This is of course a very small sample from which to draw conclusions about the semantic development of the word *castle*. However, these examples provide evidence of the way the medieval castle could be understood as a number of defensive elements in a certain relationship, rather than as an entity defined by social or political constraints. They also demonstrate that the *castella* of Biblical texts were conceived in a way perfectly consistent with the other defensive buildings of the Middle Ages.

The majority of examples I have mentioned so far are from Latin writing, with only a few examples of the use of *castel* and its variants in English. Post-Conquest England is often described as a trilingual society in which Latin, English and French jostled alongside one another. However, the relationship between these different languages is often not explored by dictionaries and studies, which confine themselves to a single language, or assume that all three are interchangeable and comment no further. It seems especially important to clarify this situation with regard to castle words in English usage, because of the suggestion that a separate, earlier and Latin-derived sense of the English word *castel* was preserved in Middle English for translating *castellum* from Biblical and Classical Latin. I have suggested above that, if Biblical (or Classical) usage of the word *castellum* suggested a village or small town, then these meanings could have been encompassed quite happily by the castle words used in England under the influence of Norman culture. Linguistically speaking, too, there is no reason to suggest the preservation of

---

[48]   Ibid., col. 303.
[49]   I discuss this possibility in more detail in Chapter 3.

a separate and archaic meaning for a word when it occurs in one particular context. Linguists agree on the polysemousness of words: their ability to absorb a number of meanings, even contradictory ones, and their tendency to preserve an older meaning while taking on a newer and changed meaning.[50]

However, it is important to realize that the concept of historical and/or obsolete meanings of a word, and of the process of semantic shift, although an accepted tenet of modern linguistics, was not part of the medieval understanding of words. The idea of semantic change is dependent on Saussure's concept of the arbitrary connection between the linguistic signifier and its referent. Before the formulation of this concept, etymology was thought to reveal not a series of linguistic associations and shifts, but the true and immutable meaning of a word.[51] The contemporary sense of a word was thought to be the meaning it had always held. Therefore medieval English readers of around the beginning of the eleventh century, coming across the word *castellum* in a Biblical or Classical text, must have accepted that this word had the same range of meanings as the *castellum* mentioned in a property charter or chronicle written in their own time.[52] This would probably not have produced many problems for medieval observers, as such words are very often employed in ambiguous contexts, under the assumption that the meaning would be clear. A medieval understanding of the word *castellum*, particularly the broad understanding of the term I have illustrated, would therefore have fitted into a great many historical texts, including Biblical and Classical ones.

In order to illustrate this suggestion, I have looked at a series of closely related texts in different languages which show interaction between Latin and English, and indeed French, castle words. These texts do not belong to the charter or chronicle evidence more usually consulted for castle vocabulary, but they do provide a unique linguistic resource of the early post-Conquest period, just as valid for linguistic information as historical records of a more conventional kind. Geoffrey of Monmouth's *Historia regum Britannie* (*History of the Kings of Britain*) was written in Latin in 1138, and rapidly achieved popularity. In 1155 the poet Wace translated and adapted Geoffrey's work into Anglo-Norman for the English court as the *Roman de Brut*, and at some point between 1189 and the middle of the thirteenth century, Wace's work was

[50] McMahon, *Understanding Language Change*, p. 176; J. Milroy, 'On the Social Origins of Language Change', in *Historical Linguistics: Problems and Perspectives*, ed. C. Jones (London, 1993), pp. 215–36.

[51] McMahon, *Understanding Language Change*, p. 177; R. Lass, *Historical Linguistics and Language Change* (Cambridge, 1997), pp. 10–11, 17.

[52] Some dictionaries suggest that the two loans of the word *castel* into English preserved the different genders of their original languages: the earlier *castel* being neuter like the Latin and the later being masculine like French *chastel*. Other sources, however, acknowledge that such a distinction was never systematically maintained, and by the twelfth century grammatical gender had anyway disappeared; J. A. Burrow and T. Turville-Petre, *A Book of Middle English* (Oxford, 1992), p. 4.

turned into an English poem, now known as the *Brut*, by Laȝamon.[53] These texts span a time of crucial importance in the development of post-Conquest language structures and relationships. Their subject-matter, the history of Britain from its earliest, legendary times, was of great importance and popularity throughout the Middle Ages, and also raises some interesting questions about medieval perceptions of the past, which are highly relevant to this investigation. As each successive text is, loosely speaking, a translation of the former, it has been possible to identify castle words in one text and search the corresponding section of the other two to examine the relationship between the different languages and authors.

Certain patterns have emerged. In many instances where the word *castellum* or *castrum* occurs in the Latin text of Geoffrey of Monmouth's *Historia regum Britannie*, Wace's work contains several more *chastels*, and Laȝamon often adds more *castels*. This numerical incidence is partly accounted for by the relative lengths of the three texts: each expands on the former version. However, on comparison of the positioning of these terms in each of the texts, the transmission of vocabulary from one text to another does seem to follow particular trends. While Geoffrey, in Latin, often uses several different words including *castellum* for fortresses, Wace and Laȝamon are much more consistent: they usually translate Geoffrey's different words only as (respectively) *chastel* and *castel*. This suggests that, at least in the minds of Wace and Laȝamon, vernacular castle words could be used as the equivalent of the Latin word *castellum*, and also of other, interchangeable Latin words; but it also shows in both authors a marked preference in the vernacular for the words *chastel* and *castel*.

For instance, in paragraph 7 of Geoffrey's text,[54] 'tria castella' are mentioned, which are the inheritance of a certain Assaracus;[55] Wace renders these into French as 'tres bons chastels';[56] Laȝamon into English as 'sele þreo castles'.[57] When Geoffrey describes in the next paragraph how Assaracus provisions these strongholds, they appear as *oppida*, and again one of these, an *oppidum*, reappears in paragraph 10.[58] However, these fortifications are described as *chastels* in Wace,[59] who, furthermore, scatters *chastels* freely around the intervening lines, adding instances where no fortress of any kind is

[53] Ibid., p. 94.
[54] I refer here to the first variant version, on which Wace based his translation: *The* Historia regum Britannie *of Geoffrey of Monmouth, 2. The First Variant Version: A Critical Edition*, ed. N. Wright (1988), pp. xi–cxiv; see *Wace's Roman de Brut: A History of the British*, ed. and transl. J. Weiss (Exeter, 1999), Introduction p. xviii.
[55] Geoffrey of Monmouth, *The First Variant Version*, paragraph 7, p. 4.
[56] Wace, *Wace's Roman de Brut*, p. 6, line 196.
[57] Laȝamon, *Brut or Hystoria Brutonum*, ed. W. R. J. Barron and S. C. Weinberg (Harlow, 1995), p. 14, line 195.
[58] Geoffrey of Monmouth, *The First Variant Version*, paragraph 8, p. 4; paragraph 10, p. 5.
[59] Wace, *Wace's Roman de Brut*, p. 6, line 215; p. 8, line 315.

mentioned by Geoffrey.[60] Laȝamon, following Wace, mentions these defences as *castlen*.[61] A similar pattern occurs when Geoffrey employs the word *castrum*. In paragraphs 19 and 20 of Geoffrey's work, the word is used in its various forms seven times.[62] Wace substitutes the word *chastel* and uses it ten times.[63] At this level of analysis, the texts provide a fairly consistent picture, showing an appreciation of the equivalence of castle words in different languages. There also seems to be a marked preference for using the words *chastel* and *castel*, rather than other terms, in French and English, which may be due to the social and linguistic prestige associated with these words in Britain since the Conquest. However, at certain points there does seem to be an attempt to differentiate between structures denoted by castle words and other kinds of defensive buildings.

Geoffrey uses several different words for fortifications, settlements and towns, but when these words occur in close proximity, it can be difficult to know whether they are used pleonastically – to denote the same structure through a pleasing variety of words – or in order to compare different types of structure. However, close examination of the context suggests that different kinds of structure are often implied.[64] Similarly, while Wace and Laȝamon add many *chastels/castels* to their narratives, they also add towns and other kinds of settlements, making it difficult to tell whether they were creating distinctions between these different forms. In Wace's *Roman de Brut*, for example, there are several ambiguous phrases which may or may not be meant pleonastically, such as 'chastels, viles e cites'; and 'Lud fist citez e fist chastels'.[65] Yet sometimes an effort is made to differentiate more clearly between different structures. For example, adapting the line I have just quoted from Wace, Laȝamon narrows down the vocabulary. He writes: 'Castles makede Lud þe king', but then goes on to explain that Lud was especially fond of London, and that there were no castles there except the tower (*tur*) built by Belinus; Lud therefore built a wall about the town (*burh*) of London, which is still to be seen there.[66] This phrasing seems to differentiate the town and fortress quite clearly, implying a careful distinction between the royal stronghold and civic defences. However, this distinction cannot in this case arise

---

60 Ibid., p. 6, lines 201, 216; p. 8, lines 264, 317.
61 Laȝamon, *Brut or Hystoria Brutonum*, p. 14, lines 217, 233.
62 Geoffrey of Monmouth, *The First Variant Version*, pp. 14–16.
63 Wace, *Wace's Roman de Brut*, pp. 25–6, lines 937, 948, 960, 965, 979, 981, 982, 999, 1022, 1024.
64 See J. S. P. Tatlock, *The Legendary History of Britain: Geoffrey of Monmouth's* Historia regum Britannie *and its Early Vernacular Versions* (Berkeley, 1950), pp. 323–6. Although Tatlock does not question the definition of the castle generally accepted at the time he was writing, his analysis of Geoffrey's use of the word *castellum* is attentive and stands on its own merits.
65 Wace, *Wace's Roman de Brut*, p. 40, line 1589; p. 94, line 3745.
66 Laȝamon, *Brut or Hystoria Brutonum*, p. 182, lines 3528–33.

from the perceived difference between a Norman castle and a town wall. The whole train of events Laȝamon describes is set far back into the legendary, pre-medieval, past, so it seems logical to suppose that the tower he mentions must be imagined as an ancient one.

On the other hand, the identification of a tower as the sole castle of London, and the specific mention of Belinus, do suggest that the familiar post-Conquest fortress is implied. The White Tower, the central bulwark of the Tower of London, was in fact built on the orders of William the Conqueror around 1070–80,[67] yet Geoffrey of Monmouth (along with other authors following him) describes the construction of the Tower of London by the legendary king Belinus,[68] who is supposed to have reigned in Britain well before the time of Christ.[69] The distinctive nomenclature of the Tower (as opposed to the Castle) of London is based on a medieval appreciation of the symbolic importance of the White Tower, at the heart of the fortress. As early was 1141, the White Tower is referred to in a charter of Matilda as 'turris Londoniae',[70] and this phrase seems to have been transferred, by the time of Laȝamon's text, to the whole castle. Because the naming of London's castle is so specifically connected to its medieval architecture, the conclusion must be that Laȝamon imagined the White Tower as a much older structure than it actually was, or imagined that the medieval building had an ancient predecessor of a very similar form. The same is true for Geoffrey of Monmouth, who, only about fifty years after its construction, projects the building back into Britain's legendary past.

London is in fact only one of several fortresses mentioned by Geoffrey, Wace and Laȝamon which match up to actual medieval castles. It seems clear that all three authors were influenced by ancient remains which could be seen standing at many of the sites they mention,[71] so it may be that some of their references were to ancient buildings replaced by later castles. However, in some of these cases, as with London, there seems to be an implication that structures either very like or identical to the medieval ones were already present there in the periods the texts describe, and castle words are often used to describe them. These references do seem to indicate that the buildings of the remote past were sometimes, in the medieval imagination, very similar or identical to the buildings of the Middle Ages, and could be named in the same way.[72]

Two important conclusions follow. Firstly, the apparent references to medieval buildings, transposed back into ancient, legendary times, suggest

---

[67] G. Parnell, *English Heritage Book of the Tower of London* (London, 1993), p. 19.
[68] Discussed in Chapter 2, p. 74; Wace, *Wace's Roman de Brut*, p. 82, lines 3217–18; Laȝamon, *Brut or Hystoria Brutonum*, p. 156, lines 3018–19.
[69] The Belinus reference occurs in paragraph 44 of Geoffrey's roughly chronological account; Christ appears in paragraph 64; see Chapter 2, p. 73, n. 147, p. 58, n. 86.
[70] Round, 'Tower and Castle', p. 328.
[71] Tatlock, *The Legendary History of Britain*, p. 323.
[72] See Chapter 4 for a fuller discussion.

that architectural forms could be understood as having existed through historical time without change, just like the medieval understanding of language which precluded the concept of linguistic change over time. Castle-like structures were clearly envisaged as having existed long before the arrival of the Normans, even by the time Geoffrey was writing in 1138, and could be given the same name as the Norman imports. It seems to follow that instances of the word *castellum* in historical texts set similarly in the ancient past – the Bible and Classical authors – were understood as referring to buildings in some ways similar to medieval castles. No special and archaic meaning of *castellum* would have been needed if Biblical and Classical *castella* were imagined in this way. Secondly, the use of castle words to describe ancient remains pushes the medieval understanding of the castle into another dimension. It expands its meanings back across the architecture of the past, to include all fortresses from the fall of Troy, through the ages of the prophets and of Christ, down to the age of Arthur and beyond.

This realization is difficult for modern readers to grasp, partly, I suspect, because we are brought up with a clear archaeological appreciation of ancient history, especially the Roman and Biblical cultures to which the texts in question belong. We know that, when a Classical author described a *castellum* he had in mind some kind of military encampment, and that when Jerome chose the word *castellum* to describe Bethany[73] or Emmaus,[74] he had in mind a village or small town. Modern English speakers, trained by O'Neil and Brown to think of the word *castle* as intrinsically feudal and post-Conquest, cannot accept the idea that, in a medieval context, it could be applied to Biblical or Roman buildings. To us the idea is linguistically and archaeologically anachronistic. The preceding examples show that this is merely received wisdom, yet it has influenced the narrow definition of the castle, and led to the exclusion of Biblical and Classical *castella* from the mainstream medieval meanings of the English word.

There are plenty of additional examples to press home this point. The following passages also begin to illustrate the ways in which the medieval understanding of the English word *castle* changed over the years. They suggest that the word often did become more specifically linked to lordly fortresses, even in Biblical and Classical contexts, but still retained the more general meaning common in earlier usage.

---

[73]   Referred to in Luke 10. 38 (quoted above, n. 43) and John 11. 1: 'Erat autem quidam languens Lazarus a Bethania, de castello Mariae et Marthae soror eius' ('Now there was a certain man sick, named Lazarus, of Bethania, of the *town* of Mary and of Martha her sister').

[74]   Luke 24. 13: 'Et ecce duo ex illis ibant ipsa die in castellum, quod erat in spatio stadiorum sexaginta ab Ierusalem, nomine Emmaus' ('And behold, two of them went, the same day, to a *town* which was sixty furlongs from Jerusalem, named Emmaus').

The first homily in Lambeth MS 487 (*c.*1225) includes a translation of the text of Matthew 21. 2:[75]

> Goth in than castel thet is ongein you, and ye findeth redliche thar ane asse ye-bounden[76]

In this particular instance the *castel* is not in any way specified, and could be imagined by the author of the homily either as a defended town or as a lordly residence of some description. Even though the Biblical text must originally have been meant to refer to a village or town, there is no indication that it must necessarily do so here. *The Southern Passion* (*c.*1325) treats the same text similarly, rendering it:

> Wendeth forth . . . To a castel that agen yow is, and ye shulleth anon fynde an asse[77]

Again, there is nothing in this text to suggest what particular kind of *castel* is envisaged, but neither is there anything to indicate that a village or town is specifically implied. However, in the middle portion of a Life of Christ of around 1300, the context surrounding the word *castel* has shifted somewhat, suggesting rather a specific meaning for the word. In this case the Biblical text is John 11. 1,[78] and the translation is not a literal one: instead the text links Lazarus, through his supposed sisters Mary and Martha, to the *castellum* of Bethany:

> Hit bifel that Lazar the knight In grete siknesse lai In is castel bi side Betanie[79]

Here, Lazarus is glossed as a knight, and his castle is at Bethany, implying that it is envisaged as a lordly residence rather than as a defended town. A similar treatment of the text occurs in *Cursor Mundi* (*c.*1300), which describes how Lazarus and his sisters have jointly inherited a *castel* where Jesus goes to enjoy their hospitality:

> This lazarus o betani
> Had sisters martha and mari,
> Mikel he luved his sisters both,
> Ne soght he never man wit loth,

---

[75] Matthew 21. 2: 'Ite in castellum quod contra vos est et statim invenietis asinam alligatam et pullum cum ea: solvite et adducite mihi' ('Go ye into the *village* that is over against you, and immediately you shall find an ass tied, and a colt with her: loose them and bring them to me').

[76] *Old English Homilies and Homiletic Treatises of the Twelfth and Thirteenth Centuries*, ed. R. Morris, Early English Text Society, original series 34 (1867–73), p. 3, lines 5–6.

[77] *The Southern Passion*, ed. B. D. Brown, Early English Text Society, original series 169 (1927), p. 2, lines 48–50.

[78] Quoted above, n. 73.

[79] *The Middle Portion of the Life of Christ*, ed. C. Horstmann (Münster, 1873), line 679.

> A castel was both his and theirs,
> Thoru eldres ther-of war thei airs.
> To this castel was iesus cald
> Til herberi, als I for-wit tald[80]

This, too, has the air of a lordly fortress, owned jointly by three siblings who offer hospitality there.

Luke 24. 13,[81] a text describing the visit of the disciples to Emmaus, is also consistently rendered into English using the word *castel*.[82] An early fourteenth-century lyric, also emphasizing this castle's function in offering hospitality to the weary traveller, says allegorically of Mary, 'Thou art Emaus, the riche castel,/ Thar resteth alle werie'.[83] Again, this suggests a lordly residence or monastic enclosure more readily than the village intended in the original, Biblical text. These examples continue to demonstrate the links between Biblical castle texts and sites, and medieval defensive architecture. Clearly, the word *castel* could be applied to the *castella* of the Bible without any dramatic change in meaning. Nevertheless, a general shift in the meaning of the word, away from the more general fortified enclosure and towards the lordly fortress, is apparent in some of these later examples. A sermon by Wyclif on the text of Matthew 9. 35[84] demonstrates this succinctly. Wyclif's wording implies that, around 1425, the more general sense had not disappeared completely from the understanding of the castle. However, by this time it might have to be specially explained:

> The gospel seiþ how, *Jesus wente aboute in the cuntre*, both to more places and lesse, *as citees and castellis* . . . Castels ben undirstonden litil tounes, but wallid, as Jerusalem is clepid a cite by Mathew; and sich grete castels ben clepid citees.[85]

The sense of this passage follows the Biblical text, relating that Jesus spread his preaching around amongst different kinds and degrees of place. Wyclif seems at pains to clarify the relationship between the *castellis* and the *citees*, and to justify their comparison in this passage, by reminding his audience of

---

[80] *Cursor Mundi*, ed. R. Morris, Early English Text Society, original series 57, 59, 62, 66 (1874–7, repr. 1961), lines 14128–35.

[81] Quoted above, n. 74.

[82] Further examples are cited in Chapter 3.

[83] (?)William of Shoreham, 'A Song to Mary', in *Medieval English Lyrics: A Critical Anthology*, ed. R. T. Davies (London, 1966, repr. 1971), pp. 103–5 (line 57, p. 105).

[84] Matthew 9. 35: 'Et circuibat Iesus omnes civitates et castella, docens in synagogis eorum, et praedicans evangelium regni, et curans omnem languorem et omnem infirmitatem' ('And Jesus went about all the cities, and *towns*, teaching in their synagogues, and preaching the gospel of the kingdom, and healing every disease, and every infirmity').

[85] John Wyclif, 'Sermon LXIV', in *Select English Works of John Wyclif*, ed. T. Arnold, 3 vols. (Oxford, 1869), I, 197–201 (p. 197).

the formal physical resemblance between the walled defences of towns and the smaller, but similar, castles. This emphasis implies that this was not the foremost sense of the word *castel* at this time, but demonstrates that this meaning could still be revived if the occasion arose.

Notwithstanding a gradual shift in emphasis over time, then, these examples all show (a) that a broad definition of the castle was in fairly extensive use into the later Middle Ages, and (b) that Biblical *castella* participated fully in this meaning. However, this last point also applies to the *castella* of Classical texts. A linguistic and semantic relationship between Latin *castellum* and English *castel* is highlighted in a Middle English translation of the Classical text, Vegetius' *De re Militari*. A chapter with the heading 'Quod civitates & castella aut natura aut opere aut utroque modo debent muniri' is, understandably, rendered as follows: 'How alle townes & castelles beth warded or with kynde or with craft or with bothe'.[86] This is a fairly straightforward translation. Once again the original text suggests to the medieval translator the similarities of form shared by the walled town and the lordly fortress, the main difference being that of scale. Having observed this comparison, the translator sticks to it, introducing *castels* into his translation at several other points where the original text mentions defences for *urbes*, but not for *castella*.[87] Clearly for this medieval translator, as for Wyclif, it was still possible to understand a lordly fortress as a smaller version of a defended town. All these later passages, whether of Biblical or Classical origins, acknowledge the continued possibility of a range of meanings for castle words, while demonstrating that their foremost meaning at this later period had become more specialized towards more private, lordly fortresses.

So far, this chapter has focused on the varying meaning of castle words in their different contexts, investigating examples that seem to demonstrate meanings well beyond the limits often set by modern definitions of the castle. This has sometimes involved discussion of complex cultural attitudes towards language, architecture and the past, but has for the moment mainly avoided wider cultural and artistic questions. In the following section, I will begin to explore some of the broader implications of the range of meanings I have suggested for medieval castle words. This process will continue throughout the book. However, I will continue to tie my argument securely to particular examples, as these display the richness and importance of the medieval idea of the castle whilst discouraging generalization.

*

---

[86] *The Earliest English Translation of Vegetius'* De re militari, ed. G. Lester (Heidelberg, 1988), pp. 160, 123.

[87] Vegetius, *Flavi Vegeti Renati Epitoma Rei Militaris*, ed. C. Lang (Leipzig, 1885), p. 131: compare with Lester, *The Earliest English Translation*, p. 162; also Lang p. 130 with Lester pp. 160–1.

In the Introduction, which discussed the phenomenon of the medieval castle, this book argued that defensive architecture of the periods before and after the Conquest was not as different as has often been assumed. In the previous section of this chapter, this exercise was repeated in linguistic terms, to suggest that the meaning of medieval castle words was broader than has usually been recognized. While they often referred to the new Norman fortresses, castle words were also used for a wide variety of other defences, both medieval and ancient. Both these arguments challenge accepted ideas of the castle, expanding it from a neat and distinctive phenomenon into a broader and less manageable concept. They encroach into the social realm, disproving the idea that the castle was necessarily a private, feudal fortress, and showing instead that it could also be a communal structure such as a fortified town or a monastery. They reach into the past, demonstrating that Roman fortresses and Biblical sites could be gathered into the castle category. They also extend into religion, showing that Biblical and Classical instances of the word *castellum* relate precisely to the mainstream medieval concept of the castle, rather than to an obscure and archaic sub-category.

The three chapters that follow tackle these issues, separating out different themes with which the castle was associated: 'The Urban Castle', 'The Spiritual Castle' and 'The Imperial Castle'. There are, nevertheless, many points of contact between the ideas in these chapters. The main section of this chapter has concentrated on textual analysis and borrowed much of its methodology from linguistics. By contrast, subsequent chapters explore examples from a wide variety of sources and media and employ the apparatus of several different disciplines, in order to assemble a composite image of perceptions of the castle across medieval English culture. In order to introduce this change of approach, and as a summary of the main ideas in this chapter, I will end with an example that crosses all these boundaries. It demonstrates the cultural currency of all the various connotations I have noted for the medieval castle, but also shows the infinite flexibility and richness of the castle as a cultural icon, combining all three of this book's main themes in one image.

The example is provided by a fifteenth-century civic seal of Colchester (Plate 1). The round seal shows on its obverse side an architectural screen or façade of canopies and niches, inhabited by images of St Helena, Christ and several angels and shields. The reverse of the seal shows a collection of buildings surrounded by crenellated walls with towers, standing behind flowing water. Within the walls a variety of roofs and towers can be seen. The inscription around the edge of the obverse side reads:

SIGILLU . COMMUNE . BALLIVORU . 7 . COMMUNITATIS . VILLE . DOMINI . REGIS . COLCESTRIE .

(Common seal of the bailiffs and of the community of Colchester, town of our Lord the King) while that on the reverse reads:

INTRAVIT . IHC . IN . QUODDAM . CASTELLUM . ET . MULIER . QUEDAM . EXCEPIT . ILLUM .

(Jesus entered into a certain castle and a certain woman received him)

The significance of the obverse image is fairly clear from a basic knowledge of Colchester's civic paraphernalia. St Helena was believed to be the daughter of Cole, the legendary ancient king of Colchester, celebrated in nursery rhyme and thought to have provided the city with its name. Cole reputedly married his daughter to the Roman emperor Constantius, when the latter arrived in Britain with imperial aims. Helena was thus a member of the British royalty in her own right, as well as an empress by marriage; by Constantius she was also the mother of Constantine the Great, the first Christian emperor. Helena's piety was legendary; it was associated with the conversion of her son as well as with her own pilgrimage to the Holy Land, during which she supposedly discovered the remains of the True Cross.[88] This accounts for the imagery on the obverse of the seal: St Helena, daughter of Cole and Colchester's patron saint, holds the True Cross. Christ appears above, authenticating his saint's holy achievements. The supporting angels hold the arms of St George and England, while another shield underneath the saint displays the arms of the city, denoting the royal and national status of both Helena and Colchester. The inscription on this side of the seal (quoted above) reinforces the references in the imagery to the royal status of the town of Colchester, and also introduces a link between the elite and the community of the place. It declares that the seal is shared by the bailiffs – the local agents of royal administration, often put in charge of castles – and by the people of the town.

The imagery on the reverse of the seal has been seen as somewhat problematic. However, I believe this side of the seal is equally suggestive of links between the town's elite and its community. Experts on civic seals have not been able to agree on the significance of the architectural image depicted here. Some see 'the whole town' of Colchester.[89] Another describes 'a castle

---

[88] See G. Rosser, 'Myth, Image and Social Process in the English Medieval Town', *Urban History* 23.1 (1996), 5–25 (p. 8); Jacobus de Voragine, *The Golden Legend, Readings on the Saints*, ed. and transl. W. G. Ryan, 2 vols. (Princeton, 1993. repr. 1995), I, 278. Accounts of Helena's origins are various, but often suggest that she is the daughter of a British king: de Voragine, *The Golden Legend*, I, 281. See also E. D. Hunt, 'Constantine and the Holy Land (ii) Helena – History and Legend', in *Holy Land and Pilgrimage in the Later Roman Empire, AD 312–460* ed. E. D. Hunt (Oxford, 1982), pp. 28–49 (pp. 28–9); J. F. Matthews, 'Macsen, Maximus, and Constantine', *Welsh History Review* 11 (1982–3), 431–48 (pp. 439, 441–6 *and passim*).

[89] P. D. A. Harvey and A. McGuinness, *A Guide to British Medieval Seals* (London, 1996), p. 109.

or castellated town', although he later suggests that 'this design was probably intended as a bird's-eye view of the town', and tentatively identifies 'the lofty tower' as representing Colchester Castle.[90] This seems to me another case where distinctions between public and private defences, and public and private interests, are deliberately avoided. The inscription on the obverse of the seal hints at the co-operation between the town and castle when it mentions both the town community and the bailiffs. The imagery of the reverse side is a continuation of this theme, depicting a structure that fuses walled town and walled castle into one, to symbolize the common interests represented by the seal.[91]

The imagery of the town and castle also interacts in other respects with the depiction of St Helena on the obverse. Helena's birthplace of Colchester has connections with the Roman empire through its archaeology and architecture. Both the town and castle of Colchester are founded on the remains of a Roman city that was once large and prosperous. In parts of the town walls the standing Roman material is not only visible but formidable, standing over six feet high for extensive stretches. Colchester Castle keep was built by the Normans on the plinth of the largest temple of the city, and Roman materials were re-used throughout the building (see Plates IV and V).[92] The antiquity of some of this material was well understood by medieval observers. A volume of civic annals, compiled following the inauguration of a new civic constitution in 1372, identified the Roman plinth as the remains of King Cole's ancient palace.[93] Colchester Castle, then, represented continuity between the ancient past and the medieval present, joining together in one building the aspirations of the Roman empire and the royal and architectural prestige of medieval England. The material remains of Colchester's ancient royal family were thus localized in an important monument, but were also deployed for the glory of the town as a whole. The ambiguous architectural image of the seal provides a visual analogue to this fusion of civic and royal symbolism.[94]

The inscription encircling the reverse of the seal (quoted above) has not until now been discussed by commentators, due, I suppose, to its seeming incongruence with the rest of the imagery of this seal and of other seals in general. It is in fact an adaptation of the Biblical text, Luke 10. 38. I noted earlier in this chapter that, although this text literally refers to Jesus' entry into the village of Bethany to meet Mary and her sister Martha, it was understood in medieval exegesis to refer allegorically to the Incarnation, at which Jesus

---

[90] G. Pedrick, *Borough Seals of the Gothic Period* (London, 1904), p. 55.
[91] Similar architectural imagery occurs on many civic seals of the Middle Ages, in Continental Europe as well as Britain. I discuss this more fully in Chapter 2, pp. 64–70.
[92] See P. J. Drury, 'Aspects of the Origin and Development of Colchester Castle', *The Archaeological Journal* 139 (1983), 302–419.
[93] Rosser, 'Myth, Image and Social Process', p. 8.
[94] I discuss these themes in more detail in Chapter 4.

entered into the body of the Virgin Mary. The inscription on the seal seems to invite readers to incorporate this textual and allegorical tradition into their understanding of the seal. It acknowledges the potential for religious symbolism in the medieval castle – not just in the textual castles described in theological treatises, but also in a solid, specific, stone-and-mortar castle set within the English medieval landscape. The way this particular text is used on the Colchester seal, unintroduced and unglossed, also suggests that this potential was widely understood. The text is dropped in casually, on the assumption that observers will understand the connection between the inscription and the architectural image on the reverse of the seal.

However, the text and its religious symbolism also relate to Colchester's legendary history in a similar way to the rest of the seal's imagery. Medieval figurative interpretations of Luke 10. 38 focus on the hospitality offered by Mary and Martha at their castle in Bethany, extending this into a gendered allegory of the castle as the Virgin's body and, specifically, her womb, into which Christ entered at the Incarnation.[95] The use of this text on the Colchester seal seems to me to allude to a similar figurative transformation of a castle into a female body, this time that of Colchester Castle into the body of Helena. One version of Colchester's legendary history records that Constantine was born to Helena, his royal English mother, in Colchester,[96] and what better location for this than her father's supposed palace, Colchester Castle? Helena is thus typologically another Mary, Constantine another Christ, and Colchester another Bethany, becoming through its legendary history the site of one of the significant events of Christian history. It is, perhaps, significant that the seal inscription abbreviates the Biblical text, so as not to include the name of the *mulier* (woman) to which it refers: this seems to invite comparison with the famous Christian woman depicted on the other side of the seal. Although the Biblical text specifies Martha, Helena could be supplied here, to fill the gap. In the imagery of the Colchester seal, then, the castle is deliberately associated with the community and the civic defences; it is connected to imperial Rome both materially and in local legends; it is also claimed as a participant in the Christian imagery and history of the age.

All three of these possibilities – urban, imperial and spiritual – are ignored by the standard definition of the castle in modern scholarship. However, I have set out to show, by just one example, that modifications to the accepted view are essential in attempting to understand the medieval castle in its contemporary cultural, linguistic and material setting. The castles that came over with the Norman Conquest were to some extent innovations, but their novelty was not necessarily their defining concept. Castles were indeed associated with the arrival of the Norman culture and language in Britain, but

---

95 See Chapter 3, p. 80 and *passim*.
96 Rosser, 'Myth, Image and Social Process', p. 8.

they also carried associations with a range of other defences and with the ancient architecture of Roman and Biblical times. These diverse and perhaps unexpected associations can be discerned by linguistic analysis. However, I have also begun to show how these resonances can be traced in textual and visual representations of castles, as well as in the buildings themselves.

CHAPTER TWO

The Urban Castle

> And also this present boke is necessarye to alle cytezens & haby-
> taunts in townes and castellis/ for they shal see, How somtyme troye
> the graunte/ and many other places stronge and inexpugnable, have
> ben be-sieged sharpely & assayled, And also coragyously and
> valyauntly defended/ and the sayd boke is att this present tyme
> moche necesarye/ for to enstructe smale and grete, for everyche in
> his ryght/ to kepe and defende[1]

In the previous chapter I showed that the medieval understanding of castle
words allowed for a wide degree of overlap between private fortifications and
fortified communal and urban enclosures. I used linguistic arguments to explore
this link mainly at the level of verbal usage and understanding. However, in this
chapter I concentrate on the ways in which the relationship between castle and
town was explored symbolically, in medieval literature and art, and in the spatial and political juxtaposition of urban castles and town defences.

The quotation cited above, from Caxton's preface to his *Eneydos*, serves as
introduction to a number of key ideas about the relationship between the
medieval castle and town. Phrases such as Wyclif's 'litil tounes . . . wallid'[2]
invoke the affinities between castles and towns. However, Caxton gives
a broader and more nuanced appreciation of this relationship. The subject-
matter of the text – the siege of Troy – is given an exemplary function 'to
enstructe', directed towards dwellers in both 'townes and castellis'. Both
communal and private defences are thus united in their joint duty 'to kepe
and defend'; but this collective responsibility is defined by social divisions.
Two groups, respectively of the city and of the castle, are contrasted socially
as 'citizens and habytaunts' and as 'smale and grete'. Their common purpose
is expressed through carefully differentiated hierarchies of person.

Yet Troy is ultimately an example of failure as well as of heroic joint
endeavour. It was sacked by the Greeks through the treachery of one of its

---

[1] William Caxton, *Caxton's* Eneydos, *1490, Englished from the French* Livre des
Eneydes, *1483*, ed. W. T. Cutley and F. J. Furnivall, Early English Text Society, extra
series 57 (1890, repr. 1962), p. 10, lines 9–17.

[2] John Wyclif, 'Sermon LXIV', in *Select English Works of John Wyclif*, ed. T. Arnold,
3 vols. (Oxford, 1869), I, 197–201 (p. 197), discussed in the previous chapter,
pp. 37–8.

own citizens, in a war brought about by the selfish lust of a member of its aristocracy. The knowledge of this ultimate failure lies behind the exhortations of Caxton's preface, adding poignancy to the exemplary united efforts in its defence. Troy might, then, be interpreted as a negative exemplar: a proof of the ultimate incompatibility of the interests of commons and elite and of the futility of struggling for the common good. Yet the positive example is also a strong part of the medieval Troy tradition.

As I will argue later, medieval legends renewed Troy, recreating its people, its customs and even physical echoes of its famous defences, in the cities and citadels of medieval Europe. This idea is perhaps acknowledged by the phrase 'troy the graunte' ('Troy the great') in the extract from Caxton: this seems to refer to the original Troy, differentiating it from the newer Troys founded all over medieval Europe.[3] Troy's renewal is the reward for the communal efforts of the vast majority of its inhabitants: their positive example is commemorated in the new cities. However, the negative overtones of the Troy story, expressed in treachery and discord, also make their appearance at regular intervals.[4] It seems to me that this dual example, of heroic success and of failure through treachery, echoes the dynamics of social relations in contemporary cities, where co-operation between the different groups within the class hierarchy was the ideal, even though conflict and mistrust might be the reality.[5]

This duality is a recognized feature of Britain's urban foundation myths and their performance in medieval society. Civic legends and pageants explored publicly the dynamics of urban identity and power, negotiating the relationship between civic community, governing elite and royal power.[6] Social bonding is recognized as an important function of foundation legends throughout Europe from the seventh century down to the beginning of the

---

[3] J. Clark, 'Trinovantum – the Evolution of a Legend', *Journal of Medieval History* 7 (1981), 135–51 (pp. 144–5).

[4] S. Federico, 'A Fourteenth-Century Erotics of Politics: London as a Feminine New Troy', *Studies in the Age of Chaucer* 19 (1997), 121–55 (pp. 121–4 and *passim*).

[5] See S. Reynolds, *Kingdoms and Communities in Western Europe, 900–1300*, 2nd edn (Oxford, 1997), pp. 153–4.

[6] G. Rosser, 'Myth, Image and Social Process in the English Medieval Town', *Urban History* 23.1 (1996), 5–25; S. Lindenbaum, 'Ceremony and Oligarchy: The London Midsummer Watch' and L. Attreed, 'The Politics of Welcome: Ceremonies and Constitutional Development in Later Medieval English Towns', both in *City and Spectacle in Medieval Europe*, ed. B. A. Hanawalt and K. L. Reyerson (Minneapolis, 1994), pp. 171–88, 208–231. Studies such as these question the reading of pageants and their legends by scholars such as Charles Phythian-Adams, who argued that they expressed only social cohesion: C. Phythian-Adams, 'Ceremony and the Citizen: The Communal Year at Coventry, 1450–1550', in *Crisis and Order in English Towns, 1500–1700*, ed. P. Clark and P. Slack (London, 1972), pp. 57–85; discussion in Lindenbaum, 'Ceremony and Oligarchy: The London Midsummer Watch', p. 172.

fourteenth.[7] However, these myths could also become political instruments in conflicts between different classes or nationalities.[8] Civic seals have been the subject of similar discussions, addressing their capacity to overcome the uncertainties of urban power-relations through the selection and publication of a communal civic identity. These seals often portray urban harmony,[9] but idealized images of social cohesion cannot be read as a simple reflection of the civic reality. Rather, they are a projection of the effort to resolve the multiple conflicts of the medieval urban situation.[10] With some seals, the depiction of a central castle in relation to its surrounding town wall expresses not a lack of conflict between the ruling aristocracy and the powerful civic interests, but its painstaking resolution.[11]

Non-defensive architecture of medieval civic government, including town halls and guild halls, has been the subject of careful social analysis, considering its spatial, commercial and political implications, and investigating its place in this dual dynamic.[12] Castle imagery also has its part to play in these negotiations. Several prominent medieval castles feature in foundation legends, from Colchester Castle (supposedly founded by King Cole)[13] to Arundel Castle (legendarily built by the hero Bevis of Hamtoun).[14] Depictions of these legends in literature and civic record had their positive and negative sides. However, scholarly discussion of castles themselves, as participants in the negotiation of urban power relations, has been overwhelmingly negative. The usual definition of castles as exclusively private and feudal establishments has placed them in diametrical opposition to communal and urban interests for many modern castle scholars. Christopher Drage's article on urban castles characterizes this view of the relationship succinctly:

---

[7] S. Reynolds, 'Medieval *Origines Gentium* and the Community of the Realm', *History* 68 (1983), 375–90 (p. 390).

[8] For example, with Edward I's invocation of the Brutus myth to prove his right to the overlordship of Scotland; ibid., p. 377.

[9] B. Bedos-Rezak, 'Towns and Seals: Representation and Signification in Medieval France', *Bulletin of the John Rylands Library* 72.3 (1990), 35–48 (pp. 35, 46).

[10] Ibid., p. 39 and *passim*.

[11] Ibid., p. 45.

[12] See for example, R. Tittler, *Architecture and Power: The Town Hall and the English Urban Community c.1500–1640* (Oxford, 1991); G. Sheeran, *Medieval Yorkshire Towns: People, Buildings, Spaces* (Edinburgh, 1998).

[13] Rosser, 'Myth, Image and Social Process in the English Medieval Town', p. 8; discussed in Chapter 1, pp. 40–1.

[14] J. Fellows, 'Sir Bevis of Hamtoun in Popular Tradition', *Proceedings of the Hampshire Archaeological and Natural History Society* 42 (1986), 139–45 (pp. 139, 142, 143–4). Helen Fulton has recently explored a number of other texts in which castle and town are represented in a harmonious relationship, or even symbolically fused together. She identifies Rome, Troy and Jerusalem as important models for idealized depictions of medieval cities: H. Fulton, 'The Medieval Town as Allegory', in *Representations of Urban Culture in Medieval Literature* (forthcoming). I am most grateful to Helen Fulton for access to draft copies of these pieces.

The familiar association of town and castle conceals a dichotomy that exists between them. A town is a community living off commerce . . . with a considerable potential for self-organization, which could lead to outstanding corporate and individual liberty. A castle is essentially a private institution, 'the fortified residence of a lord'.[15]

Castle and town are here contrasted in economic, social and administrative terms: the differences between them do indeed appear great from this perspective. It is not necessary to reiterate the arguments I presented earlier for a more flexible definition of the castle. However, it is worth noting here that there are as many problems in attempting to define, translate and understand medieval town words as there are for castle words, especially for the early period around and after the Conquest.[16]

Nevertheless, this kind of definition has set the pattern in castle studies. Contrasting relationships have been proposed between two different types of medieval castles and their towns, depending on whether the castles are seen as 'urban' or 'primary'. The former are defined as castles imposed on existing urban centres, often by the disruptive means of extensive demolition of existing buildings; the latter are explained as castles built in non-urban areas which then attracted towns to settle at their gates, to exploit commercial opportunities.[17] The division between urban and primary castles is based on evidence of the foundation circumstances of the castle and/or the new borough. The urban castle is read as an instrument of oppression, thrust upon a community for the purposes of intimidation and administrative and legal control, and hostile to its attempts to gain economic rights. The primary castle, by contrast, is seen to provide employment and protection for the community, from which it in turn requires services and revenues.[18] This reading

[15] C. Drage, 'Urban Castles', in *Urban Archaeology in Britain*, ed. J. Schofield and R. Leech, Council for British Archaeology Research Report 61 (1987), pp. 117–32 (p. 117). Cantor takes a similar approach: 'Fortified towns have been a common and well-established military practice throughout history and, as in the case of the A-S *burh*, were communal in nature. Castles and fortified houses, on the other hand, belonged uniquely to the Middle Ages and were distinguished by their private character': L. Cantor, *The English Medieval Landscape* (London, 1982), p. 127.

[16] See for example A.-M. Svensson, *Middle English Words for 'Town': A Study of Changes in a Semantic Field* (Göteborg, 1997); S. Reynolds, *An Introduction to the History of Medieval Towns* (Oxford, 1977), pp. 24, 31, 33–4; Reynolds, *Kingdoms and Communities in Western Europe*, p. 157; Bedos-Rezak, 'Towns and Seals', p. 39.

[17] Drage, 'Urban Castles', p. 117 and *passim*; Schofield and Vince repeat this distinction: J. Schofield and A. Vince, *Medieval Towns* (London, 1994), p. 42; Pounds describes a similar dual scheme, maintaining a distinction between the 'castle-gate town' and castles imposed during conquest on existing towns: N. J. G. Pounds, *The Medieval Castle in England and Wales: A Social and Political History* (Cambridge, 1990, repr. 1994), pp. 207–21.

[18] Pounds, *The Medieval Castle in England and Wales*, pp. 215–16; Drage, 'Urban Castles', p. 117.

is even extended to the spatial arrangement of castles in the urban setting. A marginal location is seen as an important characteristic of the urban castle, manifesting spatially its uneasy relationship with the urban populace. This supposedly ensured a quick escape route to the surrounding countryside for the castle's inhabitants, should the town turn against them.[19] With primary castles, on the other hand, the castle could face into and be surrounded by its friendly urban community without cause for concern. The twin states of conflict and harmony, which were combined in the medieval understanding of an exemplary city like Troy, are thus split between two different kinds of urban context which apparently have little in common with one another.

This binary categorization of urban/primary castle/town relations reveals much about the foundation circumstances of different sites. Yet the origin, constitution or economy of a town does not define its development.[20] In the everyday experience of its inhabitants, things might end up being very similar for a town at the gate of a primary or an urban castle. The burgesses of secondary castle boroughs certainly profited from their economic rights. However, an urban castle too could stimulate growth in the local community, through demands for craftwork and commerce and through opportunities for employment in the administrative machinery based in the castle.[21] Social advantages, such as some degree of self-government, could also be granted to both kinds of town. Both sorts of communities were under the obligation to perform various duties for the castle, but these too could vary enormously according to different circumstances and might be of a similar nature, such as the obligation to bake at the lord's oven.[22] Spatial layout might not, in the end, be so different either.[23] While foundation circumstances could influence the layout and initial growth of towns,[24] they did not permanently determine their form or orientation.[25] The following examples set out some of the types of evidence that have been seized on in this debate, but also show how these can be viewed from a contrary perspective. They are by no means typical or comprehensive examples, but they raise some important points, and provide a useful basis for later discussion.

---

[19] Drage, 'Urban Castles', pp. 117–19; Pounds, *The Medieval Castle in England and Wales*, p. 207. This idea goes back as early as E. S. Armitage, *The Early Norman Castles of the British Isles* (London, 1912), p. 96.

[20] Reynolds, *An Introduction to the History of Medieval Towns*, p. 52.

[21] Pounds, *The Medieval Castle in England and Wales*, p. 215; Reynolds, *An Introduction to the History of Medieval Towns*, p. 43.

[22] Pounds, *The Medieval Castle in England and Wales*, p. 221.

[23] Schofield and Vince, *Medieval Towns*, p. 43.

[24] See Schofield and Vince, *Medieval Towns*, pp. 35–46; Hindle's case study of Ludlow shows the complications revealed by detailed analysis of urban spatial relationships over time: B. P. Hindle, *Medieval Town Plans* (Princes Risborough, 1990), pp. 57–61.

[25] Hindle, *Medieval Town Plans*, pp. 55–6.

The Tower of London has been called 'the most complete of urban castles'.[26] William of Poitiers famously records that in 1067 William the Conqueror left London for a few days while several fortifications were erected in the city, including one on the site of the Tower of London, to protect him from hostile population.[27] The defences consisted at this stage of an enclosure thrown up hastily against the south-east corner of the extant Roman city wall.[28] The siting, the hostility of the local populace and the speed of construction all accord with expectations of an urban castle, imposed on an existing town and its population as an instrument of conquest and oppression. The royal status of the Tower also fits this model. More than half the royal castles built before 1100 were sited in pre-existing towns,[29] and although this may have been a deliberate strategy for terrifying the urban populace into submission, it seems likely that urban sites were primarily chosen as a way of ensuring some continuity with the existing system of local administration.[30] Royal castles were situated at the centre of many of the old Anglo-Saxon shires and became official bases for the new sheriffs who administered these counties.[31] In about half of royal castles (as for a time at London) the sheriff also held the post of constable of the castle, a more permanent royally-appointed post, which often became hereditary.[32] The administrative role of royal castles under these officers varied, but they were certainly part of a system of social and economic control. The Tower of London provides a vivid, though exceptional, demonstration of the range of uses to which an urban castle might be put. It housed part of the king's wardrobe, an arsenal, a mint and many administrative staff and became the main storage site for administrative records.[33] It was also a repository for the national treasure and a distribution depot for the national wine trade.[34] Like other pre-existing urban sites taken over at the Conquest, urban self-determination was well established in London with a regular meeting of the Folkmoot and Husting.[35] It is

---

[26] Pounds, *The Medieval Castle in England and Wales*, pp. 213, 207. See also Drage, 'Urban Castles', p. 121.

[27] William of Poitiers, *Gesta Guillelmi: The Deeds of William*, ed. and transl. R. C. H. Davis and M. Chibnall (Oxford, 1998), Book 2, paragraph 34, pp. 160–3.

[28] S. Thurley, E. Impey and P. Hammond, *The Tower of London* (London, 1996), pp. 45–6; *A History of the King's Works*, ed. H. M. Colvin, A. Taylor and R. A. Brown, 6 vols. (London, 1963), II, 707.

[29] Pounds, *The Medieval Castle in England and Wales*, p. 57; Drage, 'Urban Castles', p. 117.

[30] Pounds, *The Medieval Castle in England and Wales*, pp. 57–8, 92; Drage, 'Urban Castles', p. 121.

[31] Pounds, *The Medieval Castle in England and Wales*, pp. 91–101.

[32] Ibid., pp. 87–90, 96.

[33] Ibid., pp. 90, 98, 101.

[34] Ibid., pp. 100–1.

[35] C. N. L. Brooke with G. Keir, *London 800–1216: The Shaping of a City* (London, 1975), pp. ix–xx; 53, 154, 178, 249–51.

easy to see how conflicts of jurisdiction and interest arose with the arrival of the Tower and its administrative apparatus.[36] As early as 1141 Londoners declared a commune and controversies and protests continued, for example in the riots of the 1260s.[37] Yet this unrest produced generous concessions. By the mid twelfth century, a London mayor is recorded – an officially recognized representative of the population's interests – and the violent demands for a commune gained for Londoners economic privileges much greater than those enjoyed by the communities of 'primary' castles, such as Edward I's planted Welsh boroughs.[38]

To turn to the primary castle model, Edward I's Welsh plantations are often seen as representing 'the apogee of town and castle foundation'.[39] Town and castle were undoubtedly intended to be mutually supportive in exactly the sense proposed for primary castles. In several cases – Rhuddlan, Flint, Conwy and Caernarfon – town and castle were planned and built together; the latter two were also defended together by a continuous circuit of walls, a physical relationship expressing their mutual dependence.[40] Borough charters for several of these settlements, including Flint, were based on the generous terms granted by Henry III to his own planted borough of New Montgomery, including rights to a gild merchant, two fairs and a weekly market (although, as I have noted, the citizens of London, for example, gained even greater privileges).[41] These favourable economic circumstances were intended to entice the surrounding Welsh population into peaceable trading relationships with – and/or settlement in – the planted towns.[42] The aspiration towards harmony and prosperity was also communicated in the name of one of these foundations, Beaumaris (beautiful marsh), reminiscent of the optimistic names often applied to the French bastides founded under similar circumstances.[43] However, it is clear that the expected commerce never came to the Welsh planted towns,[44] and in their early years destructive Welsh raids ensured that they were not sites of peace and prosperity, as had been hoped.[45]

---

[36] Pounds, *The Medieval Castle in England and Wales*, p. 211; Drage, 'Urban Castles', p. 117 and *passim*.

[37] Reynolds, *An Introduction to the History of Medieval Towns*, pp. 105, 107–8, 123.

[38] Ibid., p. 217.

[39] Ibid., p. 129.

[40] A. Taylor, *The Welsh Castles of Edward I* (London and Ronceverte, 1986), pp. 16–17, 45, 79; M. Beresford, *New Towns of the Middle Ages: Town Plantation in England, Wales and Gascony* (London, 1967), p. 41; Drage, 'Urban Castles', pp. 117, 128; Pounds, *The Medieval Castle in England and Wales*, pp. 218–20.

[41] Beresford, *New Towns of the Middle Ages*, p. 41.

[42] Ibid., p. 35; Schofield and Vince, *Medieval Towns*, p. 29.

[43] For example, Beaulieu (beautiful place), Monségur (safe mount), Sauveterre (safe land), Bonnegarde (good defence); Beresford, *New Towns of the Middle Ages*, pp. 98, 143, 186, 187.

[44] Schofield and Vince, *Medieval Towns*, p. 32.

[45] See, for example, Taylor, *The Welsh Castles of Edward I*, pp. 30–1, 72–3, 85–7.

Spatial contrasts between these particular urban and primary castles are also difficult to justify. Caernarfon, for example, is located at one end of a continuous circuit of walls, separated from the town by a gate facing into the borough. Although the different elements at Caernarfon were planned and built together, their arrangement bears several similarities to that of London, which was constructed under very different circumstances. At London, the Tower nestles in a corner of the circuit of city walls. Like Caernarfon Castle it is separated from the city by the main castle gate facing onto the town, an arrangement that does not fit the spatial politics usually attributed to the urban castle, where escape to the countryside is seen as a high priority.[46]

These examples have demonstrated some of the evidence which has led to differentiations between primary and urban castles, but have also shown that the underlying reality of the situation, spatially, economically and politically, was not clear-cut. In both kinds of foundations, conflicts could arise and privileges could be granted. There are several notable reasons why a binary view of castles and their towns has prevailed in castle studies. Apart from the unhelpfully narrow definition of the castle in common currency, Charles Coulson has identified a consistent contemporary bias in the documentary evidence dealing with conflicts between castles and their urban (and, indeed, rural neighbours), amounting to what he terms 'castle-phobia'. He has re-examined the documentary evidence often cited to demonstrate castles' socially oppressive role, and has concluded that much of it was promulgated by ecclesiastics, jealous of threats to their own powers and defences. Much of the remaining evidence can be turned on its head, as with the examples I have discussed above. It demonstrates the support as well as the control exerted by castles, in settling disputes and administrating at the heart of the community, and, through rendability (by which a castle automatically reverted back to the monarch in times of trouble), in peacekeeping and protecting the realm.[47] Coulson's arguments are complex, as befits his evidence, but demonstrate forcefully the need for a re-evaluation of previous assumptions about castles and towns:

> The paradox that 'castles', while being to some extent 'private' because individual, familial and dynastic, were at the same time institutionally (and, with varying capacity, also structurally) public places, has its counterpart in the walled boroughs. Towns, seemingly more 'public', were hardly less ambivalent. Although usually greater in area and population . . . towns were nevertheless in law 'private' collective entities'.[48]

---

[46] Pounds, *The Medieval Castle in England and Wales*, pp. 212–15.

[47] C. Coulson, 'Battlements and the Bourgeoisie: Municipal Status and the Apparatus of Urban Defence', *Medieval Knighthood* 5 (1995), 119–75; C. Coulson, *Castles in Medieval Society: Fortresses in England, France, and Ireland in the Central Middle Ages* (Oxford, 2003); for 'castle-phobia' see especially pp. 117–25; for castles' peacekeeping and administrative roles see especially pp. 128–88.

[48] Coulson, *Castles in Medieval Society*, p. 182.

With this insight, boundaries between castles and towns begin to blur, and the legal and administrative reality behind linguistic usages such as Caxton's 'litil tounes . . . wallid' is revealed. However, Coulson lays some of the blame for long years of misrepresentation of such evidence at the door of literature.[49] In this chapter I therefore concentrate on several positive depictions of the relationship between town and castle in literary and artistic representations. Like the example of Troy, the city with its castle could embody both harmony and conflict in medieval literature, as in medieval life. For both, the urban ideal was harmony and cohesion, but for both the reality might fall far short of this.

London provides the main focus for this chapter. Although of course the economic and political situation was very different to today's, the capital city was still particularly important in medieval England.[50] The control of London was a pivotal factor in the success of any would-be monarch and for this reason the Tower of London was the most important stronghold in the kingdom in political terms. Just as importantly for my purposes, the medieval mythologies and symbolisms of both the city and its main castle are particularly well documented and suggestive. London could never be claimed to exemplify the cities, or castles, of the rest of the country, but the prominence of the city, its depictions and symbolic connotations, signal the range of possibilities in perceptions of medieval castle and town relations.

I have already noted that the Tower of London has been interpreted as an archetypally oppressive castle. I have also cited historical evidence of conflict between royal control (represented by the castles) and the interests of the urban elite, but shown how this was balanced by other factors in London's design and history which align it with more positive models of the town/castle relationship. Both these positive and negative overtones are present in literary and artistic representations of London, creating a dual image of the city with direct links to the Troy exemplar discussed at the start of the chapter. At times the city is represented as orderly and harmonious and its castles are depicted as significant markers of the status and history of the whole city. At other times, social unrest comes to the fore, and the city's defences are then implicated in the fall of the city from its ideal position.

This chapter traces the development of London's depiction in medieval literature and art. It uses the city's foundation legends and civic traditions to explore medieval conventions of city depiction, showing that this whole genre is shaped by the duality found in the history of medieval castle/town

---

[49] 'Castles' traditional dark reputation is largely the product of perceptions of King Stephen's reign, of clerical propaganda, and of Romance, all inflated by mental inertia', ibid., pp. 140–1.

[50] Brooke with Keir, *London 800–1216*, p. 30.

relations. All exemplary cities of the Middle Ages had their real as well as their ideal aspects, from Jerusalem and Rome to Troy and London. In the latter case, positive and negative imagery made its way into civic seals, saints' lives, official histories of Britain and even into political propaganda and legal documents. Far from painting urban castles as instruments of oppression, the literary and artistic evidence shows how London's castles were effectively dissociated from their Norman builders and re-established as emblems of civic independence and pride, even if they were regarded at other times with suspicion or resentment.

London's most important legendary association in the Middle Ages was with the city of Troy. The myth of Britain's foundation by the Trojan hero Brutus was disseminated in British contexts from the ninth century, but, significantly, it was only applied to London after the Norman takeover of the capital at the Conquest. Brutus, a descendant of Aeneas, born into a community of Trojan refugees fleeing after the sack of Troy, is first put forward as the founder of Britain in the *Historia Brittonum*, a ninth-century Latin text usually attributed to a Welsh author called Nennius.[51] The historical value of this work has been debated as much as its authorship.[52] However, it seems clear that the author of the *Historia Brittonum* was working from earlier historical traditions[53] and aimed to provide for the British an ancestry as ancient and respectable as that of the Romans, whose culture still cast a long shadow over ninth-century Welsh history.[54] Importantly, Rome itself provides a model for the dual values I have noted in medieval urban mythography. It was the eternal city, centre of western Christianity and source of papal controls over national government and religious affairs. Its historical reputation was simultaneously that of a cruel and oppressive empire and a bringer of status and civilization. The *Historia Brittonum* marks the beginning of a long debate articulated through the legendary histories of Britain and Rome, exploring this duality, often through urban foundation legends.[55]

---

[51] A. Gransden, *Historical Writing in England c.550 to c.1307* (London, 1974), p. 6.

[52] Dumville has waged a long battle to dissociate the name of Nennius from the authorship of the work, most recently in D. N. Dumville, 'The Historical Value of the *Historia Brittonum*', *Arthurian Literature* 6 (1986), 1–26. However, P. J. C. Field has recently sought to reinstate Nennius with his article, 'Nennius and his History', *Studia Celtica* 30 (1996), 159–65.

[53] Gransden, *Historical Writing in England c.550 to c.1307*, pp. 6–7, 9.

[54] Ibid., pp. 10–11; see also D. N. Dumville, 'Sub-Roman Britain: History and Legend', *History* 62 (1977), 173–92.

[55] In Chapter 4 I explore in more detail the imagery of Rome employed in medieval castles. Here, Troy is my main interest, because of the very direct relationship which can be detected between the cities of Troy and London, and, importantly, their castles.

Britain's legend of Trojan foundation came to wider notice with Geoffrey of Monmouth's work, the *Historia regum Britannie*, finished in 1138.[56] Like the author of *Historia Brittonum*, whose work he knew,[57] Geoffrey was probably Welsh, as his toponymic suggests.[58] The Trojan foundation legend, for both Nennius and Geoffrey, expressed the greatness of Britain through the imitation of Roman claims to ancient genealogy and foundation.[59] However, Geoffrey turned this political slant to his advantage. The venerable set of predecessors Geoffrey's history provides for the English monarchy, including King Arthur, were also used to flatter the new Norman rulers of Britain, aligning them with previous powerful British rulers and bolstering their achievement in conquering and ruling such an illustrious realm.[60] Comparisons with Rome and its famous leaders were central to the self-fashioning of the Norman monarchy of Britain,[61] so this ploy was carefully calculated to suit its audience. Geoffrey's multiple dedications of his work to powerful members of the ruling Anglo-Norman aristocracy also demonstrate his intentions eloquently.[62]

The example of Roman foundation legends may also have prompted Geoffrey to make London a particular focus of the Trojan legend in his history. The stories of Aeneas and of Romulus and Remus explain the beginnings of the entire Roman state, but both start with the foundation of the city of Rome. This is exactly how Geoffrey shaped his Trojan story. The process by which Geoffrey equated Brutus's capital city, the New Troy, with London, is complex and has already been dextrously explained by other scholars. There is no need to repeat all the evidence here, but in brief, Geoffrey found the name 'Trinovantum', mentioned in the *Historia Brittonum* and other of his sources in connection with Julius Caesar's British campaign.[63] He seems to have linked

[56] *The* Historia regum Britannie *of Geoffrey of Monmouth, 1. Bern, Burgerbibliothek, MS 568*, ed. N. Wright (1985, repr. 1996), pp. xv–xvi.

[57] Dumville, 'The Historical Value of the *Historia Brittonum*', p. 20; Gransden, *Historical Writing in England c.550 to c.1307*, p. 203; Geoffrey of Monmouth, *Bern, Burgerbibliothek, MS 568*, p. xviii.

[58] Gransden, *Historical Writing in England c.550 to c.1307*, p. 201; J. Gillingham, 'The Context and Purposes of Geoffrey of Monmouth's *History of the Kings of Britain*', *Anglo-Norman Studies* 13 (1990), 99–118 (p. 100).

[59] Gillingham, 'The Context and Purposes', pp. 104, 117; R. Waswo, 'Our Ancestors, the Trojans: Inventing Cultural Identity in the Middle Ages', *Exemplaria* 7.2 (1995), 269–90 (pp. 277, 278, 282–3); Geoffrey of Monmouth, *Bern, Burgerbibliothek, MS 568*, p. xix.

[60] Gillingham, 'The Context and Purposes', p. 101; Geoffrey of Monmouth, *Bern, Burgerbibliothek, MS 568*, p. xix and Introduction, *passim*; M. B. Shichtman and L. A. Finke, 'Profiting from the Past: History as Symbolic Capital in the *Historia regum Britannie*', *Arthurian Literature* 12 (1993), 1–35 (p. 4 and *passim*).

[61] I discuss this further in Chapter 4.

[62] Gillingham, 'The Context and Purposes', p. 101.

[63] Nennius, *British History and Welsh Annals*, ed. and transl. J. Morris (London, 1980), chapter 20, p. 64. Geoffrey may also have come across 'Trinovantum' in Caesar's

this name, presumably by the (false) etymologies of which he was so fond, to Britain's supposed Trojan origins, and concluded that 'Trinovantum' was a variant form of 'Troia Nova' or 'New Troy'. References in Geoffrey's sources connect 'Trinovantum' with a site on the North bank of the Thames, so Geoffrey was quite happy to equate the name, and the city he supposed it to represent, with London.[64]

This process of elaborating on hints in source texts is quite consistent with Geoffrey's approach to the whole of his British History.[65] By making this sort of connection, it seems likely that Geoffrey intended to boost the history and pride of his own people, the Britons, while making their legends palatable to the Norman ruling classes. It is still not clear whether he thought his stories would be understood humorously, symbolically or literally.[66] Nevertheless it is notable how seriously Geoffrey's foundation legends, and Trojan legends in general, were taken by many of his contemporaries and successors.[67] Troy's historicity was not a matter for doubt, thanks to the wide acquaintance in the Middle Ages with the supposedly eye-witness accounts of the Trojan war by Dares the Phrygian and Dictys of Crete.[68] Nor was there was any reason in the medieval period to question the story that Trojans had later settled in Western Europe.[69] So, thanks in large part to Geoffrey, Britain's Trojan foundation legend and its specific application to London were enthusiastically accepted as fact.[70] Just as Rome itself had done, London became an exemplary city through its prestigious founder. The political potential of Geoffrey's legend for the capital city soon became apparent.

De bello Gallico, 5.20, or Orosius's *Historiae*, 6.9–10: Clark, 'Trinovantum – the Evolution of a Legend', p. 139.

[64] 'Trinovantum', in historical fact a tribe rather than a city, who lived around Colchester, is associated in these texts with a battle on the north bank of the Thames, close to a crossing-point. See H. Nearing, 'The Legend of Julius Caesar's British Conquest', *Publications of the Modern Languages Association* 64 (1949), 889–929 (p. 895); the same conclusions are reached independently by John Clark, who discusses Geoffrey's role fully: Clark, 'Trinovantum – the Evolution of a Legend', pp. 141–3.

[65] Gransden, *Historical Writing in England c.550 to c.1307*, p. 204; Shichtman and Finke, 'Profiting from the Past', pp. 8–11.

[66] See all the articles on Geoffrey I have mentioned here, as well as V. J. Flint, 'The *Historia regum Britanniae* of Geoffrey of Monmouth: Parody and its Purpose. A Suggestion', *Speculum* 54 (1979), 447–68.

[67] J. C. Crick, *The* Historia regum Britannie *of Geoffrey of Monmouth, 4. Dissemination and Reception in the Later Middle Ages* (1991), p. 2.

[68] C. D. Benson, *The History of Troy in Middle English Literature: Guido delle Colonne's* 'Historia Destructionis Troiae' *in Medieval England* (Woodbridge, 1980), pp. 3–5.

[69] Reynolds, 'Medieval *Origines Gentium* and the Community of the Realm', p. 378; Benson, *The History of Troy in Middle English Literature*, pp. 3–5.

[70] Crick, *The* Historia regum Britannie *of Geoffrey of Monmouth, 4.* p. 9 and *passim*; Gransden, *Historical Writing in England c.550 to c.1307*, pp. 201–2.

William FitzStephen, who wrote a description of London in 1173, was an early emulator of the *Historia regum Britannie*.[71] He made Brutus's foundation of London central to a glowing portrait of the city's venerable Trojan customs and upright people. His description of London is aligned strongly with the formal Classical genre of city descriptions, in which foundation legends also play an important part.[72] FitzStephen makes sure that the Classical roots of his piece will be obvious to the reader, scattering his description with an astonishing number of quotations from Classical literature, which often seem to be included for bulk rather than relevance.[73] His self-consciously Classicising style is reflected in his subject-matter, too. London is compared favourably with Rome on a number of occasions, and great emphasis is placed on the assertion that Britain was founded first.[74] Like Geoffrey's claim of a Trojan founder for London, rivalling Aeneas's foundation of Rome, FitzStephen's description of London deliberately marks London out as a legendary city in its own right.[75] The overtly positive tone of the work certainly enhances this effect, though underlying political tensions can also be detected.

FitzStephen's description of London is an introduction to his main work, a life of St Thomas. FitzStephen was a secular clerk in Thomas Becket's household and seems to have been one of the bishop's few followers who witnessed his murder at first hand.[76] Unsurprisingly, FitzStephen shows some bitterness against the royal regime that had had Becket killed, though he gives it a very civic form. He heaps eulogy on the citizens and their city, often through Trojan associations, but hints occasionally at tensions between the people and their rulers.[77] He also describes the citizens of London as 'barons',[78] a traditional

---

[71] William FitzStephen, '*Descriptio nobilissimae civitatis Londoniae*', in *Materials for the History of Thomas Becket, Archbishop of Canterbury*, ed. J. C. Robertson, Rolls Series 67, 6 vols. (1877; repr. 1965), III, section 12, p. 8; section 18, p. 12; section 19, p. 12; Brooke with Keir, *London 800–1216*, p. 119.

[72] J. Scattergood, 'Misrepresenting the City: Genre, Intertextuality and William FitzStephen's *Description of London* (c.1173)', in *London and Europe in the Later Middle Ages*, ed. J. Boffey and P. King (London, 1995), pp. 1–34 (pp. 10–20); J. K. Hyde, 'Mediaeval Descriptions of Cities', *Bulletin of the John Rylands Library* 48 (1965–6), 308–40.

[73] Brooke with Keir, *London 800–1216*, p. 118.

[74] '*Urbe Roma, secundum chronicorum fidem, satis antiquior est*' ('According to the authority of the chroniclers, [London] is rather older than the city of Rome'). FitzStephen, '*Descriptio nobilissimae civitatis Londoniae*', paragraph 12, p. 8.

[75] Ibid., section 12, p. 8. See also section 17, p. 12.

[76] Gransden, *Historical Writing in England c.550 to c.1307*, pp. 299, 301; Brooke with Keir, *London 800–1216*, p. 112.

[77] One such hint can be gleaned: '*Urbs sane bona, si bonum habeat dominum*' ('Indeed a good city, if it could have a good lord'). FitzStephen, '*Descriptio nobilissimae civitatis Londoniae*', paragraph 7, p. 4.

[78] '*Habitatores aliarum urbium cives, hujus barones dicuntur*' ('The inhabitants of other cities are called citizens, but those of this [city] are called barons'). Ibid., paragraph 8, p. 4.

title symbolising their independence, but later deployed in struggles to free the city from royal control by establishing it as a commune.[79] These veiled criticisms fit well with the patterns I have noted in city depictions in other media: a harmonious form encompasses, but does not negate, underlying tensions.

FitzStephen's treatment of London's castles also follows this pattern. He includes descriptions of the Tower and London's other two castles amongst the most important landmarks of the city: 'Habet ab oriente arcem palatinam, maximam et fortissimam . . . : ab occidente duo castella munitissima' ('[London] has to the east a great and very strong palatine citadel . . . : to the west two very well fortified castles.')[80] While this description seems fairly neutral, the emphasis on the strength of the fortifications seems an implicit acknowledgement of the unrest they are designed to combat. As Brooke puts it,

> The Norman castles, and especially the Tower, were built to ensure that the citizens recognized their master. It is a symbol in the broader sense of the relationship of love and hate which always existed between the king and the patriciate of London; in a special sense of the presence of the Norman conquerors in the city.[81]

However, a subsequent treatment of London's fortresses, which seems to draw on FitzStephen's description, reclaims them for the populace by incorporating them into the legend of London's Trojan past. The passage occurs in Gervase of Tilbury's work, *Otia imperialia*:

> Brutus ad veteris Troiae recensendam memoriam condidit firmissimam urbem Trinovantum, in ipsa velut Illium ad orientem constituens, ubi Turris Londoniensis est, firmissima munitione palatium circumseptum continens, aqua Tamasis fluvii, quem cotidie ascendentis maris inundatio replet, in ambitu decurrente. Ad occidentem vero Pergama[82] construxit, duo videlicet miris aggeribus constructa castra, quorum alterum Bainardi, alterum baronum de Munfichet, est ex iure successionis.[83]

> (Brutus founded a very strong city called Trinovantum to keep alive the memory of the old Troy, placing within it a citadel like Ilium, containing

---

[79] G. A. Williams, *Medieval London: From Commune to Capital* (London, 1963), pp. 3, 44, 204 and *passim*.

[80] FitzStephen, '*Descriptio nobilissimae civitatis Londoniae*', paragraph 5, p. 3.

[81] Brooke with Keir, *London 800–1216*, p. 14.

[82] The proper noun Pergama or Pergamum is poetic usage from the Greek for the citadel of Troy, employed in several Classical authors: *A Latin Dictionary*, ed. C. T. Lewis and C. Short (Oxford, 1958). Pergama may look plural, but it is in fact an example of a Latin place-name with singular meaning and plural form, like *Athenae* (Athens).

[83] Gervase of Tilbury, *Otia Imperialia: Recreation for an Emperor*, ed. S. E. Banks and J. W. Binns, Oxford Medieval Texts Series (Oxford, 2002), Book 2, section 17, pp. 398–400.

a palace enclosed by mighty fortifications, on the eastern side of the city, where the Tower of London is, with the water of the river Thames flowing around it, which is replenished daily when the sea pours in at high tide. On the western side of the city he built Pergamum, namely, two castles constructed with magnificent ramparts, one being Baynard's Castle, while the other belongs by right of succession to the Barons of Monfiquit.[84])

Gervase here states explicitly that Brutus founded not only London's two lesser castles, Baynard's Castle and Mountfichet, but the Tower as well. This backdates London's castles drastically from their historical foundation at the Norman Conquest. According to the chronology provided by Geoffrey of Monmouth, Brutus settled in Britain at the time when the priest Eli was ruling in Judaea:[85] Brutus and his deeds are therefore dated to the period of early Biblical history before the time of Christ[86] and even before the reign of King David.[87] As I noted in Chapter 1, this dating is a nonsense for the modern scholar. The White Tower (see Plate VI), centrepiece of the Tower of London and the reason for the fortress's distinctive name, must be of a post-Conquest date, as masonry keeps of this form were only introduced to Britain with the arrival of the Normans.[88] I discussed in Chapter 1 the linguistic reasons for linking medieval castles to structures of much more ancient date in Roman and Biblical contexts. There, too, I began to explore the not uncommon literary practice of backdating medieval castles to attribute them to an ancient founder, just as Gervase does here. However, this device has the effect of breaking the link between London's fortresses and their Norman builders. Instead, Gervase transforms the castles into a point of visual, material and symbolic contact with the legendary past. They represent London's pride in its ancient heritage, and become sites at which its Trojan past can be seen, touched and understood.

It is thought Gervase of Tilbury was English, as his toponymic suggests, but in his later diplomatic career he spent much time in Europe, in the circle of the emperor Otto IV. This is probably where he composed the *Otia imperialia*, which he dedicated to the emperor on its completion at some point between

---

84 It is difficult to translate some features of this passage directly into English: the sudden changes in tense, which are a normal rhetorical feature of Latin, have no English stylistic equivalent. The precise grammatical parallels in the construction of the two sentences make an exact equation between Brutus's founding of the Tower and the other castles. The phrase 'ubi Turris Londoniensis est' should be understood as a continuous present, something like, 'where the Tower of London still stands to this day'. I have based my translation on that given by Banks and Binns, and am very grateful to Jim Binns for his advice on this passage and others in this book.

85 Geoffrey of Monmouth, *Bern, Burgerbibliothek, MS. 568*, paragraph 22, p. 15.

86 Ibid., paragraph 64, p. 42.

87 Ibid., paragraph 27, p. 17.

88 Pounds, *The Medieval Castle in England and Wales*, pp. 20–1.

1214 and 1218.[89] Gervase may have gathered his information on London and the Trojan foundation legend at a much earlier stage, when he was associated with the English court of Henry II.[90] As I will discuss in more detail in Chapter 4, Henry's court circle was responsible for a number of texts examining the Troy legend and its British connections, including Benoit de Sainte-Maure's *Roman de Troie* and Wace's *Roman de Brut*.[91] This background provides precedents for Gervase's use of the Trojan foundation legend to reconcile the Anglo-Norman royal family with its British people. It may also provide some clues as to why Gervase chose to mark London's legendary history onto the fabric of the city in such a particularly precise, topographical manner.

The wording of the passage by Gervase implies that Brutus chose the layout of his defences specifically to recreate the plan of the old city of Troy on the site of London, the New Troy. The medieval visitor to London, equipped with this knowledge, could experience not only architectural relics from the foundation period of the city and country, but also a topographical recreation of the ancient city of Troy and the relationships it set up between its citizens and its citadel. However, this experience was not just one-way. A medieval reader, encountering a description of Troy, might well reflect on the similarity of its layout to a fortified medieval town such as London. Medieval descriptions of Troy written in British contexts, from several decades before Gervase was writing, laid out the legendary city very precisely and in a form highly suggestive of a fortified medieval city. This process seems to begin with Benoit de Sainte-Maure.

Benoit de Sainte-Maure's Anglo-Norman poem, known as the *Roman de Troie*, was written between 1160 and 1170 for the court of Henry II[92] and was based closely on the accounts of the Trojan war provided by its supposed eyewitnesses, Dares and Dictys. Benoit's description of Troy is adapted from these sources, but uses vocabulary calculated to suggest to his audience the familiar fortified cities and castles of the medieval landscape. The fortress of Ilium, for example, is described as 'le maistre donjon' of the city of Troy.[93] This suggestive vocabulary would have indicated to his audience a substantial keep within a city context, something very like the White Tower at the centre of London's main fortress (see Plate VI). Similar resonances can be found consistently in subsequent British adaptations of the Troy legend.

In the mid 1180s, Joseph of Exeter based his Latin account of the seige of Troy on the work of Dares.[94] His description of the city is less specific than

---

[89] J. W. Binns and S. E. Banks, *Gervase of Tilbury and the Encyclopaedic Tradition: Information Retrieval from the Middle Ages to Today* (Leicester, 1999), pp. 5–6.

[90] Ibid.

[91] See Chapter 4, pp. 134–6.

[92] See previous note.

[93] Benoit de Sainte-Maure, *Le Roman de Troie par Benoit de Sainte-Maure*, ed. L. Constans, 6 vols. (Paris, 1904, repr. 1968), 1, p. 154, line 3042.

[94] Joseph of Exeter, *The Iliad of Dares Phrygius*, transl. G. Roberts (Cape Town, 1970), pp. ix–x.

that given by Benoit, but his portrayal of Priam's citadel is suggestive. He emphasizes Ilium's immense height, comparing it with the Tower of Babel; Later in the same passage Joseph notes that the more ostentatious citizens of Troy have built their own, lesser, towers throughout the city to vie with Priam's.[95] This confirms that Joseph had a great tower in mind for Ilium itself. Later Middle English Troy texts were influenced by the Italian Guido delle Colonna's popular *Hystoria Troiana* of 1287, but this in itself followed Benoit's account, and preserved a very similar description of the city.[96] *The Seege or Batayle of Troy*, dated 1350–1400, clearly identifies Troy's citadel as a *tour*.[97] Chaucer, too, in the Dido section of *The Legend of Good Women*, calls it 'the noble tour of Ylioun/ That of the cite was the chef dongeoun'.[98] This is corroborated by the *Gest Hystoriale of the Destruction of Troy*, thought to be dated between 1385 and 1400: the author refers to Priam's favourite vantage point from the *heghest* of the castle's *toures*.[99]

Whether it is called a donjon or a tower, the implication is clear and consistent in all these texts: Ilium is the keep within the royal fortress of Troy. It is a tower in the same way that the White Tower is the centrepiece of London's main castle, the Tower of London. In this context, Gervase of Tilbury's account just takes the supposed Trojan foundation of the Tower of London to its logical conclusion, in equating the layout of the two cities' strongholds. However, by the same token, the spatial and political relationship between citadel and city in descriptions of the ancient Troy also have a bearing on perceptions and depictions of medieval London. Closer examination of the descriptions of the Trojans' capital reveals the full extent of its participation in the imagery of exemplary medieval cities, but also highlights the role of defensive architecture in articulating depictions of urban harmony and conflict.

In the group of Troy texts I have identified, the ordered hierarchy and symmetry of the city are consistently emphasized. Benoit de Sainte-Maure

---

[95] Joseph of Exeter, *Joseph Iscanus: Werke und Briefe*, ed. L. Gompf (Leiden, 1970), pp. 95–6, lines 500–1, 504–5.

[96] Benson, *The History of Troy in Middle English Literature*, pp. 4–5.

[97] *The Seege or Batayle of Troye*, ed. M. E. Barnicle, Early English Text Society, original series 172 (1927, repr. 1971), line 323, p. 27.

[98] Geoffrey Chaucer, *The Riverside Chaucer*, ed. L. D. Benson, 3rd edn (Oxford, 1987, repr. 1992), 'The Legend of Good Women', p. 609, lines 936–7.

[99] *The 'Gest Hystoriale' of the Destruction of Troy: An Alliterative Romance translated from Guido de Colonna's 'Hystoria Troiana'*, ed. G. A. Panton, Early English Text Society, original series 39, 56 (1869 and 1874; repr. 1969), p. 55, lines 1639–40, 1636. It has been suggested that this poem is the work of one Master John Clerk of Whalley in Lancashire: the evidence for the dating and authorship of this poem is reviewed briefly in J. Simpson, 'The Other Book of Troy: Guido delle Colonne's *Historia destructionis Troiae* in Fourteenth-Century England', *Speculum* 73 (1998), 397–423 (p. 405 and nn. 34, 35). See also T. Turville-Petre, 'The Author of the *Destruction of Troy*', *Medium Aevum* 57 (1988), 264–69.

describes Troy in the *Roman de Troie* as the most beautiful city on earth, emphasizing its positive, exemplary qualities.[100] The outer walls of the city are said to have large towers around their circuit;[101] the houses within the walls are then mentioned[102] and finally the citadel of Ylion (Ilium) is described, in the highest part of Troy, complete with battlements and crenellations.[103] Joseph of Exeter describes the city walls with their gates;[104] then soaring skywards, Ylios the citadel[105] and the lesser towers scattered throughout the city, homes of its inhabitants.[106] This also seems to be a symmetrical, idealized arrangement, though Joseph sounds a note of warning, reminding his readers of Troy's ultimate fate. Later Middle English descriptions based on Guido delle Colonna's account emphasize this concentric arrangement even more strongly. The image of Troy is visually and formally harmonious, arranged in ordered hierarchies, all centred on the same point. This can be illustrated by the *Gest Hystoriale of the Destruction of Troy*, a Middle English account translated directly from Guido delle Colonna:[107]

Of the walle for to wete to the wale top,	1546
20 Cubettes by coursse accounttid full evyn,	
That of marbill was most fro the middes up,	
Of divers colours to ken craftely wroght.	
That were shene for to shew & of shap noble,	1550
Mony toures up tilde the toune to defende,	
Wroght up with the walle as the werke rose,	
One negh to Another nobly devyset.	
Within the Citie, for sothe, semly to ken,	1567
Grete palis of prise, plenty of houses,	
Wele bild all aboute on the best wise.	
The werst walle for to wale, there any wegh dwelt,	1570
Was faurty cubettes by coursse, to count fro the urthe,	
And all of marbill was made with mervellus bestes,	
Of lions & Libardes & other laithe wormes.	
Priam by purpos a pales gert make	
Within the Cite full Solempne of a sete riall,	1630
Lovely and large to logge in hym selvyn,	
Ful worthely wroght & by wit caste,	
And evyn at his etlyng Ylion was cald;	

---

[100] Benoit de Sainte-Maure, *Le Roman de Troie*, p. 152, lines 2995–6.
[101] Ibid., p. 152, lines 3005, 3009.
[102] Ibid., p. 153, line 3019.
[103] Ibid., pp. 154, 156, lines 3041–2, 3047, 3085.
[104] Joseph of Exeter, *Joseph Iscanus: Werke und Briefe*, p. 95, lines 485–7.
[105] Ibid., pp. 95–6, lines 491–2, 496–7.
[106] Ibid., p. 96, lines 504–6.
[107] Benson, *The History of Troy in Middle English Literature*, p. 35.

Closit with a clene wall crustrit with towres,
Evyn round as a ryng richely wroght, –   1635
Fyve hundrith fete fully the heght: –
Withoute, toures full tore torret above,
That were of heght so hoge, as I here fynde,
That the clowdes hom clede in unclene aire.
In the heghest to houve and behold over,   1640
All the lond for to loke when hym lefe thought.

Of crafty colours to know, all in course set,
Made of marbyll with mason devyse,   1645
With imagry full honest openly wroght.[108]

The precious materials mentioned in this description provide a touch of exoticism,[109] but apart from this the Troy described by the author is clearly comparable in form to any medieval castle within a walled town. The city wall is first described (line 1546) along with its 'mony toures ... the toune to defende' (line 1551). Within the city wall lie the houses of the citizens, but more importantly, the 'grete palice' (line 1568) built as King Priam's residence: 'closit with a clene wall crustrit with towres,/ Evyn round as a ryng richely wroght' (lines 1634–5), it is called Ylion (line 1633).[110]

The relationship between the great tower and its surrounding fortress and city is precisely but economically evoked in the *Destruction of Troy*. Successive lines of defence are graded carefully by the author in order of height. The city walls are twenty cubits high (line 1547), the wall of Priam's fortress is five hundred feet tall (line 1636) and its most important tower, the keep, is even higher to provide a vantage point over the city and surrounding countryside (lines 1640–1). The houses of the citizens also fit into this hierarchy. From forty cubits high (line 1571), they are taller than the city walls but considerably lower than the palace complex. In addition to this hierarchy of height, the city walls, the houses within the city and of the palace and its defences are all made of marble: the city walls are marble from halfway up (line 1548), the houses of the citizens have walls all of marble

---

[108] *The 'Gest Hystoriale' of the Destruction of Troy*, ed. Panton, lines 1546–53, 1567–73, 1629–41, 1644–6, pp. 52–5. I have included the line numbering for ease of reference.

[109] There is a long tradition in medieval romance of associating precious stones, especially incorporated into buildings, with exotic or fantastic locations: examples such as the description of the palace at Constantinople in the *Pelerinage de Charlemagne* and Prester John's palace can be found in P. Frankl, *The Gothic: Literary Sources and Interpretations through Eight Centuries* (Princeton, 1960), pp. 161–9. In many of these texts, as with Benoit's, there is also a hint of the Heavenly Jerusalem, with its foundation layers of semi-precious stones, but exoticism is the keynote.

[110] The description of Priam's stronghold as a 'palace' should not divert modern readers from its obvious affinity to a medieval castle: Gervase of Tilbury also uses the noun *palatium* to describe the Tower of London in a similar usage when clearly referring to a castle complex (see above).

(line 1572) and the palace itself is made of marble dressed with different precious metals and stones.[111]

The author establishes on the one hand a decorative unity among the greatest and least buildings, all being built with marble, yet on the other hand a strict hierarchy of increasing proportions of precious materials and increasing height. The architectural forms are also arranged in a repeating pattern: the towered wall of the city is echoed in the towered wall of the castle within and the houses of the citizens are mirrored by Priam's residence, the palace. Even more emphatically, a three-way relationship is set up between the towered walls of the city, the towered walls of the fortress and the highest tower of the citadel. The symmetry and ordered hierarchy of this arrangement creates the idea of a concentric city, centred on the great tower of the citadel.

This concentric arrangement is easy to translate into pictorial terms, as it bears a strong resemblance to many medieval depictions of cities and their castles, which show several tiers of successive defensive circuits, with a donjon at the centre. The sketch of Troyes (see Plate I) from an itinerary by Matthew Paris (*c*.1253–9) seems a perfect visual rendition of the descriptions of Troy I have discussed. Its three-tiered arrangement suggests an outer town wall, an inner palace circuit and finally a tower-keep, all carefully graded in ascending order of height. As with the descriptions of Troy, it is defences – both civic and seigneurial – that are used to describe and define the city visually. Its name is even right. However, it depicts a real medieval city – Troyes in France – and comes not from a romance but from a map. The way this image imposes ideal symmetry onto the topography of a real city may sit uneasily for modern observers. A similar juxtaposition is implied in Gervase of Tilbury's suggestion that the city of London reproduces the layout of Troy, which, as I have shown, was represented as an idealized, concentric arrangement very different from our understanding of the topography of medieval London. Yet it is interesting to note that, in the description from the *Gest Hystoriale of the Destruction of Troy*, a concentric arrangement is never explicitly stated in terms of the physical layout of the imagined city. It is the structure of the description that takes the reader through repeated architectural forms, carefully graded details of materials and height and successive rings of accommodation and defence. This seems fully deliberate: the author creates an aesthetic of spatial harmony and order, while leaving the topographical details of the city unspecified. The audience is invited to recognize the architectural elements of Troy in their own urban environment and to imagine Troy's layout accordingly. It is the perfect exemplary city, evoking lofty urban ideals but resembling every city equally. It is this quality that invited Gervase to shape London in Troy's image, and enabled Caxton to call on Troy as a universal exemplar of the urban experience.

---

[111] *The 'Gest Hystoriale' of the Destruction of Troy*, ed. Panton, lines 1648–59. p. 55.

Nevertheless, symmetry and formal harmony were important elements in civic planning and pride in the Middle Ages, and were consistently focused on and expressed through images and ideas of the urban castle. I will return later in this chapter to show how these ideas are expressed in the case of London, but make a diversion here to consider the place of symmetry and order in medieval urban ideology. Recent research has shown the extent to which planning, order and symmetry were built in to medieval urban environments (even those that appear to modern observers to have grown organically or haphazardly).[112] This reflected beliefs about the divinely ordered nature of geometry which were also expressed in medieval ideology, art and architecture and may well have been planned into medieval townscapes by the same architect-designers working on cathedrals, castles and other town defences. One feature of this careful ordering, not always apparent to the casual modern observer, is the axis set up between the town's castle and church, usually connected by the main street.[113] Careful interpretation of civic records has also shown that, while burgesses keen to defend their town with walls often invoked the need for defence, motives of civic prestige were far more pressing in many cases.[114] Town walls were important not for their physical strength, but for their symbolic value as markers of status and as a means of urban self-definition. Both these trends demonstrate the extent to which urban defences, both civic and seigneurial, and their spatial dynamics, were involved in articulating concepts of the ideal town in the Middle Ages.

The medieval ideal of urban symmetry, expressed through defensive boundaries, is not just to be found theological texts, but also in the visual media that had most influence on depictions of cities. As I have shown Matthew Paris's image of Troyes draws together elements from a number of important sources of medieval civic imagery. For example, Matthew Paris was certainly familiar with images of Rome depicted on imperial *bullae*, and his interpretations of these show that he had in mind for the Eternal City a concentric arrangement rather like his Troyes image.[115] Once again, the defensive elements of the city are key components in this depiction, as the crenellations of the outermost and innermost towers show. Imperial seals of exactly this type had an important influence on the depiction of towns in a British context. Medieval urban seals made their appearance in Europe in the mid-twelfth century, starting at the seat of the Holy Roman Empire at Cologne and spreading out to France, Italy and England towards the end of the

---

[112] See K. D. Lilley, *Urban Life in the Middle Ages, 1000–1450* (Houndmills, 2002), pp. 138–77, especially pp. 157–68.

[113] Ibid., p. 164.

[114] See Coulson, 'Battlements and Bourgeoisie'.

[115] Matthew Paris's drawing of the seal of Frederick II (1229–53), in Cambridge, Corpus Christi College, MS 12, fol. 72v, is illustrated in S. Lewis, *The Art of Matthew Paris in the Chronica Majora* (Aldershot, 1987), fig. 37, p. 76.

twelfth century.[116] These civic seals display a wide variety of devices, amongst which architectural motifs form an important group.[117] Since the time of Charlemagne the seal of the Holy Roman Emperor had displayed on its reverse the image of Rome, so it is likely this was the ultimate source of these architectural devices.[118]

From the earliest stage there was, then, an ideal quality to the architectural imagery of the seal, and an appreciation that the symbolism of one, exemplary city could be overlaid on to other urban contexts. The round format of seals also facilitated the assimilation of concentric city images used for portraying Jerusalem on medieval maps.[119] Jerusalem, while embodying a set of civic connotations rather different to the Trojan foundation legends, was of course the supreme exemplary city for the Middle Ages and is probably the ultimate source for medieval representations of urban spatial and symbolic harmony.[120] However, its dual identity as an ideal and a real city was a fundamental tenet of Augustinian thought.[121] With visual depictions of Jerusalem, as with Rome, symmetry and spatial harmony were crucial. While some plans of the city, made to direct pilgrims around its streets, aimed at a schematic topography of the city's streets and landmarks, perfectly circular walls defined the outer boundary of the city.[122] Others, such as the image of Jerusalem on the Mappa Mundi in Hereford Cathedral, formalized the entire city into a symmetrical pattern more reminiscent of descriptions of the perfect, heavenly city (see Plate II).

Civic seals of medieval Britain often show a close visual similarity to the Troyes or Rome type of image, with the tiered castle within its town walls, as I will show shortly. Here too the concentric and harmonious depiction is symbolically important for the image of the city,[123] overcoming civic divisions in

---

[116] Bedos-Rezak, 'Towns and Seals', p. 39; J. Cherry, 'Imago Castelli: The Depiction of Castles on Medieval Seals', *Château Gaillard* 15 (1990), 83–90 (p. 84).

[117] Bedos-Rezak, 'Towns and Seals', p. 46; Cherry, 'Imago Castelli', p. 84; Harvey and McGuinness, *A Guide to British Medieval Seals*, p. 109.

[118] Cherry, 'Imago Castelli', p. 83.

[119] Bedos-Rezak, 'Towns and Seals', pp. 44–5.

[120] P. Lavedan, *Répresentation des villes dans l'art du Moyen Âge* (Paris, 1954), pp. 11–12; C. Frugoni, *A Distant City: Images of Urban Experience in the Medieval World* (Princeton, 1991), p. 4 and *passim*.

[121] Helen Fulton gives a useful summary of the development of this imagery in 'The Medieval Town as Allegory', chapter 2 of her forthcoming book, *The Medieval Town Imagined*. I also touch on the example of Rome more fully in Chapter 4. However, I have chosen Troy as the main exemplar of this chapter because of its supposedly direct connections with London and English politics in general, and because of the emphasis on Troy's citadel, which brings it fully into the debate on castle/town relations.

[122] For example, the plan of Jerusalem shown on the *Situs Hierusalem*, one of the first Crusader maps, c.1100, Brussels, Bibliothèque Royale Albert 1er MS 9823–9824, fol. 157; reproduced in colour in *The Atlas of the Crusades*, ed. J. Riley-Smith (London, 1990), inset p. 44.

[123] Bedos-Rezak, 'Towns and Seals', pp. 45–6.

a display of communal civic identity expressed through defensive boundaries. For example, the civic seal of York dating from the thirteenth century uses on its obverse a tall fortified structure rising up from enclosing fortified walls (see Plate 2). It shares a certain formal resemblance with images such as Matthew Paris uses to represent both Troyes and Rome, as can be seen in the way the central element rises up from behind the lower wall, and the way in which this front wall seems to project backwards behind the central tower to enclose it, going up the picture plane. This kind of architectural image was a fairly early development in English seal iconography. This particular example dates from the thirteenth century, but is a copy of an earlier seal of York Minster which dates from the late twelfth century.[124]

Like the fifteenth-century seal of Colchester I discussed in the previous chapter, the iconography of the York seal has been described differently by different scholars, who have interpreted the structure shown on the obverse as representing different combinations of town and castle. John Cherry suggests that the seal 'shows a tall keep, with double windows, rising up behind a town wall with three gates'.[125] Pedrick, on the other hand, sees 'an ornate castle, with three pointed and tiled towers and an embattled keep of peculiar form, all masoned';[126] J. H. Bloom also describes 'a castle . . . of early design'.[127] However, with the York seal image, as with Matthew Paris's Troyes and the city descriptions, it seems to me that a deliberate resemblance is created between the form of the castle and that of the city as a whole. In all these cases, the central castle becomes the innermost in repeated rings of similar defences – a smaller version of the city walls which surround it – very much like Wyclif's idea of castles as miniature towns, or 'litil tounes, but wallid'.[128] Yet these images also work outwards as well as inwards: just as the central castle

---

[124] The earlier seal is dated to some point after 1191 by D. M. Palliser, 'The Birth of York's Civic Liberties, c.1200–1354', in *The Government of Medieval York: Essays in Commemoration of the 1396 Royal Charter*, ed. S. Rees Jones (York, 1997), pp. 88–107 (p. 92 and n. 23); the seal is illustrated in W. de G. Birch, *Catalogue of Seals in the Department of Manuscripts in the British Museum*, 6 vols. (London, 1892), II, pl.1. This seal bears on its obverse an architectural image notably similar to that on the later civic seal. However, the inscription around the obverse reveals that this image represents the cathedral, rather than the town:+ [SI]GILLVM : ECL'E : SAN[CTI : PET]RI : CAT . . . EBORAC . . . It may be that a merging of martial and ecclesiastical architecture is the intended message of this image, a rich topic I discuss more fully in Chapter 3. However, it may also be that church and state powers are shown united in this architectural image. The reverse of the seal confirms this kind of reading, as its inscription mentions the town: + SIGILLVM . CIVIVM . EBORACI . FIDELES . R[EG]IS. The image on this side of the seal also shows unity with the cathedral, showing St Peter, to whom both the city and cathedral are dedicated.

[125] Cherry, 'Imago Castelli', p. 84.

[126] G. Pedrick, *Borough Seals of the Gothic Period* (London, 1904) p. 135.

[127] J. H. Bloom, *English Seals* (London, 1906), p. 223.

[128] Discussed in Chapter 1, pp. 37–8.

1. Civic seal of Colchester, obverse (left) and reverse (right). Fifteenth century. Reproduced with kind permission of Colchester Museums.

2. Civic seal of York, obverse (left) and reverse (right). Thirteenth century. Reproduced with kind permission of York City Archives.

3. Seal of the barons of London, obverse (left) and reverse (right). 1191–1219. By permission of the Society of Antiquaries of London.

represents the city in miniature, so the enclosing city walls represent an extension of the castle – the outermost of the baileys and defences with which the citadel surrounds itself. With the visual images there is a clear sense that the architectural device could be read as a single unit: this is probably why scholars have often read such structures as castles without reading in the outer, notionally civic, boundaries.

As with the Colchester seal (discussed in Chapter 1; see Plate 1), I think that this ambiguity of form is fully deliberate, fusing elements of town and castle into one to represent the exemplary harmony of the urban community. These urban castles are an expression and symbol of their towns and the two entities can be exchanged and identified in this symbolic discourse.[129] Despite the fact that York had its own share of conflict between urban factions,[130] the castle is portrayed very much as a citadel – a stronghold which overlooks and protects the town surrounding it – rather than as an elite preserve or as a source of oppression. This fits closely with the trends I have already identified in the use of urban foundation legends. In some cases there is even evidence for the transfer of motifs and ideas between these different genres. This confirms that the foundation legends and city descriptions performed something of a similar social and symbolic function to the seals, in drawing together the conflicting factions of the urban community through a formalized and harmonious representation of it.[131]

The seal of the 'barons' or citizens of London, thought to be of the late twelfth or early thirteenth century, depicts a large figure of St Paul on the obverse, and St Thomas of Canterbury on the reverse, both towering above small cityscapes of London (see Plate 3). The cityscapes show spires, towers and lesser buildings surrounded by walls: they are arranged symmetrically and imply some of the characteristics of concentricity I have identified in images such as the York seal. However, in this case a certain degree of topographical accuracy seems to be an aim. The city is viewed from the south on the larger, obverse depiction, with a wall and gate in the foreground, the river underneath (indicated by a wavy line just visible below the wall), St Paul's Cathedral in the centre, and castles at either end of the enclosed space. St Paul himself looms behind his cathedral, supporting a heraldic flag of the arms of England. On the reverse, underneath St Thomas, St Paul's Cathedral again takes the central position, with castles at either end, but the enclosing wall shows no river in the foreground: the viewpoint for this image must be north of the city.

---

[129] For general comments on the unifying qualities of defences portrayed on seals, see Bedos-Rezak, 'Towns and Seals', p. 45.

[130] Palliser, 'The Birth of York's Civic Liberties', pp. 88–107.

[131] Bedos-Rezak makes a connection between city descriptions and seals: 'Towns and Seals', p. 35; Cherry makes a more specific link between FitzStephen's description of London and a London seal, which I will discuss more fully later in this chapter: Cherry, 'Imago Castelli', p. 85.

When John Cherry discusses this image he suggests that the two castle structures shown represent the Tower at one end of the city and either Baynard's Castle or Mountfichet Castle at the other. The respective positions of the Tower and, for example, Baynard's castle at east and west ends of the city respectively, support this reading,[132] but other elements of the depiction are not so easy to explain from the medieval topography of the city. For example, the river wall in the foreground of the city on the obverse of the seal did not exist in the Middle Ages. Interestingly, Cherry looks to London's legendary history for an explanation, proposing that the wall shown in the obverse view depicts the Roman river wall mentioned in FitzStephen's account and that it thus represents a past and legendary, rather than a medieval, reality.[133]

This interpretation accords very well with the symbolic strategies I have identified in other medieval representations of London, including, of course, FitzStephen's own description of the city. In all these cases, famous landmarks are linked to the city's ancient heritage and are used to map the legendary past of the city on to its medieval present. The seal's very unusual attempt to combine the harmonious, symmetrical arrangement with a schematic topography of the city also places the seal in a very interesting relationship to the literary accounts of the city which were circulating at around the time when the seal was made. Again, the dating of this seal is ambiguous: the surviving seal was engraved around 1219, but its design may date from the brief period in 1191 when the citizens of London were recognized as a commune.[134] Around the obverse of the seal is inscribed: 'SIGILLUM . BARONVM . LONDONIARVM.' ('seal of the barons of London').[135] These 'barons' are not in fact aristocrats, but the proud citizens of the independent city.[136] I have already discussed briefly some of the political tensions which medieval Londoners experienced. Struggles were ongoing to retain the large degree of autonomy that must already have existed amongst London's elite citizens well before this date.[137] From the period of the Conquest onwards, London's castles, with their administrative and military roles within the city, must have been understood as representing these tensions to some degree.[138] It is particularly significant that in the mid-twelfth century London's castles were involved in attempts to curtail such civic freedoms, when King Stephen used the constables of the Tower and Baynard's Castle as instruments of royal authority and control in the capital.[139] The inclusion of the castles in the ideal city

---

[132] Cherry, 'Imago Castelli', p. 85.

[133] Ibid.; William FitzStephen, '*Descriptio nobilissimae civitatis Londoniae*', section 5, p. 3.

[134] Harvey and McGuinness, *A Guide to British Medieval Seals*, p. 107, fig. 104.

[135] Pedrick, *Borough Seals of the Gothic Period*, p. 84.

[136] Williams, *Medieval London: From Commune to Capital*, p. 3.

[137] S. Reynolds, 'The Rulers of London in the Twelfth Century', *History* 57 (1972), 337–57 (pp. 338–9 and *passim*).

[138] Brooke with Keir, *London 800–1216*, pp. 13–14.

[139] Reynolds, 'The Rulers of London in the Twelfth Century', pp. 340–1.

depicted on the seals thus has particular force, signalling opposing royal and civic interests, but drawing them together into a harmonious formal relationship. The depiction of London's castles mediates crucially between the general and the specific, the legendary past and the contemporary medieval realities of the city.

Dating difficulties make it impossible to suggest a specific relationship between the seal and the passage on London's ancient topography in Gervase of Tilbury. It is suggestive, however, that in both the seal and Gervase's account, London's castles are an important feature, in their topographical relation to each other, to the river, and to the city walls, all of which are precisely located on the seal. If this interpretation is correct, the seal is a much more remarkable piece of iconography than has previously been supposed. It may be the first town seal used in medieval England, and is certainly the earliest surviving one. It is not only very early in attempting to reproduce some account of the city's topography, but manages to combine this with a formalized and symmetrical view, suggesting the archetypal nature of the city of London. Whatever the relationship between the seal and Gervase of Tilbury's Trojan description of the Tower, the presence in the seal of the non-existent river wall from FitzStephen's description[140] confirms that the legendary Trojan foundation of the city must have been known to its designer. The role of Troy as the exemplary city, famous both for its harmony and its treachery, is thus also behind this depiction.

The enduring importance of the barons' seal in translating these ideas into visual form is confirmed by several subsequent images which seem to be derived from it. These later depictions support the legendary allusions which have been detected in the barons' seal, but they also emphasize the position of the Tower within the image of London, as a central feature which carries connotations both of past events and present realities. The ideogram devised for London in one of Matthew Paris's mid-thirteenth-century itineraries or pilgrim maps[141] (Plate III) bears a close formal resemblance to the smaller view of London on the reverse of the barons' seal, seen from the north. This image similarly shows the city wall and two gates in the foreground, St Paul's in the centre of the enclosed space and 'la tur' to the left on the river which forms the further boundary of the city. As with the seal, the Tower is portrayed as a squarish crenellated tower surrounded by enclosing walls (compare with Plate VI), and this time is the only castle included, emphasizing its pre-eminent importance as a city landmark. This city is more diagrammatic than the cityscape of the seal: the city gates are placed symmetrically along the walls, and the monuments included are dispersed spaciously, with no attempt to portray the crowded and populous nature of the city which the

---

[140] Cherry, 'Imago Castelli', p. 85.

[141] In this case the one prefacing his *Historia Anglorum*, London, British Library MS Royal 14.C VII.

jostling spires and crenellations of the seal achieve. However, the link between these landmarks and the legendary past of the city is made explicit by the inscription over the city:

> La cite de lundres ki est chef dengleterre. Brutus ki primere enhabita engleterre la funda. Et lapella troie la nuvele.

> (The city of London which is capital of England. Brutus who first colonized England founded it. And called it the new Troy.)

As an image, this depiction of London, along with its individual components, is similar to Matthew Paris's London ideograms in other versions of his itinerary.[142] However, in this particular case the similarity of the layout to the image on the reverse of the barons' seal seems to me to demonstrate the seal's enduring iconographic impact on medieval perceptions of London, and to reiterate the importance of the founding myth within this construction. Rather like the barons' seal, this image manages to juxtapose the city's true topography with the ideal of symmetry, in a reconciliation of the exemplary, Trojan city and its more fallible, irregular counterpart. Once again in these images, the Tower's presence in London is consistently emphasized, underlining its role in mediating between the ideal and the real city.

A further use of parallel iconography is found in some illustrations for a late thirteenth- to early fourteenth-century copy of the *Historia regum Britannie*, the legendary history of Britain by Geoffrey of Monmouth.[143] Sketches survive in the lower margins of the manuscript, one of which shows a view of London to illustrate the passage in the text describing the Trojan foundation of the city (see Plate 4).[144] The Tower here corresponds to its place in the cityscape of the barons' seal, at the far right of the picture, portrayed similarly as a squarish block surrounded by an outer wall. The artist has also added extra distinguishing features such as the carefully differentiated corner towers and the arched windows (compare with Plate VI). As in the seal, churches again take up the centre and left of the view, with St Paul's, again, in the middle. Several tall, thin banners, reminiscent of the one St Paul supports on the seal, stick up into the city's skyline to identify their respective churches. The similar viewpoints, the similar portrayal of two of the main buildings, and the similar arrangement of the tall, thin banners convince me that the artist of the *Historia regum Britannie* knew of the depiction on the barons' seal and emulated its symbolic depiction of London.[145]

---

[142] For example, Cambridge, Corpus Christi College MS 26, fol. 1, illustrated in Lewis, *The Art of Matthew Paris*, pl. 14.

[143] London, British Library MS Royal 13.A III.

[144] Fol. 14.

[145] The date of the sketches in this manuscript is by no means certain. It has been suggested that they are by the scribe of the manuscript: C. Caine, 'Our Cities: Sketched 500 Years Ago', *Journal of the British Archaeological Association* 4 (1898),

4. View of London from the *Historia regum Britannie*. Manuscript late thirteenth century, drawings ?fourteenth century. London, British Library Additional MS Royal 13.A.III, fol. 14. By permission of the British Library.

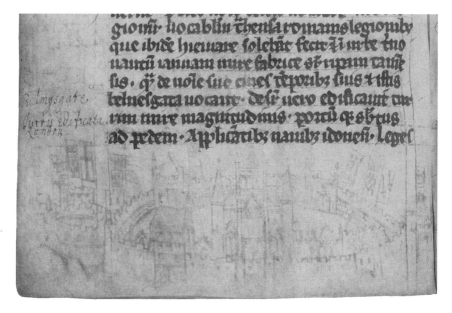

5. Bird's eye view of London from the *Historia regum Britannie*. Manuscript late thirteenth century, drawings ?fourteenth century. London, British Library Additional MS Royal 13.A.III, fol. 28v. By permission of the British Library.

I. The city of Troyes by Matthew Paris, from his Itinerary from London to Apulia. *c.*1253–9. Cambridge, Corpus Christi College MS 26, fol. 1v. © The Master and Fellows of Corpus Christi College, Cambridge.

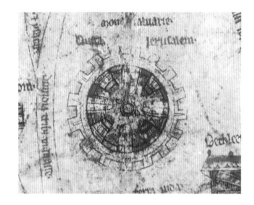

II. Detail of Jerusalem on the Mappa Mundi. Late thirteenth century. © The Dean and Chapter of Hereford Cathedral and the Hereford Mappa Mundi Trust.

III. Plan of London by Matthew Paris from his Itinerary from London to the Holy Land. *c.*1253–9. London, British Library MS Royal 14.C.VII, fol. 2. By permission of the British Library.

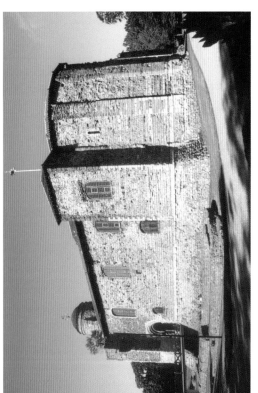

IV. Colchester Castle keep from the southeast. Castle 1074–6, Roman plinth AD 49–60.

V. Colchester Castle keep, southeast corner tower, showing detail of rubble, limestone and tile banding, above Roman plinth. Wall 1074–6, Roman plinth AD 49–60.

VI. The White Tower, Tower of London, south face. Begun *c.*1078.

VII. London's Roman city wall at Tower Hill, showing detail of banded masonry. AD 190–220.

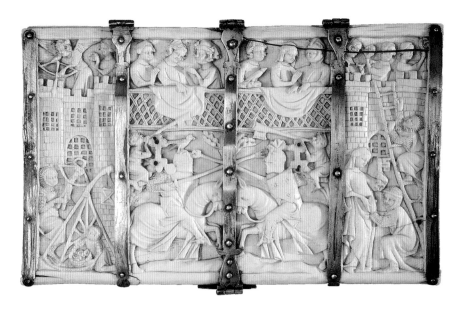

VIII. French ivory casket depicting the siege of the Castle of Love (far right-hand and far left-hand panels) and jousting (central panels). *c*.1325. © The British Museum.

IX. Detail of the Castle of Love from the Luttrell Psalter. *c*.1340. London, British Library MS Additional 42130, fol. 75v. By permission of the British Library.

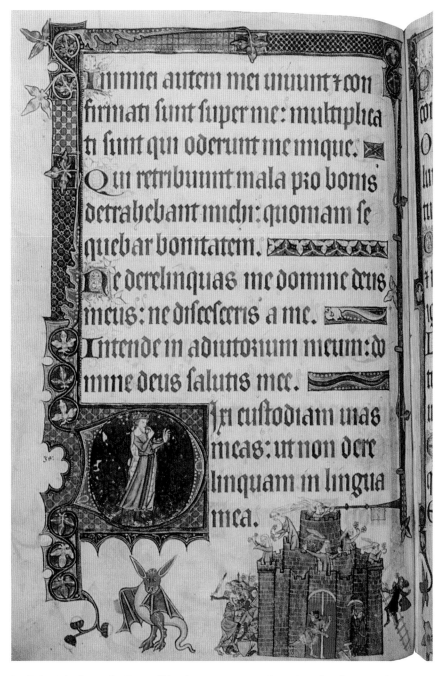

inimici autem mei inuunt ꝛ con
firmati sunt super me: multiplica
ti sunt qui oderunt me inique.
Qui retribuunt mala pro bonis
detrahebant michi: quoniam se
quebar bonitatem.
Ne derelinquas me domine deus
meus: ne discesseris a me.
Intende in adiutorium meum: do
mine deus salutis mee.

in custodiam uias
meas: ut non dere
linquam in lingua
mea.

X. Folio 75v from the Luttrell Psalter. *c.*1340. London, British Library MS
Additional 42130. By permission of the British Library.

XI. Southern bay of the west front, Lincoln Cathedral, showing machicolation slot. Eleventh century.

XII. The Great Tower, Chepstow Castle, from the east. 1067–75. Welsh Historic Monuments. Crown Copyright.

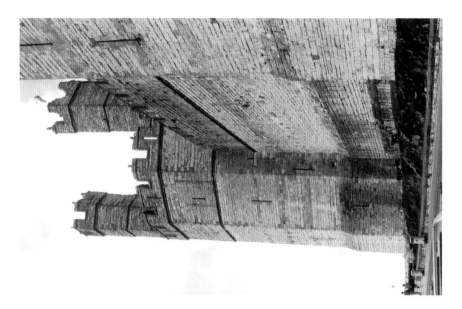

XIII. Caernarfon Castle from the southwest; Eagle Tower to the left. Begun 1283.

XIV. Eagle Tower, Caernarfon Castle, from the south, showing detail of masonry banding. Begun 1283.

XV. Dover Castle keep, from the northwest. Begun 1183.

XVI. Dover Castle keep, from the northwest, central buttress, showing detail of masonry banding. Begun 1283.

XVII. Roman *pharos* at Dover Castle, from the southeast, showing banded masonry. First century AD.

Even more convincing evidence comes from another illustration in the same manuscript (see Plate 5).[146] This sketch accompanies the section of Geoffrey's text describing Belinus's river gate (identified by Geoffrey with Billingsgate) and the tower he built near it.[147] The picture echoes quite precisely the view of London on the obverse of the barons' seal, with the curve of the city walls enclosing St Paul's and various other buildings, and a castle at either end of the composition. The two castles included on the sketch also differ from their seal counterparts in being portrayed outside (though apparently attached to) the city walls. Once again there are the characteristic slim banners above the buildings. All these elements suggest that the artist of the sketch must have studied the barons' seal quite closely. The river wall in the foreground, taken from FitzStephen's description of London, marks the ancient content of this image, and confirms that the buildings depicted are invoked as architectural survivors from an earlier age. The foreground sections of both the seal and the sketch are conjectural reconstructions, and their similarities must therefore confirm the connection between the two images, as well as their joint legendary content.

In this particular case, the sketch from the *Historia regum Britannie* seems to be used to invoke a different foundation legend for the Tower, as it is placed

---

319–21 (p. 319). However, this seems unlikely, as they are squashed into the margins of the text, rather than placed in specially reserved spaces. They have alternatively been dated to the fourteenth century through the identification of certain specific buildings: H. J. D. Astley, 'Mediaeval Colchester – Town, Castle and Abbey – from MSS. in the British Museum', *Transactions of the Essex Archaeological Association* 8 (1903), 117–35 (pp. 117–18). The relevant British Museum Catalogue suggests that the drawings are inserted and belong to the early fourteenth century: G. F. Warner and J. P. Gilson, *Catalogue of the Western MSS in the Old Royal and King's Collections in the British Museum* 4 vols. (London, 1921), II, 75. However the sketches seem to me more complicated than these simple datings allow. Close inspection shows that they often made up of two layers: under-drawing in a fine, silvery line, and over-drawing in brown line (presumably originally black) which is often slightly thicker. There are several places where discrepancies occur between these two lines, for example in the depiction of London I have discussed, where the silver under-drawing often shows Romanesque type features such as windows, and the over-drawing changes these to a Gothic style (it is very hard to see these details in reproductions of these images, but they are clear in the manuscript itself). Such changes may suggest that the images are the production of two different artists, working at different periods and reflecting architectural changes which have taken place. The images are also identified very differently in various commentaries on them. I have made my own identifications of their subject-matter based on my research, but, for example, the image I have just discussed is identified in the British Library Photographic Index as Jerusalem. This does at least show that the sketches are appreciated as depicting exemplary cities, even by modern observers.

[146] Fol. 28v.

[147] Geoffrey of Monouth, *Bern, Burgerbibliothek, MS. 568*, paragraph 44, p. 30.

under Geoffrey's description of the achievements of the legendary British king, Belinus. The passage describes Belinus's foundation of a gate and a tower which has been identified as the Tower of London.[148] The decision to place this image here suggests that the artist supported this reading, although this did not prevent him or her including the Tower in the earlier illustration of London, accompanying the text describing Brutus's foundation of the city. Again, as with both the seal and Matthew Paris's illustrations, these depictions use the medieval monuments of the city to illustrate foundation legends, hinting at the correspondences between the surviving buildings and those built by ancient founders. There is a blurring of past and present, just as there is a fusion of the identities of castle and town, expressing the unity of the city and its powerful traditions. The Tower again takes its prominent position, a visual symbol of the special status of London and of continuity between the old and the new.

I have emphasized the parallels between these depictions and positive images of the exemplary cities of Rome, Jerusalem and Troy. However, I have also noted that such idealized images necessarily admit to a gap between ideal image and urban reality. There are, on the other hand, plenty of cases where the legendary Trojan heritage of London, with its sad beginnings in the sack and treachery at Troy, takes on a mainly negative and divisive function. I will end my discussion with some of these examples, which demonstrate that the negative connotations of the Trojan foundation legend could sometimes come to the fore.

This was perhaps illustrated most forcefully by events that occurred in 1388, when the Lords Appellant convicted a former London mayor of treason. Nicholas Brembre, the former mayor in question was hanged; his crime, which the Lords Appellant had thought so dangerous, was reputedly a plan to rename London 'Little Troy' and to declare himself its duke.[149] The general reasons for such a violent reaction to an invocation of London's legendary connections are perhaps explained by Troy's negative connotations, which could sometimes outweigh its positive example. The war with the Greeks was, after all, caused by lust and ended by treachery, so Trojan connections were thus potentially dangerous in implying that such qualities could be transferred, by inheritance or by comparison, to the citizens of medieval London.[150] Invocations of the Trojan foundation legend in connection to the

---

[148] J. S. P. Tatlock, *The Legendary History of Britain: Geoffrey of Monmouth's* Historia regum Britannie *and its Early Vernacular Versions* (Berkeley, 1950), p. 31; Gransden, *Historical Writing in England c.550 to c.1307*, p. 207.

[149] See Thomas Walsingham, *Historia Anglicana*, ed. H. T. Riley, 2 vols. Rolls Series 28 (1863), II, 174. Discussed in Federico, 'London as a Feminine New Troy', pp. 121–5 and *passim*.

[150] Federico, 'London as a Feminine New Troy', pp. 121–5, and *passim*.

aftermath of the Peasants' Revolt of 1381 illustrate this model of a degenerate, feminized and reviled New Troy. These may explain the violent reaction to Brembre's invocation of the legend, seven years later.

Gower's *Vox clamantis* is one of these examples. What is now the first section of *Vox clamantis* was added by Gower to his existing poem, probably shortly after the Peasants' Revolt, as a condemnation of the rebels' actions and an exoneration of the young King Richard's role.[151] It depicts London as the New Troy, in a gendered position of female submissiveness as a vulnerable widow, defenceless against the unnatural depredations of the revolting peasants. This imagery is overlaid on to the architectural features of the medieval city. The city walls in particular are associated with the Trojan heritage in one of these passages:

> A dextrisque novam me tunc vidisse putabam
> Troiam, que vidue languida more fuit:
> Que solet ex muris cingi patuit sine muro,
> Nec potuit seras claudere porta suas[152]

> (On my right I then thought I saw New Troy, which was powerless as a widow. Ordinarily surrounded by walls, it lay exposed without any wall, and the city gate could not shut its bars[153])

The lack of walls leaves the city vulnerable and symbolizes here the destructive power of social conflict. However, the association between the city walls and the legendary past still remains, with the inevitable implication that, when the walls stood intact, the city was a happy and unified one. The exemplary qualities of the city of London are further reinforced by echoes in this passage of the Biblical Lamentations of Jeremiah, which describe the ruin of the city of Jerusalem in terms notably similar to those used here by Gower.[154] Such Biblical imagery is entirely suitable for a poem whose very name is a Biblical quotation applied as a commentary on Britain's contemporary political troubles.[155]

---

[151] John Gower, *The Major Latin Works of John Gower*, transl. E. W. Stockton (Seattle, 1962), pp. 11–13.

[152] John Gower, *The Complete Works of John Gower*, ed. G. C. Macaulay, 4 vols. (Oxford, 1902), IV, lines 879–82, pp. 46–7.

[153] Gower, *The Major Latin Works*, p. 69.

[154] Lamentations, 1. 1: 'Quomodo sedet sola civitas plena populo! facta est quasi vidua domina gentium' ('How doth the city sit solitary that was full of people! how is the mistress of the Gentiles become as a widow'); 2. 8: 'Cogitavit Dominus dissipare murum filiae Sion; . . . luxitque antemurale, et murus pariter dissipatus est' ('The Lord hath purposed to destroy the wall of the daughter of Sion; . . . and the bulwark hath mourned, and the wall hath been destroyed together'); 2. 9: 'Defixae sunt in terra portae eius, perdidit et contrivit vectes eius' ('Her gates are sunk into the ground: he hath destroyed, and broken her bars').

[155] Gower, *The Major Latin Works*, p. 11.

The imagery of feminization and violation can also be found in connection with events supposed to have taken place at the Tower during the Peasants' Revolt, extending this imagery to London's citadel. Passages in the works of Froissart and Thomas Walsingham describe the penetration of the Tower by the rebels, and their assault on the king's mother, Joan of Kent, using heavily gendered imagery of assault and violation.[156] As with Gower's poem, it is a widow whom the peasants attack, and the Tower forms the location for this scene, with its walls, doors and rooms carefully enumerated. Once again, defensive boundaries define the state of social relations in the city – in this case, they are violated, like the walls and gates of *Vox clamantis* and Lamentations.

However, gendered invocations of the New Troy could also be used in the period following the Peasants' Revolt as a means of re-establishing London's social harmony. In the pageant that celebrated Richard II's reconciliation with London, performed in 1392, the New Troy in its gendered and submissive role constantly recurs.[157] The Tower is not left out , but makes a placatory appearance in the pageant as the Trojan citadel, as the queen begs the king to accept the capitulation of the citizens. Richard Maydiston's description of the pageant announces:

> quod se reddent modo cives –
> Corpora, divicias, Pergama, queque sua
>
> (that the citizens now yield themselves
> bodies, riches, the Trojan citadel, their all)[158]

Again, the gender connotations of this appeal are unmissable, but there is also the implication that the capital's castle, and its Trojan heritage, play an integral part in the restoration and preservation of social and political harmony

---

[156] Discussed illuminatingly in W. M. Ormrod, 'In Bed with Joan of Kent: The King's Mother and the Peasants' Revolt', in *Medieval Women: Texts and Contexts in Late Medieval Britain: Essays for Felicity Riddy*, ed. J. Wogan-Browne, R. Voaden, A. Diamond, A. Hutchinson, C. M. Meale and L. Johnson (Turnhout, 2000), pp. 277–92.

[157] 'Hic licet accensus foret in te, Troja, parumper,/ Grata modo facies se docet esse piam./ Non poterat mordax detractans lingua tenere,/ Quin cuperet thalamum sponsus adire suum' ('Although he was angry with you for a while, O Troy, his kind face now radiates parental affection. No detractor's tongue could overcome the bride-groom's longing to enter his bridal chamber'): G. Wickham, *Early English Stages 1300–1660*, 3 vols. (London, 1980), I, 65–6, reproduced from Oxford, Bodleian Library MS E. Museo. 94.

[158] This quotation and translation are cited in Federico, 'London as a Feminine New Troy', p. 146, from '*Concordia Facta inter Regem Ricardum II et Civitatem Londonie*', ed. and transl. C. R. Smith (unpublished Ph.D. dissertation, Princeton University, 1972), lines 213–14 and p. 189. This passage is not included in the extract from Maydiston's account reproduced in Wickham's work and I have unfortunately been unable to obtain Smith's dissertation.

within the city. Once again, city and castle are important symbols of civic harmony, even when they are also used to illustrate the temporary breakdown of that harmony. The threat of discontent and division is always present in urban town/castle images, which juxtapose walls and citadel; the harmony of the layout, however, counteracts these divisions to affirm the medieval belief that consensual government was both desirable and possible.[159]

---

[159] Reynolds, 'Medieval *Origines Gentium*', pp. 380–1.

CHAPTER THREE

The Spiritual Castle

Ideo, fratres, praeparemus spirituale quoddam castellum, ut veniat ad nos Dominus noster. Audacter enim dico, quia nisi beata Maria hoc castellum praeparasset in se, non intrasset in uterum ejus, nec in mentem ejus Dominus Jesus, nec istud Evangelium in ejus festivitate hodie legeretur. Ergo praeparemus hoc castellum. In castello fiunt tria quaedam, ut forte sit, scilicet fossatum, murus et turris. Primo fossatum, et postea murus super fossatum, et sic turris quae est fortior et excellentior caeteris. Murus et fossatum se invicem custodiunt; quia nisi fossatum praeesset, possent per aliqod ingenium homines accedere ad murum suffodiendum; et nisi murus esset super fossatum, possent ad fossatum accedere, et illud implere. Turris omnia custodit, quia altior est omnibus. Intremus modo animam nostram, et videamus quomodo ista omnia debent in nobis spiritualiter fieri.[1]

(Therefore, brothers, let us make ready a certain castle spiritually, so that our Lord might come to us. Indeed I say to you [do it] boldly, because unless the blessed Mary had prepared this castle within herself, Lord Jesus would not have entered into her womb, nor into her mind, nor would this gospel be read today on her holyday. Therefore let us prepare this castle. Three things make up a castle, so that it might be strong, namely a ditch, a wall and a tower. First the ditch, and after that a wall over the ditch, and then the tower which is stronger and better than the others. The wall and ditch guard each other; because if the ditch were not there, men could by some device get in to undermine the wall; and if the wall were not above the ditch, they could get to the ditch and fill it in. The tower guards everything, because it is taller than everything else. So let us enter our minds, and see how all these things should be brought into being spiritually within ourselves.)

Castles and churches are without doubt the most impressive architectural achievements of the Middle Ages, yet they have traditionally been studied from different points of view and by different scholars. This approach has inevitably emphasized the contrasts between them, especially in terms of their ideological connotations. The whole of this book is an attempt to show that defensive architecture could communicate meaning in the same ways as

---

[1] Aelred of Rievaulx, '*Sermo XVII: In Assumptione beatae Mariae*', in *Patrologiae Latinae Cursus Completus*, ed. J. P. Migne (Paris, 1844–64), 195, cols. 303–4.

ecclesiastical architecture. This chapter seeks to explore in more detail some of the ideological similarities and connections between defensive and devotional buildings. Physical architectural resemblances, joint planning and patronage are implicated in these arguments. However, devotional and ideological patterns associated with castles in literature and art are the main focus of this discussion, as these have been most neglected in traditional approaches to medieval castle architecture. The examples I discuss have been chosen to illustrate the ways in which, and the extent to which, common ideological ground can be found between castle and church, the secular and the sacred in medieval thought, art and life. They make an emphatic case for the importance of the medieval castle as a spiritual and devotional concept.

Central to this argument is the understanding that, in its medieval context, the word *castle* could be applied to structures other than the private, feudal defences with which castle studies is so familiar. It is difficult to understate the importance of this in the interpretation of defensive and ecclesiastical architecture. It means not only that monastic and ecclesiastical defensive complexes could be understood as castles in certain contexts, but also that Biblical texts containing the word *castellum* could be read as referring to structures very similar to medieval castles, in all senses of the word. This casts a completely new light on the significance of the castle motif in medieval theology. Castle imagery has often been seen as a strategy of deliberate medievalizing: of inserting a characteristically contemporary concept into a Biblical or devotional context to give a theological point an immediate relevance for the Middle Ages. For example, the imagery in the extract above, from a sermon on the Assumption of the Virgin by Aelred, abbot of Rievaulx from 1147 to 1167,[2] has been characterized as an 'allegory constructed with recognizable images of royal power', a 'combination of edifying intent and everyday imagery' which 'was in part the result of the spread of castle-building from the twelfth century'.[3] This is a logical conclusion when it is assumed that castles were understood in the Middle Ages as being characteristically medieval buildings, and that different readings were reserved for castle words used in Biblical and medieval texts.[4] However, castle imagery must now be recognized as having a much more fundamental Biblical and theological significance: as referring to structures and

---

[2] See P. Fergusson and S. Harrison, *Rievaulx Abbey: Community, Architecture, Memory* (New Haven, 1999), p. 38; M. L. Dutton, 'The Conversion and Vocation of Aelred of Rievaulx: A Historical Hypothesis', in *England in the Twelfth Century*, ed. D. Williams, Proceedings of the 1988 Harlaxton Symposium (1990), pp. 31–49 (p. 33).

[3] M. Hebron, *The Medieval Siege: Theme and Image in Middle English Romance* (Oxford, 1997), pp. 146, 164.

[4] This can, for example, be seen in Hebron's translation of a treatise by Godfrey of Admont, prefaced by the Biblical text of Luke 10. 38: ' "Intravit Jesus in quoddam castellum". Castellum ubi pro tuitione construitur . . .'. Hebron translates this: ' "Jesus entered into a certain village". When a castle is constructed for defence . . .'. Hebron, *The Medieval Siege*, p. 144.

ideas which were believed to have been written into the Bible by its original authors, seen and visited by Jesus and other Biblical figures. This shift in interpretation transforms theological castle imagery, changing it from an elaborate form of allegory or metaphor into a very direct quotation of a Biblically sanctioned architecture. Not only does Aelred shape his whole sermon around a Biblical castle text, but he also ensures this has a number of very direct applications to the devotional practices and architectural surroundings of his audience. Aelred's text offers a succinct introduction to many of the methodologies and ideas I explore in this chapter, so a brief summary of his rhetorical strategy and ideological and architectural context will form an introduction to later discussions.

In Chapter 1, I noted that the castle in this excerpt from Aelred's sermon is described as an association of certain defensive elements, rather than being defined by particular social or political constraints. Aelred's concept of the castle could be applied equally to lordly, ecclesiastical and urban defences, and so illustrates the broad understanding of the castle I have set out through linguistic analysis of medieval sources. This demonstrates from the outset the broad relevance Aelred intended his architectural allegory to have. However, the architectural elements Aelred pinpoints also have specific allegorical and devotional functions to perform within his sermon. Each is accorded a particular spiritual significance: the ditch is humility, the wall chastity and the tower charity.[5] Just as these defensive elements combine to form the castle, so the individual allegorical elements are used to construct the meaning of an entire symbolic edifice. Aelred constructs his castle out of a number of Biblical texts, which he quotes explicitly. His sermon is based on Luke 10. 38, which he renders as: 'Intravit Jesus in quoddam castellum'.[6] This text describes Jesus's entry into Bethany to visit Martha and Mary, but Aelred interprets this as referring figuratively to the Incarnation. The castle of the Biblical text is understood as an allegorical representation of the body of the Virgin, into which Jesus entered to be born as a man.[7] Aelred makes a further Biblical reference to Ezekiel 44. 2, a text that describes the closed east gate of the Temple of Jerusalem.[8] He interprets this text, describing the closure of the east gate and its exclusive use by the Lord, as signifying the intact state of the Virgin's

---

[5]   Aelred of Rievaulx, '*Sermo XVII: In Assumptione beatae Mariae*', cols. 304–5.

[6]   Ibid., col. 303. Luke 10. 38 reads: 'Factum est autem dum irent, et ipse intravit in quoddam castellum; et mulier quaedam, Martha nomine, excepit illum in domum suam' ('Now it came to pass as they went, that he entered into a certain castle: and a certain woman named Martha, received him into her house'). This text recurs throughout this chapter, so I will not cite it in full or translate it each time. Because of my arguments in Chapter 1 to show that the word *castellum* has a meaning consistent with the normal medieval use of the word *castle*, I will translate the use in this text as *castle* throughout this chapter, without further justification.

[7]   Aelred of Rievaulx, '*Sermo XVII: In Assumptione beatae Mariae*', col. 305.

[8]   Ibid.

body before and after Jesus's birth. The castle of Aelred's sermon is therefore constructed out of important tenets of the Christian faith: three virtues and the Incarnation and Virgin Birth. These elements combine to create the allegorical significance of the whole castle, which represents the Virgin herself.

In expounding and combining Biblical texts in this way, Aelred is drawing on established exegetical readings and methods. Luke 10. 38 seems to have been connected with the Virgin since the seventh century, and interpreted as an architectural image of the Virgin as a castle (*castellum*) from the ninth.[9] Ezekiel 44. 2 had also been interpreted allegorically as referring to the Virgin Birth since before the fourth century.[10] Aelred was, then, following approved readings of these texts, agreed by medieval theologians over many years to represent their essential meanings. Similarly, Aelred's method of architectural allegory is derived from the interrelationships and resonances written into these texts in their original, Biblical context. I Peter 2. 5[11] sees the faithful as living stones, built into a spiritual edifice, notably similar in conception to Aelred's idea of his listeners constructing a spiritual castle for the reception of God. For other allegorical buildings with carefully delineated components, each given a particular symbolic meaning, Aelred needed to look no further than the temple of Ezekiel with its twelve gates named after the tribes of Israel (Ezekiel 48. 31ff) and the twelve foundation layers of the Heavenly Jerusalem, named after the apostles (Revelation 21. 14).[12] These texts outline a number of specific elements in a particular relationship (such as the four walls with twelve gates of Jerusalem, the easternmost of which is closed) implying, and in some cases providing, the symbolic and spiritual rationale for such arrangements. More significantly, they also create complex interrelationships with the other architectural texts of the Bible, combining and recombining different elements to create new symbolic and spiritual edifices.[13]

---

[9]   R. D. Cornelius, *The Figurative Castle: A Study in the Mediaeval Allegory of the Edifice with Especial Reference to Religious Writings: A Dissertation* (Bryn Mawr, 1930), pp. 37–50; Hebron, *The Medieval Siege*, pp. 142–5; B. E. Kurtz, ' "The Small Castle of the Soul": Mysticism and Metaphor in the European Middle Ages', *Studia Mystica* 15.4 (1992), 19–39 (pp. 24–6); J. Mann, 'Allegorical Buildings in Mediaeval Literature', *Medium Aevum* 63 (1994), 191–210 (p. 198).

[10]   Mann, 'Allegorical Buildings in Mediaeval Literature', p. 193 and *passim*.

[11]   I Peter 2. 5: 'Et ipsi tamquam lapides vivi superedificamini, domus spiritualis, sacerdotium sanctum' ('Be you also as living stones built up, a spiritual house, a holy priesthood').

[12]   Ezekiel 48. 31: 'portae civitatis in nominibus tribuum Israhel portae tres a septentrione porta Ruben una porta Iudae una porta Levi una porta' ('And the gates of the city, according to the names of the tribes of Israel, three gates on the north side, the gate of Reuben one, the gate of Juda one, the gate of Levi one'); Revelation 21. 14: 'Et murus civitatis habens fundamenta duodecim, et in ipsis duodecim nomina duodecim apostolorum agni' ('And the wall of the city had twelve foundations, and in them the twelve names of the twelve apostles of the Lamb').

[13]   Mann, 'Allegorical Buildings in Mediaeval Literature', pp. 192–6.

The temple of Ezekiel's vision is derived in many of its features from Solomon's temple (I Kings 6–7), not least in the way every element is carefully measured and enumerated. The Heavenly Jerusalem of Revelation in turn builds upon Ezekiel's temple, repeating once more the motif of measuring out each part of the building. The twelve gates of Ezekiel's temple, named after the tribes of Israel, are also reflected in the twelve foundation layers of the Heavenly Jerusalem, named after the apostles (discussed and cited above). Aelred's sermon is, then, not just citing Biblical texts but recombining them according to patterns set by the texts themselves. The image of the castle, the central idea of Aelred's text, is perfectly in tune with this very canonical use of architectural texts and methodologies. It is not a medievalizing interpolation into the architectural framework so carefully created out of Biblical texts. Itself derived from the text of Luke 10. 38, it takes its place in Aelred's sermon amongst similar images and allegorical components, all derived from Biblical buildings understood both allegorically – in terms of the spiritual value of their structures – and literally – as buildings whose structures were seen and comprehended by their Biblical describers.

Aelred also transforms his castle into a spiritual exercise for his fellow monks, when he recommends the spiritual construction of a castle in the mind of each of them. This is part of a rhetorical and spiritual strategy that puts castle architecture and Biblical castle texts at the heart of the medieval understanding and practice of exegesis and devotion. The description of the castle is enumerated in a specific order, with the ditch first, then the wall and then the tower. When Aelred advises his listeners to prepare this castle spiritually, he is asking them to construct each feature mentally, in the precise order and relationship in which they are described. He goes through this process more fully in the passage immediately following this extract, describing in detail the spiritual significance of each of the elements.[14] It is only with the inward construction of the spiritual castle, Aelred advises, that the mind can be prepared for the spiritual and mental reception of God.

This spiritual exercise bears a strong resemblance to an architectural mnemonic. Architectural mnemonics were derived ultimately from Classical models, passed on to the medieval period through various treatises, the most famous of which was known as the *Rhetorica ad Herennium*, often attributed to Cicero.[15] This work advises that items to be remembered should be located at various points within a familiar architectural framework, so that they can be recalled in order, as the subject progresses mentally through the building.

---

[14] Aelred of Rievaulx, '*Sermo XVII: In Assumptione beatae Mariae*', cols. 304–5.

[15] For descriptions of the mnemonic technique transmitted to the Middle Ages through the text of the *Rhetorica ad Herennium*, sometimes attributed to Cicero, see F. A. Yates, *The Art of Memory* (London, 1966), pp. 5–8 and *passim*; M. J. Carruthers, *The Book of Memory: A Study of Memory in Medieval Culture* (Cambridge, 1990), especially pp. 71–3.

This kind of spiritual apparatus was well known and used for mnemonic and devotional purposes, to assist in recall and inward contemplation of important spiritual tenets in monastic circles up to about 1200. Indeed, such schemes were particularly associated with Cistercian contexts,[16] making it more than probable that Aelred would have been fully aware of the exegetical and mnemonic traditions associated with Biblical architectural texts.

The key principle of the architectural mnemonic is the familiarity of the architectural setting selected. If the setting is not very well known, the thinker will not be able to remember it with sufficient precision for the mnemonic to be effective. Some convincing work has been done on the usefulness of ecclesiastical architecture for this purpose. Indeed, Mary Carruthers has identified patterns and traits specifically in Cistercian monastic buildings of the twelfth century which seem designed for mnemonic use.[17] In a similar way, the castle of Aelred's sermon seems specially configured to reflect certain aspects of monastic architecture that would be familiar to his monastic brothers. At the most basic level, the spiritual attributes he attaches to its architectural elements make this connection smoothly. He equates the ditch with humility, the walls with chastity and the tower with the virtue of charity which is above all the others. These architectural elements, and their spiritual meanings, bear certain obvious resemblances to the monastic setting.[18] The motif of construction – which is not part of the conventional architectural mnemonic, but which Aelred makes into an integral part of his sermon, inviting the monks to build the castle as part of their devotional exercise – also seems specifically designed to reflect monastic architecture and its construction. It was by no means unusual for monks to assist in the physical labour of building their own monastery;[19] indeed, documentary evidence suggests that Aelred himself was involved in such tasks during his early years at Rievaulx.[20] A very practical understanding of the architecture of monasticism therefore forms the basis for Aelred's spiritual imagery.[21] The castle image cannot be seen merely as a metaphorical trope. It is applied directly to the monastic setting, emphasizing the symbolic qualities of its architecture.

---

[16] M. Carruthers, *The Craft of Thought: Meditation, Rhetoric, and the Making of Images, 400–1200*, Cambridge Studies in Medieval Literature 34 (1998), especially pp. 5, 257–69.

[17] Ibid., pp. 257–76.

[18] Cornelius, *The Figurative Castle*, pp. 49–50.

[19] Fergusson and Harrison, *Rievaulx Abbey: Community, Architecture, Memory*, p. 62.

[20] Ibid.; see also Walter Daniel, *Walter Daniel's Life of Aelred, Abbot of Rievaulx*, ed. F. M. Powicke (London, 1950), p. 22.

[21] The importance of labour as a spiritual virtue and its connection to the roles of Mary and Martha in Aelred's Marian sermons, are discussed in D. La Corte, 'The Abbatial Concerns of Aelred of Rievaulx Based on his Sermons of Mary', *Cistercian Studies Quarterly* 30 (1995), 267–73 (pp. 268–70).

Nevertheless, there also seem to be hints in Aelred's sermon to look beyond the architecture of Cistercian monasticism. The tower of Aelred's sermon-castle represents the monastic virtue of charity, and its Marian associations make it generally appropriate to an ecclesiastical setting.[22] However, Aelred places repeated emphasis on the distinctive form of the tower, making its pre-eminent height an integral part of its spiritual symbolism. This is harder to relate to Cistercian architecture than the other elements Aelred singles out, such as ditch and walls, especially given the statute of 1157 which forbade the building of towers by the order.[23] Perhaps, however, the tower can be interpreted as a specific invitation to Aelred's listeners to look outside the Cistercian monastic environment for mnemonic settings, towards architecture with a more specialist defensive form.

Examination of Aelred's wider social, spiritual and architectural context reveals the full extent to which the monastic life was enmeshed in defensive architecture and military connections, not just in terms of imagery or rhetoric, but in the most practical ways possible. This area will repay a brief examination, as it will lead, in the end, to a better understanding of the context of Aelred's writings. Like many other monasteries of its time, Aelred's own abbey of Rievaulx[24] was founded on land in Yorkshire granted to the Cistercian order by Walter Espec, lord of Helmsley Castle.[25] Important connections continued between this temporal lord and his monastic protégés. Helmsley Castle was only three kilometres away from Rievaulx, and so offered protection as well as patronage to the community:[26] an important consideration in the unstable north of England during this period of the anarchy. It is possible that the castle of Aelred's sermon refers obliquely to Helmsley. No traces now survive of Helmsley's original timber buildings, but Espec's castle is known to have been built in the form of a ringwork. It is likely to have been equipped, like other ringworks of the period, with a substantial ditch, a palisade wall at the crown of its ramparts, and a timber tower of some sort.[27] It is clear from Aelred's personal involvement in Espec's political and military affairs that Rievaulx and Helmsley were perceived very much as complementary establishments with duties of mutual support.

[22] Cornelius, *The Figurative Castle*, p. 49.

[23] *Cistercian Art and Architecture in the British Isles*, ed. E. C. Norton and D. Park (Cambridge, 1986), p. 328.

[24] Although my remarks so far have been directed towards the monastic life in general, it seems natural to turn to Rievaulx when considering the environment of which Aelred may have been thinking. Rievaulx reportedly inspired Aelred's conversion to the monastic life, and although he travelled widely during his life and was briefly appointed as founder abbot of Revesby in Lincoln, Rievaulx was his home for the rest of his life. See Fergusson and Harrison, *Rievaulx Abbey: Community, Architecture, Memory*, pp. 61–6.

[25] Ibid., p. 37.

[26] Ibid.

[27] G. Coppack, *Helmsley Castle*, 2nd edn (London, 1997), p. 23.

Aelred used his political influence in the North of England to mediate between King David of Scotland's court and the magnates of the North, including Walter Espec. For example, in 1138 he travelled to the Scottish border to assist in the transfer of Wark Castle from David to Walter.[28] This political and military involvement was expressed in Aelred's writing when in 1155–7 he composed the martial poem *Relatio de Standardo* to commemorate Espec's role in the decisive Battle of the Standard in 1138, when Walter had rallied the northern troops to defeat the Scots.[29] Within this context it would not be unexpected or inappropriate for Aelred to apply martial metaphors in his sermons, or to allude to military architecture, which was involved in various ways so closely in the abbey's own affairs.

Military attitudes and duties were inseparable from the monastic situation both physically and spiritually, as the foundation texts of the Cistercian order confirm. The Cistercian rule refers to its monks as 'novi milites Christi' ('new knights of Christ')[30] and Bernard of Clairvaux applied this martial imagery specifically to Rievaulx at its foundation in 1131.[31] This language is a deliberate reflection of phrases which had by this time become synonymous with the religious armies mobilized on the Crusades. Pope Urban II's call for the First Crusade in 1095 was couched in terms which deliberately elided the religious and the military. As subsequent campaigns progressed, especially with the capture of Jerusalem in July 1099, the religious rhetoric became more and more emphatic, with terms such as *milites Christi* (knights of Christ), *exercitus Dei* and *exercitus Domini* (army of God, army of the Lord) springing up.[32] Just as with Aelred's sermon, these ideas derived ultimately from Biblical texts. St Paul's writings are a fertile source of both military and architectural metaphors of the Christian faith which he conceived as spiritual armour for the faithful,[33] while

---

28 Dutton, 'The Conversion and Vocation of Aelred of Rievaulx', p. 33.

29 D. Baker, 'Aelred of Rievaulx and Walter Espec', *Haskins Society Journal* 1 (1989), 91–8 (pp. 91–3).

30 Fergusson and Harrison, *Rievaulx Abbey: Community, Architecture, Memory*, p. 37.

31 Ibid., pp. 37–8.

32 Ibid., pp. 8, 37; J. Riley-Smith, *The First Crusade and the Idea of Crusading* (Cambridge, 1986), pp. 16–17.

33 For example, Ephesians 6. 13–17: 'Propterea accipite armaturam Dei ut possitis resistere in die malo et in omnibus perfecti stare. State ergo succincti lumbos vestros in veritate et induti loricam iustitiae et calceati pedes in praeparatione evangelii pacis, in omnibus sumentes scutum fidei, in quo possitis omnia tela nequissimi ignea extinguere; et galeam salutis assumite et gladium spiritus, quod est verbum Dei' ('Therefore take unto you the armour of God, that you may be able to resist in the evil day . . . Stand therefore, having your loins girt about with truth, and having on the breastplate of justice, And your feet shod with the preparation of the gospel of peace: In all things taking the shield of faith, wherewith you may be able to extinguish all the fiery darts of the most wicked one. And take unto you the helmet of salvation, and the sword of the spirit (which is the word of God)'); 1 Thessalonians 5. 8: 'Nos autem qui diei sumus, sobrii simus, induti loricam fidei et caritatis et galeam

in the Psalms God is frequently described as a defender or refuge of the faithful from their enemies.[34] The application of these powerful metaphors spread, just as the label of 'Crusade' was spreading, to describe monastic and ecclesiastical campaigns and ideas, as well as military ones.[35] It is within this context, I suggest, that Aelred's sermon should be understood. Its imagery, drawn similarly from Biblical texts, presents exactly this sort of fusion of the military and the religious, demonstrating the venerable, Biblical roots of the idea of the Church militant. However, the architectural fusion of the defensive and the ecclesiastical, as expressed through the Crusades, also provides models which may have inspired Aelred in the creation of his spiritual sermon-castle.

The churches of the Crusaders reflected the integral relationship of religious and military principles in the Crusaders' mission. They had to be strongly defended in this environment of militant Christianity and so combined defensive and ecclesiastical architecture. The twelfth-century cathedral of Tortosa, for example, had thick walls, small windows and arrow-loops.[36] The Church of the Ascension on the Mount of Olives was also fortified.[37] Chapels were a large and central facility in Crusader castles, especially those of the religious orders, reflecting the importance of spiritual concerns to their inhabitants.[38] Castles themselves were, of course, essential to the Crusaders' tactics of conquest and occupation and had an important part to play in the developing symbolism of the holy war.[39] In the hostile, rocky and parched terrain in which they were often built, the Crusader castles are still some of the most impressive technical achievements of the Middle Ages, and stand as monuments of faith like its cathedrals, as well as of aggression. This military architecture was accompanied by huge building campaigns at Christianity's holiest

---

spem salutis' ('But let us, who are of the day, be sober, having on the breastplate of faith and charity, and for a helmet the hope of salvation'); 2 Timothy 2. 3: 'Labora sicut bonus miles Christi Iesu' ('Labour as a good soldier of Christ Jesus').

[34] For example, Psalm 59. 2: 'Eripe me de inimicis meis, Deus meus, et ab insurgentibus in me libera me' (Deliver me from mine enemies, O my God; and defend me from them that rise up against me); Psalm 71. 3: 'Esto mihi in Deum protectorem et in locum munitum, ut salvum me facias, quoniam firmamentum meum et refugium meum es tu' ('Be thou unto me a God, a protector, and a place of strength: that thou mayst make me safe. For thou art my firmament and my refuge'). See also Psalms 18. 2; 31. 3; 91. 2; 144. 2 for similar imagery. I use the Vulgate numbering for the Psalms.

[35] J. Riley-Smith, *The Crusades: A Short History* (London, 1987, repr. 1992), pp. 37, 88 and *passim*.

[36] S. Bonde, *Fortress Churches of Languedoc: Architecture, Religion and Conflict in the High Middle Ages* (Cambridge, 1994), p. 13; A. J. Boas, *Crusader Archaeology: The Material Culture of the Latin East* (London, 1999), p. 124.

[37] D. Pringle, 'Templar Castles on the Road to Jerusalem', in *The Military Orders: Fighting for the Faith and Caring for the Sick*, ed. M. Barber (Aldershot, 1994), p. 151.

[38] See, for example, H. Kennedy, *Crusader Castles* (Cambridge, 1994), p. 127.

[39] Riley-Smith, *The Crusades*, p. 77.

sites: the Holy Sepulchre, the Temple, Calvary, and so on.[40] Famous Biblical fortress sites were also important in the Christians' symbolic reclamation of the Holy Land. Godfrey of Bouillon moved straight into the Tower of David after the capture of Jerusalem, restoring its Biblical use as the royal residence. He publicized his acquisition of this important Biblical landmark by having it depicted on his royal seal and on coinage, emphasising the symbolic impact of his action.[41]

The sites associated with Biblical *castellum* texts also came in for their share of new building.[42] For example, in the twelfth century Queen Melisende built a convent at Bethany in the form of a great tower surrounded by a wall with projecting towers.[43] It seems to me more than probable that this structure was intended to relate to the *castellum* of Luke 10. 38 and John 11. 1, both in its form and function. Its appearance seems to have been distinctively defensive, while its monastic function can be related to Martha and Mary, whom Christ visited at Bethany, and who represented in medieval exegesis the active and contemplative principles essential to the monastic calling.[44] The dedication of this convent to St Lazarus[45] further emphasizes these connections, as he was believed to have been the brother of Martha and Mary, living with them at Bethany.[46] This construction at Bethany was not an isolated case. A similar project was also underway in the twelfth century at Abu Gosh, a site identified at this time as Emmaus, where Christ supped with his disciples.[47] Emmaus, too, is a Biblical castle, referred to in Luke 24. 13 as a *castellum*.[48] The extremely strong construction of the basilica church on this site,[49] like the central tower with perimeter defences at Bethany, converted Emmaus once more into a castle-like structure, in accordance with the Biblical text. I have already provided

---

[40] Boas, *Crusader Archaeology, passim*; Riley-Smith, *The Crusades*, pp. 43–4; J. Riley-Smith, *The First Crusaders, 1095–1131* (Cambridge, 1997), pp. 23ff.

[41] Boas, *Crusader Archaeology*, pp. 18–19; Riley-Smith, *The Crusades*, p. 42; E. B. Smith, *Architectural Symbolism of Imperial Rome and the Middle Ages* (Princeton, 1956), p. 104. The Tower of David became an enduring image on the Crusader seal and coin issues of Jerusalem, especially at moments of crisis: see C. J. Sabine, 'Numismatic Iconography of the Tower of David and the Holy Sepulchre: An Emergency Coinage Struck during the Siege of Jerusalem, 1187', *Numismatic Chronicle* 19.7 (1979), 122–32. See also Kennedy, *Crusader Castles*, pp. 22–3.

[42] That is, the sites associated with Biblical texts containing the word *castellum* or its variants, and so probably interpreted in the Middle Ages as referring to defensive structures. I discussed several of these texts in Chapter 1, pp. 35–8.

[43] Pringle, 'Templar Castles on the Road to Jerusalem', p. 151.

[44] This imagery goes back as far as Augustine: Cornelius, *The Figurative Castle*, p. 42.

[45] Boas, *Crusader Archaeology*, p. 142.

[46] See Chapter 1, p. 36.

[47] Ibid., p. 129.

[48] Luke 24. 13: 'Et ecce duo ex illis ibant ipsa die in castellum, quod erat in spatio stadiorum sexaginta ab Ierusalem, nomine Emmaus' ('And behold, two of them went, the same day, to a *town* which was sixty furlongs from Jerusalem, named Emmaus').

[49] Boas, *Crusader Archaeology*, pp. 124, 129–30.

evidence in the first chapter to show that both Emmaus and Bethany were referred to as castles quite straightforwardly in medieval texts.[50] These sites have not been much discussed in terms of their symbolic or Biblical significance, as far as I know. However, it seems to me highly probable that Crusader building schemes at such sites were meant to recreate symbolically the castles believed to have occupied them in Biblical times. As such, these building projects are every bit as significant as those undertaken at sites such as the Holy Sepulchre. They all express in their form and symbolism a veneration of Biblical architecture, and a desire by the Crusaders to reconstruct it.

This context demonstrates effectively that the kinds of hybrid spiritual/ military building Aelred creates in his sermon on the Assumption of the Virgin are not confined to the realms of allegory. It is possible Aelred knew of the towered monastery at Bethany, and constructed his sermon-castle deliberately in its image.[51] If this was not the case, however, he had plenty of other models for architecture with strong symbolic significance in which the military and the religious were equally weighted. The Crusades articulate this fusion of architectural functions and meanings with particular clarity, but their influence on military and religious ideas throughout the medieval world is hard to underestimate.[52] It is modern critics who have emphasized the divide between what they perceive as secular and spiritual in medieval life and in medieval architecture.

Aelred's sermon provides a masterful demonstration of the integration of the idea of the castle into all aspects of medieval monasticism. It participates in venerable traditions of exegesis and so invokes some of the most important figures and ideas of medieval Christianity in the Virgin Mary and the sisters Mary and Martha, the Incarnation and the Virgin Birth. However, it is also given a more direct relevance to the life of the medieval monk. The castle represents the defences which protect the monk both spiritually and physically, both in the monastic enclosure and in the lordly fortresses which guards its interests. The castle is presented to the monk as an embodiment of both the spiritual and the physical virtues of the monastic profession. It is a mnemonic image of his spiritual and mental life which the monk is exhorted to carry with him, and at the same time a description of the monk's physical and spiritual relationship with his architectural surroundings. This introduction has shown some of the ways in which these ideas could be received, articulated and understood in a twelfth-century English context. The main

---

[50] I have looked only for references in texts from an English context, as these are most relevant to this project.

[51] Until more archaeological findings on the structure are published, it will be impossible to ascertain the full significance of this building and its implications for twelfth-century theology and the idea of the castle. This would certainly be a worthwhile subject for further study.

[52] See, for example, Riley-Smith, *The First Crusade*, Riley-Smith, *The Crusades*; Riley-Smith, *The First Crusaders*.

part of this chapter sets out to explore other English medieval contexts which demonstrate a similar emphasis on the spiritual application of the idea of the castle in literature, art and architecture. However, it begins with a brief survey of the religious and military background of post-Conquest Britain, to set out the background against which these ideas of the castle can be understood.

The Crusades provide manifest evidence of the interdependence of medieval military and religious aims and practices. This chapter sets out to show, however, that this close relationship is not confined to this specialist context: it is a fundamental dynamic of medieval life and thought, and can be found reflected in many and various aspects of medieval culture. The intimate links between the martial and the spiritual have often been obscured by modern historical perspectives, particularly those that see the architecture and ideology of castle and church as diametrically opposed: the one built as a symbolic celebration of the spiritual role of medieval society's *oratores* (those who pray), the other as a manifestation of the practical and violent concerns of its *bellatores* (those who fight). I discussed some of the implications of this perceived division in the Introduction. Nevertheless, there has been enough discussion of crossovers between the two fields in an English context to provide a background for ideas and images such as Aelred's.

Castles were the military tool by which the Normans achieved the Conquest, but ecclesiastical foundation was just as important to the establishment of a political and moral mandate for the kingdom. In this sense, like the fortified Christian sites of the Crusaders, the churches of Norman England were strong-holds of religious power.[53] From the earliest stages of the Conquest, ecclesiasti-cal and military power and architecture were deployed side by side. As well as the castles that marked prominent military sites of the Conquest, like Pevensey and Hastings,[54] William founded an abbey on the field of Battle. This was an unusual gesture, but may have been intended to underline God's supposed support of the Norman victory.[55] In the post-Conquest reorganization of Britain's government and administration, bishops held positions of great political as well as spiritual power, and were often given the highest temporal honours, such as earldoms, alongside their spiritual authorities.[56] Diocesan sees were re-sited in strategic positions, their bishops swore feudal oaths and were

---

[53] F. Barlow, *The Feudal Kingdom of England, 1042–1216* (London, 1974), p. 131.

[54] N. J. G. Pounds, *The Medieval Castle in England and Wales: A Social and Political History* (Cambridge, 1990, repr. 1994), pp. 6–7.

[55] See E. M. Hallam, 'Monasteries as "War Memorials": Battle Abbey and La Victoire', in *The Church and War*, ed. W. J. Shiels, Studies in Church History 20 (1983), pp. 47–57.

[56] Barlow, *The Feudal Kingdom of England, 1042–1216*, pp. 93–4.

granted baronial rights to armed retinues.[57] Their role in setting up the new government was crucial: Lanfranc, archbishop of Canterbury, was behind the introduction of canon law and the overhaul of the English legal system,[58] while William of St Calais, bishop of Durham from 1081, may have been in charge of the whole Domesday survey.[59] With such political and economic power came architectural patronage, as the top clerics rebuilt their churches and monasteries, and made themselves palaces and castles to live in. Here too, the combination of military and ecclesiastical was key.

At Durham the new bishop, Walcher, took over the earlier defences on the Durham peninsula and was the first among his clerical peers to construct a castle for his protection, with the new cathedral positioned in the south bailey. The prudence of this defensive siting, prompted by Durham's vulnerable position near the Scottish border, was underlined when Bishop Walcher was murdered during a raid at Gateshead in 1080.[60] A comparable situation can be seen at Lincoln, where an existing church, within the extensive early Norman castle, was turned into the cathedral when the see was relocated there in 1072–5.[61] However, even in less turbulent parts of the country, cathedrals were sited within fortifications. The Iron Age hillfort of Old Sarum became the site for the foundation of a royal castle and a cathedral. This situation caused some conflicts between garrison and chapter, but also served to emphasize the close relationship that could exist between them.[62]

Twinned defensive and ecclesiastical architectural projects were also generated by the lay aristocracy, when they built monastic or collegiate foundations along with their castles. The first lord of Hastings founded a college of secular canons within the bailey of the castle itself.[63] A similar foundation was made just below Bramber Castle in similar circumstances.[64] Under the Conqueror's successor, William Rufus, such examples multiplied, with joint

---

[57] Ibid., pp. 116–23.

[58] Ibid., pp. 123–6.

[59] W. M. Aird, 'An Absent Friend: The Career of Bishop William of St Calais', in *Anglo-Norman Durham 1093–1193*, ed. D. Rollason, M. Harvey and M. Prestwich (Woodbridge, 1994), pp. 283–97 (pp. 290–1).

[60] Ibid., p. 289.

[61] R. Gem, 'Lincoln Minster: *Ecclesia Pulchra, Ecclesia Fortis*', in *Medieval Art and Architecture at Lincoln Cathedral*, ed. T. A. Heslop and V. A. Sekules, British Archaeological Association Conference Transactions 8 (1986), pp. 9–28 (p. 9); D. Stocker, 'The Two Early Castles of Lincoln', in *Lincoln Castle*, ed. P. Lindley, Society for Lincolnshire History and Archaeology Occasional Monographs 11 (forthcoming). I am most grateful to David Stocker for giving me access to draft documents from this forthcoming volume.

[62] See P. Brimacombe, *A Tale of Two Cathedrals: Old Sarum, New Salisbury* (London, 1997), especially pp. 12–13, 22–3; T. Cocke and P. Kidson, *Salisbury Cathedral: Perspectives on the Architectural History* (London, 1993), especially pp. 3, 37.

[63] Pounds, *The Medieval Castle in England and Wales*, p. 233.

[64] Ibid., p. 234.

castle and ecclesiastical foundations at Chepstow,[65] Lewes and its offshoot Castle Acre,[66] Colchester[67] and Pembroke:[68] altogether forty-five joint establishments were founded in the eleventh century.[69] Castles also helped to define the practicalities of worship for ordinary lay people from 1066, as the Normans adapted the Anglo-Saxon parochial system, which had placed the parish church in the care of the local landholder.[70] The church was often located near a new castle, and sometimes within its confines, and the local patron and his family might be buried within the church ground. As church reforms took hold,[71] the castle chapel became a more important focus of aristocratic worship, though it too occasionally filled a quasi-parochial role for the local populace, especially in cases such as the chapel of St Michael at Clitheroe Castle, where the parish church proper was ten kilometres away, too distant for ease of travel.[72]

This much overlap between the castle and the church in early post-Conquest England is clear from the briefest historical overview. However, new critical approaches have recently begun to identify new exchanges between the two in architectural planning and execution. Even in the mainstream of castle studies, it has been recognized in recent years that two prestigious kinds of architecture in one society will inevitably have certain overlaps in siting, patronage, scale, design detail, or in construction personnel and procedures.[73] More detailed studies along these lines make the case persuasively. The castle and cathedral at Norwich have been identified 'as a "pair"' planned and executed together: masons' marks from the buildings match, suggesting an overlap in date and workforce between the two.[74] It is also clear that both were planned in a similar way, employing the same architectural techniques and detailing motifs, to achieve a harmonious overall

---

[65] M. W. Thompson, *The Rise of the Castle* (Cambridge, 1991), p. 139.

[66] Pounds, *The Medieval Castle in England and Wales*, p. 232; Thompson, *The Rise of the Castle*, p. 141.

[67] Thompson, *The Rise of the Castle*, p. 140.

[68] Ibid.

[69] Pounds, *The Medieval Castle in England and Wales*, p. 233; see also M. W. Thompson, 'Associated Monasteries and Castles in the Middle Ages: A Tentative List', *The Archaeological Journal* 143 (1986), pp. 305–21.

[70] See R. Morris, *Churches in the Landscape* (London, 1989), pp. 227–74.

[71] Pounds, *The Medieval Castle in England and Wales*, p. 224.

[72] Ibid., p. 230; J. McNulty, 'The Endowment of the Chapel of St. Michael in Clitheroe Castle', *Transactions of the Historical Society of Lancashire and Cheshire* 91 (1939), 159–63; J. McNulty, 'Clitheroe Castle and its Chapel: Their Origins', *Transactions of the Historical Society of Lancashire and Cheshire* 93 (1942), 45–53. Other examples of castle chapels with quasi-parochial functions include those of Farleigh Hungerford and Caerphilly: Pounds, *The Medieval Castle in England and Wales*, p. 230.

[73] For example, see the section devoted to 'Castle and church' in Pounds, *The Medieval Castle in England and Wales*, pp. 222–45.

[74] T. A. Heslop, *Norwich Castle Keep: Romanesque Architecture and Social Context* (Norwich, 1994), pp. 7, 12.

effect.[75] The architectural patronage of the earls of Warwick has attracted similar attention and the similarities between the detailing of their ecclesiastical and defensive commissions noted.[76] Other structural crossovers have become grounds for heated debate. The structure at Rochester Cathedral known as 'Gundulf's Tower' has been identified alternatively as a mid-twelfth-century bell tower and as an early post-Conquest defensive structure.[77] Similar controversy rages over the apparent machicolation slots visible on the west front of Lincoln Cathedral, which I discuss later in this chapter.

A more explicitly ideological approach to crossovers between defensive and ecclesiastical architecture has been used convincingly to explore the use of military architectural devices, such as crenellations, in ecclesiastical architecture. Charles Coulson has examined this topic with characteristic rigour and insight, detecting many important social and ideological motivations in such displays of defence, as well as practical and legal considerations.[78] He sees this not as a medievalizing strategy of making religious architecture appropriate to the contemporary military concerns of medieval society, but as a manifestation of the assimilation of the religious and defensive in medieval thought:

> To the medieval mind, God was almost a feudal lord, albeit of transcendent order, whose glory was manifested by the buildings of his vassal cathedral and conventual establishments, in much the same way as were the honour, power and renown of any earthly *seigneur* and king by the castles of his feudatories. Quintessentially, it was the precinct walls and buildings of religious houses which displayed the divine lordship. The great church was its main focus, of course, but the exclusive and walled close as a whole had a symbolism as eloquent as that of the castellated gentry-residence.[79]

This model of close integration is a helpful one for the purposes of this chapter. However, studies looking for the medieval ideology of defence in more

---

[75] Ibid., and pp. 63–5. See also R. Gilchrist, 'Norwich Cathedral: A Biography of the North Transept', *Journal of the British Archaeological Association* 151 (1998), 107–36 (pp. 128–9).

[76] R. K. Morris, 'The Architecture of the Earls of Warwick in the Fourteenth Century', in *England in the Fourteenth Century*, ed. W. M. Ormrod, Proceedings of the 1985 Harlaxton Symposium (1986), pp. 161–74.

[77] See T. Tatton-Brown, ' "Gundulf"s' Tower', *Friends of Rochester Cathedral: Report for 1990/1* (Rochester, 1991), 7–12; J. P. McAleer, 'Rochester Cathedral: The North Choir Aisle and the Space between it and "Gundulf's' Tower", *Archaeologia Cantiana* 112 (1993), 127–65; J. P. McAleer, 'The So-called Gundulf's Tower at Rochester Cathedral. A Reconsideration of its History, Date and Function', *The Antiquaries Journal* 78 (1998), 111–76.

[78] C. Coulson, 'Structural Symbolism in Medieval Castle Architecture', *Journal of the British Archaeological Association* 132 (1979), 73–90; C. Coulson, 'Hierarchism in Conventual Crenellation', *Medieval Archaeology* 26 (1982), 69–100.

[79] Coulson, 'Hierarchism in Conventual Crenellation', p. 72.

complex architectural structures have often found less compelling connections.[80] The contrasting approaches used in architectural and ideological discussions of castle symbolism cannot have helped. While castle scholars have attempted to explore the ideological possibilities of certain clearly identified features of specific buildings,[81] literary scholars have been revelling in the instability and multiplicity of theological castle imagery. Roberta Cornelius's work *The Figurative Castle*, published in 1930, is still the definitive collation and study.[82] It is arranged thematically, but readers quickly become aware of the ease with which different paradigms of the figurative castle mutate into others and boundaries blur between what might be thought of as sacred and profane imagery and genres. Editions of several crucial texts related to figurative castles[83] and a small but fairly steady flow of studies on the subject have only added to the dazzling variety of these exemplars.[84]

In this chapter I seek to show that the spiritual ideology associated with medieval castles in an English context is similarly complex, shifting and multiplicitous. Because literary methodologies facilitate this approach, what follows is led by textual examples. However, as with the discussion of Aelred's sermon at the start of this chapter, these texts are tied closely to physical architecture

[80] See for example R. Gilchrist, *Gender and Material Culture: The Archaeology of Religious Women* (London, 1994); R. Gilchrist, 'Medieval Bodies in the Material World: Gender, Stigma and the Body', in *Framing Medieval Bodies*, ed. S. Kay and M. Rubin (Manchester, 1994), pp. 43–61; R. Gilchrist, 'The Contested Garden: Gender, Space and Metaphor in the Medieval English Castle', in R. Gilchrist, *Gender and Archaeology: Contesting the Past* (London, 1999), pp. 109–45.

[81] P. Dixon and B. Lott, 'The Courtyard and the Tower: Contexts and Symbols in the Development of the Late Medieval Great House', *Journal of the British Archaeological Association* 146 (1993), 93–101; P. Dixon 'The Donjon of Knaresborough: The Castle as Theatre', *Château Gaillard* 14 (1988), 121–40; P. Dixon and P. Marshall, 'The Great Keep at Hedingham Castle: A Reassessment', *Fortress* 18 (August 1993), 16–23; P. Dixon, and P. Marshall, 'The Great Tower in the Twelfth Century: The Case of Norham Castle', *The Archaeological Journal* 150 (1993), 410–32.

[82] Cornelius, *The Figurative Castle*.

[83] William Nevill, *The Castell of Pleasure by William Nevill: The Text of the First Issue with Variant Readings from the Reprint of 1518*, ed. R. D. Cornelius, Early English Text Society, original series 179 (1930, repr. 1971); *Sawles Warde: An Early English Homily Edited from the Bodley, Royal and Cotton MSS*, ed. R. M. Wilson, Leeds School of English Language Texts and Monographs 3 (1938); *The Middle English Translations of Robert Grosseteste's Château d'Amour*, ed. K. Sajavaara, *Mémoires de la Société Néophilologique de Helsinki* 32 (1967).

[84] From the specific: J. Chorpenning, 'The Literary and Theological Method of the *Castillo Interior*', *Journal of Hispanic Philology* 3 (1979), 121–33; J. Chorpenning, 'The Monastery, Paradise, and the Castle: Literary Images and Spiritual Development in St Teresa of Ávila', *Bulletin of Hispanic Studies* 62 (1985), 245–57; to the more general: G. R. Owst, *Literature and the Pulpit in Medieval England*, 2nd edn (Oxford, 1961); Kurtz, ' "The Small Castle of the Soul" '; Mann, 'Allegorical Buildings in Mediaeval Literature'; J. Wogan-Browne, 'Chaste Bodies: Frames and Experiences', in *Framing Medieval Bodies*, ed. Kay and Rubin, pp. 24–42; Hebron, *The Medieval Siege*, pp. 136–65.

and its practical historical context. This link only becomes obvious when it is recognized that the medieval castle was understood as a characteristically Biblical architecture, fraught with spiritual significance, and that castle words in all languages could be used to denote defended ecclesiastical enclosures as well as temporal fortresses.

Robert Grosseteste, bishop of Lincoln, was probably the most influential English figure in the spread of the spiritual castle motif. The Marian castle forms the central image in an Anglo-Norman poem written by him at some point between 1215 and 1253, sometimes called *Carmen de Creatione Mundi* (Poem on the Creation of the World), and sometimes *Château d'Amour* (Castle of Love).[85] This work has been identified as 'the culmination of [the] allegory of the castle as the Virgin',[86] and many of its details seem to be original to Grosseteste.[87] The image is, however, derived from Luke 10. 38 and shares some notable features with the sermon by Aelred discussed earlier. Grosseteste's work, like Aelred's, enumerates the features of the castle, explicating their spiritual significance, to create a complex edifice embodying many of the important tenets of the faith. Grosseteste's Castle of Love also has some relevance to the architectural, spiritual and political surroundings of its author, as I will show.

Grosseteste enumerates the features of the Castle of Love twice during his poem: once to describe its construction and appearance (lines 571–666), and a second time to explicate the symbolic significance of each part of the edifice (lines 671–827).[88] These elements are linked in each case by a shared characteristic. For example, Grosseteste's seven barbicans (lines 727–31 and ff) reflect the number of the seven virtues, one of which is ascribed to each of the

[85] The authorship of the poem has been discputed, but Kari Sajavaara points to parallels between the *Château d'Amour* and other writings by Grosseteste, and concludes that, 'as no absolutely negative evidence has so far been presented and all the evidence available confirms it, Grossesteste's authorship of the *Château d'Amour* cannot be denied': *The Middle English Translations of Robert Grosseteste's* Château d'Amour, ed. Sajavaara, p. 43. See also Sajavaara's discussion of the poem's dating on the same page.

[86] Cornelius, *The Figurative Castle*, p. 44; see also *The Middle English Translations of Robert Grosseteste's* Château d'Amour, ed. Sajavaara, p. 100.

[87] 'No direct source for Grosseteste's castle has been found. Grosseteste may well have developed the allegory himself, but he may, as well, have found it, like the exemplar of the allegory of the *Four Daughters of God*, in some Latin manuscript so far untraced. The only link between Grosseteste's castle and other allegorical castles could be the similarity of the symbols, but so far, no other castle bearing these symbols has been found. As long as no source is discovered, the "castle of love" must be considered Grosseteste's invention': *The Middle English Translations of Robert Grosseteste's* Château d'Amour, ed. Sajavaara, pp. 93–4.

[88] Robert Grosseteste, *Le Château d'Amour de Robert Grosseteste, Evêque de Lincoln*, ed. J. Murray (Paris, 1918), pp. 105–12. I cite this edition throughout, unless otherwise specified.

structures; and the three concentric baileys (lines 709–24 and ff) represent the Virgin's concentric virtues of maidenhood, chastity and holy marriage. Once again this type of architectural symbolism can be recognized as echoing the treatment of Biblical buildings, such as Ezekiel's vision of the temple, with a particular emphasis in Grosseteste's case on the numerological correspondences found in such examples.

Many of the architectural features mentioned by Grosseteste also seem deliberately included as references to Biblical texts concerned with symbolic architecture. The closed gate through which Christ enters the Castle of Love (lines 785–6) refers to the east gate of the temple in Ezekiel, 44. 2.[89] As in Aelred's sermon this motif is used to express Mary's virginity in an architectural form. The foundation of the castle upon the firm rock of the Virgin's heart (lines 671–72) is also reminiscent of the wise man of Matthew 7. 24 who built his house upon a rock.[90] Scenes in the narrative surrounding the castle are also reminiscent of Biblical texts. At the end of the explanatory, second description of the castle, the narrator momentarily interacts with the architecture, beating on the castle gate for sanctuary against his attackers – the world, the flesh and the devil (lines 789–804). This action seems to refer to a number of Biblical texts with different nuances. The narrator here may be cast as the Christ of Revelation 3. 20, 'Behold, I stand at the gate and knock. If any man shall hear my voice and open to me the door, I will come in to him',[91] knocking to be admitted to the castle of the human soul, embodied in the Virgin Mary. This passage also recalls Canticles 5. 2, 'the voice of my beloved knocking: Open to me, my sister, my love'.[92] The narrator in this case is the lover, knocking to rouse his beloved, also interpreted in medieval exegesis as Christ calling to Holy Church.

Grosseteste's Castle of Love, then, articulates a set of moral attributes, whilst it also indexes a series of Biblical architectural texts in an allegorical narrative. Aelred's version of the Marian castle emphasized the process of

---

[89] Grosseteste, *Le Château d'Amour*, lines 785–6: 'Par la porte close entra / A l'issir close la lessa.' Ezekiel 44. 2 'Et dixit dominus ad me: Porta haec clausa erit, non aperietur, et vir non transibit per eam, quoniam Dominus Deus Israel ingressus est per eam' ('And the Lord said to me: This gate shall be shut, it shall not be opened, and no man shall pass through it: because the Lord the God of Israel hath entered in by it').

[90] Grosseteste, *Le Château d'Amour*, lines 671–72: 'La roche k'est si bien polie, / C'est le cuer la duce Marie'; Matthew 7. 24 'Omnis ergo qui audit verba mea haec, et facit ea, assimilabitur viro sapienti qui aedificavit domum suam supra petram' ('Every one therefore that heareth these my words, and doth them, shall be likened to a wise man that built his house upon a rock').

[91] Revelation 3. 20: 'Ecce sto ad ostium et pulso; si quis audierit vocem meam et aperuerit mihi ianuam, intrabo ad illum' ('Behold, I stand at the gate, and knock. If any man hear my voice, and open to me the door, I will come in to him').

[92] Song of Songs 5. 2: 'Ego dormio, et cor meum vigilat. Vox dilecti mei pulsantis: Aperi mihi soror mea, amica mea' ('I sleep, and my heart watcheth: the voice of my beloved knocking: Open to me, my sister, my love').

construction and the need to recreate this spiritually. Grosseteste's castle seems similarly designed for the mental contemplation of both the building and the texts associated with it, in a highly sophisticated series of verbal echoes and allegorical linkages. The whole structure of the poem, and especially of the Castle of Love section, seems, like Aelred's sermon, to be designed as an elaborate mnemonic, constructed to facilitate the recall of a series of sacred texts and devotional precepts. Like Aelred's use of mnemonics, too, Grosseteste's has an important theological purpose. *Château d'Amour* shares many characteristic features with the new wave of vernacular poems, embodying spiritual and devotional truths in the form of chivalric or visionary narratives, which emerged around 1220.[93] They were created in response to the Fourth Lateran Council, held in 1215, which called for the first time for the cultivation of inward contemplation amongst the lay Christian population. The increasing use of mnemonic devices in religious literature from this time onwards is linked directly to this call:

> What were the things which the pious Middle Ages wished chiefly to remember? Surely they were the things belonging to salvation or damnation, the articles of the faith, the roads to heaven through virtues and to hell through vices. These were the things . . . which it wished chiefly to remember by the art of memory, which was to fix in memory the complex material of medieval didactic thought.[94]

These values seem to apply particularly aptly to the *Château d'Amour*, which narrates the story of the salvation of mankind from the beginning of the world (as witnessed by the title sometimes used, *Carmen de Creatione Mundi*). Numerological elements in the poem's symbolism have been attributed to the influence of the Fourth Lateran Council, which also encouraged such allegorical schemes.[95] Grosseteste's choice of Anglo-Norman (the vernacular language of the court) as opposed to his usual Latin for this poem, marks out the *Château d'Amour* as a departure from the high theology and focused homiletic material which forms the greater part of his work. The poem is composed in

---

[93] See B. Nolan, *The Gothic Visionary Perspective* (Princeton, 1977), pp. 130–3, 144–6. She cites as an example the *Tournoiement Antechrist*, written about 1234 by Huon de Méri, a French Benedictine monk, which is rather similar in its essentials to the *Château d'Amour*: they both rely on the form of Prudentius's *Psychomachia*: Nolan, *The Gothic Visionary Perspective*, pp. 130–1; *The Middle English Translations of Robert Grosseteste's* Château d'Amour, ed. Sajavaara, pp. 96–7. Grosseteste had certainly read the *Psychomachia*: R. W. Hunt, 'The Library of Robert Grosseteste', in *Robert Grosseteste, Scholar and Bishop: Essays in Commemoration of the Seventh Centenary of his Death*, ed. D. A. Callus (Oxford, 1955, repr. 1969), pp. 121–45 (p. 142). They also both employ allegorized castles.

[94] Yates, *The Art of Memory*, p. 55.

[95] *The Middle English Translations of Robert Grosseteste's* Château d'Amour, ed. Sajavaara, p. 94; M. D. Legge, *Anglo-Norman Literature and its Background* (Oxford, 1963), p. 215.

octosyllabic couplets, a metre adopted by popular narrative literature in the twelfth century.[96] The emphasis on mnemonics in this genre[97] also seems to fit the form and function of Grosseteste's poem, and to confirm its place within this specific literary and ideological context. The identification of the poem as an architectural mnemonic has not, to my knowledge been made before. Yet it reflects the place of the figurative castle, and Biblical castle texts, at the heart of medieval architectural exegesis, and the developing apparatus of devotional contemplation from the thirteenth century onwards.

The chivalric imagery of this new group of texts is usually interpreted as a medievalizing strategy of the kind I discussed earlier, aimed at making difficult theological ideas accessible in characteristically contemporary imagery.[98] However, while Aelred's sermon-castle seemed carefully formulated to resemble a range of different defensive structures that would have been familiar to his audience, Grosseteste's Castle of Love does not resemble any real building of the Middle Ages. I have already mentioned its seven barbicans and three concentric baileys, for example. The emphasis in these details is obviously on number symbolism rather than architectural accuracy. However, these unreal qualities present the castle as a spiritual architecture which can take its place alongside the Heavenly Jerusalem and Ezekiel's Temple, as sacred buildings which could never exist in earthly logic, yet are ever present in the medieval Christian's mind as spiritual goals. Far from representing the mediation of difficult theology through an essentially lay

---

[96] R. W. Southern, *Robert Grosseteste: The Growth of an English Mind in Medieval Europe*, 2nd edn (Oxford, 1992), pp. 225–9; *The Middle English Translations of Robert Grosseteste's* Château d'Amour, ed. Sajavaara, p. 41 and *passim*.

[97] The more mundane details of Grosseteste's studies also seem to confirm his interest in and use of mnemonic schemes for both personal and didactic purposes. Many extant manuscripts from Grosseteste's own collection bear witness to his system for indexing works by means of several hundred different symbols which he noted in the margins to mark the occurrence of particular topics. It is clear that this was a highly complex system, providing cross-referencing far more sophisticated than the marginal *notae* often made by less organized readers. Mary Carruthers in fact identifies it as a mnemonic scheme, developed to assist Grosseteste in his memorization of the material: a scheme similar to, but more sophisticated than, many strategies that emerged across Europe around 1220, and which only gained common acceptance in the 1280s, after Grosseteste's death. Grosseteste, then, was a pioneer of mnemonic methods and their devotional application. See Hunt, 'The Library of Robert Grosseteste', pp. 121–45; Southern, *Robert Grosseteste*, pp. 186–98; Carruthers, *The Book of Memory*, pp. 110, 117–19. It may be significant that Hugh of St Victor, the only twelfth-century author whose work Grosseteste includes in his index, suggested the use of such a scheme for mnemonic marking of texts, both physical and mental (although not in the text cited by Grosseteste). See Southern, *Robert Grosseteste*, p. 187; Hunt, 'The Library of Robert Grosseteste', p. 144, and Carruthers, *The Book of Memory*, pp. 94, 108, 110, 124 and *passim*.

[98] *The Middle English Translations of Robert Grosseteste's* Château d'Amour, ed. Sajavaara, pp. 41–2; Southern, *Robert Grosseteste*, pp. 225–9.

and medieval symbol, Grosseteste's *Château d'Amour* expresses the strength of the castle as a Biblical type and a religious image. The exegetical tradition of the castle of Bethany is central to the medieval understanding of this symbolism. The castle of the Virgin Mary, derived, as I have shown, from exegesis of the text of Luke 10. 38, was not only applied in spiritual texts, but also found a context in the buildings of the period. Indeed, Lincoln Cathedral itself, where Grosseteste was bishop between the years 1235 and 1253,[99] was dedicated to the Blessed Virgin from an early stage.[100]

Critical attention has recently turned to Lincoln, and the question of whether, and to what extent, the cathedral was a fortified church at any stage of its medieval history. This debate has focused largely on the apparent evidence of machicolation slots in the arched bays at the west end of the church (see Plate XI). However, the terms used to describe the cathedral in certain crucial medieval documents also align it strongly with ideas of the castle of the Virgin and so provide their own evidence of the ways in which the building was perceived and understood.

As with the defended cathedral sites of Durham, Rochester and Old Sarum, discussed earlier, defensive precautions had to be considered from the earliest establishment of the diocesan see at Lincoln, due to its vulnerable Northern location. The latest research suggests that the present castle, in the southwest of the upper city, covers only a small proportion of the ground occupied by the earliest Norman one. This seems to have encompassed the whole area of the Roman upper city, within the standing Roman defences.[101] This area contained a number of Anglo-Saxon churches, including the Anglo-Saxon Minster of St Mary, which later became the cathedral when the see of the bishopric of Lincoln was moved from Dorchester-on-Thames around 1072–5.[102] This period is, of course, much too early to have been directly noted by Bishop Grosseteste, but it established the later dynamics of Lincoln's upper city, and demonstrates once again that castles and churches could readily occupy the same defensive enclosure in medieval Britain. The close relationship between the new bishopric and the castle at Lincoln is emphasized by the bishop's duty to provide the castle guard from the foundation of the bishopric until the 1130s.[103]

---

[99] P. Kidson, 'Architectural History', in *A History of Lincoln Minster*, ed. D. Owen (Cambridge, 1994), pp. 14–46 (p. 31).

[100] D. Owen, 'Introduction: The English Church in Eastern England, 1066–1100', in D. Owen, *A History of Lincoln Minster*, pp. 1–13 (pp. 12–13); D. M. Owen, *Church and Society in Medieval Lincolnshire* (Lincoln, 1971), p. 37.

[101] D. Stocker and A. Vince, 'The Early Norman Castle at Lincoln and a Re-evaluation of the Original West Tower of Lincoln Cathedral', *Medieval Archaeology* 41 (1997), 223–33 (p. 224).

[102] Gem, 'Lincoln Minster: *Ecclesia Pulchra, Ecclesia Fortis*', p. 9; Stocker, 'The Two Early Castles of Lincoln'.

[103] Stocker and Vince, 'The Early Norman Castle at Lincoln', pp. 226–7.

The proximity of the castle motte and tower and the cathedral has been a crucial factor in explanations of the apparent fortifications in the west façade of the cathedral. The two machicolation-like slots in the arches over the two outer recessed bays along the front of the building have been interpreted as belonging to the eleventh-century fortification of the cathedral[104] mentioned by Henry of Huntingdon (writing between 1129 and 1154)[105] (as quoted in the title of Gem's paper) and also by William of Malmesbury in his *Historia Novella* (1140–3).[106] The rest of the west front of the cathedral has been altered since, but it is suggested that these slots remain from the eleventh-century phase designed to oppose the defensive capabilities of the castle during the unstable period of the anarchy.[107] Alternatively, it has been argued that what is now the west end of the cathedral was in the eleventh century a separate tower keep, constructed as a residence for Bishop Remigius on his arrival from Dorchester-on-Thames and later incorporated into the fabric of the cathedral. The machicolation slots, it is suggested, are a remnant of this defensive tower.[108] The architectural context surrounding these slots is complex and problematic, and does not prove definitively that they were ever intended to have a defensive function.[109] However, suggestions of alternative functions are equally without architectural precedent.[110]

What cannot be disputed is that the slots have been clearly visible on the west front of the cathedral, probably since the eleventh century. A certain number of medieval visitors must have looked up and noticed the slots as they entered the cathedral through the west door and they must have been reminded of the fully functional machicolation slots they could observe on other defensive structures.[111] In the absence of definitive architectural evidence of the origin and function of the slots at the west end, the best guidance comes from the texts cited in this debate. These make it clear that the cathedral was at some point fortified, so it seems most likely that the slots were originally related

---

[104] Gem, 'Lincoln Minster: *Ecclesia Pulchra, Ecclesia Fortis*'; Kidson, 'Architectural History', pp. 21–4; Bonde, *Fortress Churches of Languedoc*, pp. 36–7.

[105] See A. Gransden, *Historical Writing in England c.550 to 1307* (London, 1974), p. 194.

[106] See William of Malmesbury, *Historia Novella, The Contemporary History*, ed. E. King, transl. K. R. Potter (Oxford, 1998), p. xxxiii.

[107] Gem, 'Lincoln Minster: *Ecclesia Pulchra, Ecclesia Fortis*', pp. 10–11 and *passim*.

[108] See Stocker and Vince, 'The Early Norman Castle at Lincoln'; Stocker, 'The Two Early Castles of Lincoln'.

[109] Kidson, 'Architectural History', p. 20.

[110] Peter Kidson suggests (ibid.), that 'one can imagine ornamental hangings being lowered through them on special ecclesiastical occasions'. As there is no evidence for this function, it is hardly an improvement on the military suggestions Kidson dismisses.

[111] Gem suggests the east gate house of Exeter Castle, built around 1068, as the closest parallel for the arrangement of the arches and slots on the west front of Lincoln Cathedral; Gem, 'Lincoln Minster: *Ecclesia Pulchra, Ecclesia Fortis*', p. 22; illustrated pl. IXB.

to these defences. The wording of these documents also places consistent emphasis on the Marian associations of the church, showing, I will argue, that it was perceived as a Castle of the Virgin by contemporary observers. Such connotations can only have made it more likely that the slots on the west front would have carried martial associations for medieval observers.

William of Malmesbury's reference identifies King Stephen's role in the cathedral's fortification:

ecclesiam beatae Dei genetricis de Lindocolino incastellaverat[112]

(he had fortified the Church of the blessed mother of God at Lincoln)

This reference is brief, but it is notable that William of Malmesbury identifies the church as that of Mary rather than just as the cathedral of Lincoln. Of course, as I have noted, the cathedral was dedicated to Mary, but William specifically mentions Mary in her role as the mother of God, rather than simply by name, as in the dedication of the church, or by her other roles, for example as intercessor or queen of Heaven. This may be a deliberate device by William to remind his readers of the castle imagery attached to Mary's role in the Incarnation, through the traditional exegesis of the text of Luke 10. 38.

Marian castle imagery also seems to inform a passage from Henry of Huntingdon which has been quoted in discussions of the cathedral's military functions. The passage describes the foundation of the church by Bishop Remigius:

Mercatis igitur praediis, in ipso vertice urbis iuxta castellum turribus fortissimis eminens, in loco forti fortem, pulchro pulchram, virgini virginum construxit ecclesiam; quae et grata esset Deo servientibus, et, ut pro tempore oportebat, invincibilis hostibus.[113]

(And so, having bought up the estates, in the heights of the city next to the eminent castle with its very strong towers, he built a strong church on a strong site, a beautiful [church] on a beautiful [site], [a church] to the Virgin of Virgins; so that it might be pleasing to those serving God and, as was necessary for the times, invincible against enemies.)

It has recently been suggested that the 'castellum turribus fortissimis eminens' in this passage refers not to the royal castle, but to Remigius's tower keep, later incorporated into the west end of the Minster.[114] The text presents no objection to this argument, though this phrase could equally refer to the royal castle. However, it is important to emphasize the rhetorical polish of this sentence, and to draw attention to the whole of the grammatical construction.

---

[112] William of Malmesbury, *Historia Novella*, Book 3, paragraph 42, p. 82.

[113] Henry of Huntingdon, *Henrici Archidiaconi Huntendunensis: Historia Anglorum*, ed. T. Arnold, Rolls Series 74 (1879), Book 4, paragraph 41, p. 212.

[114] P. Everson, Appendix 1, in Lindley, *Lincoln Castle.*

The celebrated article on Lincoln's west front by Richard Gem may have focused attention on the phrase 'in loco forti fortem, pulchro pulchram' at the expense of its context. Yet, however the reference to the *castellum* is interpreted, the construction of the sentence is designed to emphasize the proximity and similarity of the *castellum* and the church. This juxtaposition (*iuxta*) is strengthened verbally with the repetition of *fortissimus . . . fortem* and the similar case of the words *castellum* and *ecclesiam*. The two linked adjectives describing the church as strong and beautiful have often been noted, but in fact three elements are joined here, all qualified by the same verb and subject: the church is built strong, beautiful, and to the Virgin. The triple effect is further emphasized, against the actual syntax of the sentence, by the similarity of the endings of all three pairings: 'forti fortem, pulchro pulchram, virgini virginum'.[115] Although the last two words perform different functions to the first four, all appear by their arrangement and fortuitous similarities of ending to be exactly parallel terms, suggesting an integral link between architectural beauty, strength, and the Virgin: just those qualities combined in the image of the Marian castle of the Incarnation. This reference is concise, yet crafted with considerable rhetorical polish. The structuring of the triple phrase does not make great sense, unless its readers have a context in which they can understand this combination of elements. This suggests that Henry of Huntingdon understood the fortification of the cathedral and its dedication to the Virgin as a natural grouping, which would be understood easily as such by his readers. Without the context of the Marian castle and its exegesis, Henry's rhetorical flourish falls flat. The brevity of this reference, and the general misunderstanding of medieval interpretations of the text of Luke 10. 38, has meant that this imagery has not been understood before, either in the context of Henry of Huntingdon's choice of words or in the symbolism of the *ecclesia fortis*, Lincoln Cathedral. Yet, as with the use of the text of Luke 10. 38 around the outside of the seal of Colchester, which I discussed in Chapter 1, the very brevity of the reference also implies an easy familiarity with the text and its application to medieval defended buildings amongst at least the literate sector of the population.

These two historical references to Lincoln Cathedral help to demonstrate, I believe, the ubiquity of the imagery of the Marian castle. But more importantly for my argument, they show, as Aelred's sermon did, that this imagery was applicable not just to the symbolic castles of rhetoric and sermon, but to the built architecture of the medieval church. Defended ecclesiastical structures were clearly comparable to lordly fortresses, as linguistic evidence, cited in Chapter 1, demonstrates. But the imagery of the Marian castle shows that they were also comparable in symbolic and religious terms, and that this

---

[115] 'Forti' and 'pulchro' are masculine ablative singular, agreeing with the ablative 'loco'; 'fortem' and 'pulchram' are feminine accusative singular, and agree with 'ecclesiam'. 'Virgini' is feminine dative singular, referring to 'ecclesiam' but not in the same case, and 'virginum' is feminine genitive plural, qualifying 'virgini' itself.

comparison had an important significance for the individual Christian. Mnemonic exercises based on the architecture of the castle of Bethany of Luke 10. 38, such as those written by Aelred and, later, Grosseteste, would have helped to fix the significance of the spiritual castle in the awareness of clerics and laity respectively, sensitizing the medieval mind to defensive architectural elements as conveyors of spiritual meaning. The descriptions of Lincoln Cathedral I have just discussed seem to result from, and to allude to, exactly this kind of learned association between certain military/ecclesiastical architectural elements and their Marian exegesis.

The ongoing importance of military trappings at Lincoln Cathedral also tends to support these readings. During the thirteenth and fourteenth centuries, several building campaigns in Lincoln's cathedral complex emphasized the church's resemblance to a fortress. These are symptomatic of a wider trend in the crenellation of ecclesiastical enclosures.[116] However, the grant of royal licences for many of these structures indicates a seeking of status rather than a defensive need. At Lincoln, four royal licences to enclose and crenellate the cathedral complex were granted between 1285 and 1316.[117] Charles Coulson confirms the symbolic intent behind these fortifications, noting that 'the cathedral close by gradual degrees expanded and assumed a more pronouncedly castle-like appearance'.[118] Once again, this is a generic development, not restricted to Lincoln Cathedral. But it does demonstrate the ongoing presence of ecclesiastical contexts in which the mnemonic exercise of the castle of Luke 10. 38 might be called to mind. Like the other ideological aspects of the castle to which I have drawn attention, I believe such connotations are easy to miss, or to dismiss, when the conventional wisdom does not acknowledge them. I hope the importance of the text Luke 10. 38, and its exegesis, is no longer in doubt. However, it would be instructive to look for further evidence of its application to ecclesiastical and defensive architecture. At the simplest level, it would be useful to see whether any correlation can be found between the use of defensive architectural elements – such as crenellations – in an ecclesiastical context, and buildings – like Lincoln Cathedral – with Marian dedications.

Robert Grossteste's *Château d'Amour* may have had some ongoing role in spreading theological castle imagery in an English context. His poem was very popular in its day, as attested by the sixteen surviving manuscripts, and was translated into Middle English four times between 1300 and 1450.[119] During the thirteenth and fourteenth centuries, as I will show, the Castle of Love grew in popularity as an image, and spread from devotional treatises to

---

[116] Coulson, 'Hierarchism in Conventual Crenellation', p. 72.
[117] Ibid., p. 75.
[118] Ibid.
[119] *A Manual of the Writings in Middle English 1050–1500*, ed. A. E. Hartung, 10 vols. (New Haven, 1967–98), VII, 23–37.

many other forms of sacred and secular use. Interestingly, Grosseteste's circle has been identified as the source of another military/religious device, the shield of faith.[120] This was also amongst the defensive motifs deployed at this period in ecclesiastical decoration,[121] and displays the same concern with expressing important religious tenets through a mnemonic object that was both familiar in a medieval context and enshrined in Biblical imagery.[122] Whatever the precise nature of Grosseteste's influence, later developments in the Castle of Love certainly show the popularity of the motif and demonstrate that, by the later Middle Ages, it had became far more widespread and had many modes of application, both serious and light-hearted in intent. However, the parodic use of the Marian castle confirms the understanding and reception not only of the image itself, but of its mnemonic properties. From the earliest stages, such architectural allegories could be imitated to secular as well as sacred ends. Andreas Capellanus in the fourth century could, for example, rework the temple of Ezekiel parodically as the Court of Love, playing on the sexual imagery of the closed east gate (representing the Virgin Birth of Christ).[123] I detect a similar attempt at parody, and indeed a similar experimentation with sexual architectural symbolism, in certain manifestations of the Castle of Love.

The first account of the pageant of the Castle of Love is recorded in 1214 in Treviso, Italy.[124] Rolandino of Padua describes how a model castle, defended by ladies wielding flowers, fruit and nuts, was attacked by knights bearing similarly playful weapons. This pageant siege was to be repeated throughout medieval Europe, and even survived in parts of Switzerland up until the eighteenth century.[125] This enacted siege can be found portrayed in its various stages on ivory mirror-backs and caskets of the early fourteenth century, which found their way from their manufacture, probably in Paris, round most of medieval Western Europe.[126] These ivories portray the different stages of the siege, from the initial assault to the parley, the payment of a ransom in kisses, and finally the knights' entry of the castle and eventual exit, paired off

---

[120] P. Binski, *Westminster Abbey and the Plantagenets: Kingship and the Representation of Power, 1200–1400* (New Haven, 1995), p. 81.

[121] Ibid.

[122] For example, Song of Songs 4. 4: 'Sicut turris David collum tuum, quae aedificata est cum propugnaculis; mille clypei pendent ex ea, omnis armatura fortium' ('Thy neck is as the tower of David, which is built with bulwarks: a thousand bucklers hang upon it, all the armour of valiant men').

[123] Mann, 'Allegorical Buildings', p. 193.

[124] R. S. Loomis, 'The Allegorical Siege in the Art of the Middle Ages', *American Journal of Archaeology* 23.3 (1919), 255–69 (p. 255).

[125] Ibid., pp. 255–8.

[126] Ibid., pp. 258–9; see also R. Koechlin, *Les Ivoires gothiques français* (Paris, 1924); M. H. Longhurst, *Victoria and Albert Museum Department of Architecture and Sculpture Catalogue of Carvings in Ivory* (London, 1929); J. Nathanson, *Gothic Ivories of the 13th and 14th Centuries* (London, 1951).

with the erstwhile defenders (Plate VIII, an ivory casket, shows the siege to the left and the capitulation to the right). Subsequently the image of the Castle of Love also found its way into other media, appearing in illuminated manuscripts, on tapestries and in elaborately crafted table decorations.

The date of the first recorded enactment of this Siege of Love is, interestingly, one year before the earliest possible date given for Grosseteste's *Château d'Amour*. If there is a connection in the origins of these two traditions, then, it must go back further. Some basic similarities can immediately be appreciated between both these castles in terms of the gender symbolism expressed by metaphors of defensive bodily architecture – either of the besieged ladies, or of the Virgin's body. Scholars of Grosseteste unanimously dismiss any connection between the two phenomena, yet the descendants of both the Treviso pageant and the Grosseteste castle show evidence of having shared in an exchange in later years. There are certain examples of the Castle of Love motif which display obviously religious elements. R. S. Loomis, for example, describes one such depiction on a fourteenth-century casket, where the castle motif 'is surmounted by a church, and the battlements are held by nuns. They hurl down white pellets on the powers of the world represented by six gaily clad youths.'[127] Loomis sees this as evidence, not of the sacred connotations of the castle image, but of the medieval Church's 'canny instinct for appropriating to its uses any popular image'.[128] However, as I have shown, the castle is drawn very directly and literally from Biblical imagery and is not medievalizing in this sense. Loomis's image seems more like a transposition of the pageant siege to the monastic fortress of the castle of Bethany. Further examples demonstrate even more succinctly that the Castle of Love, even in its most flamboyant and playful depictions, was capable of reflecting the imagery of the Marian castle of theological exegesis.

Plates IX and X show the Castle of Love from British Library Additional MS 42130, otherwise known as the Luttrell Psalter (*c.*1320–40).[129] The image has enjoyed a great deal less comment than some of the other scenes from this famous manuscript, but its commentators have been very consistent in their opinion of it. Scholars of both the Luttrell Psalter and of the Castle of Love image have all agreed with Loomis in his suggestion that the enacted siege of the Castle of Love, depicted on the Parisian ivories, is the ultimate referent of this and other manuscript images.[130] There is no doubt that the Luttrell Psalter image is very similar to the Parisian ivory carvings, in particulars as well as in general appearance. At least two of the figures from the Psalter have very

[127] Loomis, 'The Allegorical Siege in the Art of the Middle Ages', p. 264.
[128] Ibid.
[129] London, British Library Additional MS 42130, fol. 75v.
[130] Loomis, 'The Allegorical Siege in the Art of the Middle Ages', pp. 259–61. See, for example, E. G. Millar, *The Luttrell Psalter: Additional Manuscript 42130 in the British Museum* (London, 1932), p. 32.

similar counterparts in ivory carvings of the subject. The knight scaling the ladder on the right of the castle and the crossbowman aiming up at the battlements just to his left, are very similar in attitude and appearance to the crossbowman and the ladder-scaler from Plate VIII, where they appear in combination in the left-hand panel of an ivory casket depicting the Castle of Love.

More recent interpretations – notably by Michael Camille – have looked more closely at the immediate context of the image within the Luttrell Psalter, opening up some interesting possibilities, but again emphasizing the motif's courtly and secular overtones.[131] Camille's most important contribution is to supply an interpretation that integrates text with illustration. He links the Castle of Love to the text above it, that of Psalm 38: 'Dixi: custodiam vias meas, ne peccem in lingua mea' ('I said: I will take heed to my ways: that I sin not with my tongue').[132] This text displays a historiated initial of King David, the authorial voice of the Psalms, pointing to his tongue in illustration of this text. For Camille, 'the castle, too, illustrates the same words in a parodic fashion since *custodiam* can mean "guard" or "watch" in a military sense.'[133] I do not wish to rule out such a reading, as I think this image can sustain a number of different associations and connotations at once. However, it seems to me that the castle image fits much more neatly the otherwise unillustrated text further up the page, that of Psalm 37. 20–23:

> Inimici autem mei viventes confortati sunt, et multiplicati sunt odientes me mendaciter; et qui reddunt malum pro bono adversabantur mihi, Ne derelinquas me, Domine Deus meus, ne elongeris a me; festina in auxilium meum, Domine salutis meae.

> (But my enemies live, and are stronger than I: and they that hate me are wrongfully multiplied. They that render evil for good, have detracted me, because I follow goodness. Forsake me not, O my Lord: do not thou depart from me. Attend unto my help, O Lord, the God of my salvation.)

The relationship of the castle image to these words makes immediate sense; the words of the Psalm seem almost to be spoken by the defenders of the castle, as they cry to God for help in their defence, just as the historiated initial on the same page also illustrates the speaker of the verse, suiting his actions to his words. This context, once understood, changes the relevance of the image. The similarities with the pageant siege still remain and are emphasized in the immediate appearance of the illumination. However an underlying meaning is encoded in the context of the image. The words of the Psalm point to the evil of the attackers, and suggest no fault but goodness in those attacked, providing a

---

[131] M. Camille, *Mirror in Parchment: The Luttrell Psalter and the Making of Medieval England* (London, 1998), pp. 118–19; M. Camille, *The Medieval Art of Love: Objects and Subjects of Desire* (London, 1998), pp. 87–93.

[132] The first of these verses is all that is included on this folio of the Psalter.

[133] Camille, *Mirror in Parchment*, p. 118.

moral complement to the sexual symbolism of the pageant siege. There is a strong resemblance here to the siege of the spiritual castle by the vices, an allegory which is implied in Grosseteste's poem,[134] and which was later elaborated by theologians and sermonists.[135] This development of castle imagery is sometimes called the Castle of Mansoul, and identified as a reference, not to Luke 10. 38 specifically, but to the text of Matthew 21. 2, 'Ite in castellum quod contra vos est', which refers literally to Jesus's instructions to the disciples on Palm Sunday to go and collect the ass for him to ride.[136] In exegetical terms, the ass stands for the evil soul of man, imprisoned within the fortress of the body and assailed by the vices and virtues.[137] This bodily imagery accounts for the ease with which its attributes are transferred to the Marian castle of Luke 10. 38.

However, the symbolism of the image in the Luttrell Psalter is not enriched simply by juxtaposition with a relevant Biblical text: significant differences from the ivory Castles of Love confirm and emphasize this spiritual reading. The winged and crowned god of love, prominently placed at the top of the castle in the vast majority of the ivory depictions (for example, at the top of the left-hand panel in Plate VIII) is missing. Had he been included, the text's plea, 'Forsake me not, O my Lord', might have seemed to be directed towards the personification of Love, so de-Christianizing the words of the Psalm and emphasizing the amorous nature of the siege. As it is, with this omission the Christian symbolism of the castle is instead brought to the fore. The main business of siege warfare, which in most of the ivory carvings is placed directly in front of the castle gate (see the far left and far right panels, Plate VIII) is moved to occupy rather an awkward corner, partially obscured by the castle wall (Plate X). Its place is taken in front of the gate by just one knight, who carries no weapons; his left hand is raised in a fist, and he seems to be knocking on the door of the castle.[138] Again, a particular relevance can be found in this re-arrangement of the scene, if Grosseteste's poem is recalled. Its narrator knocked on the door of the Castle of Love to be admitted, while he was being attacked by the world, the flesh and the devil. No other depiction of the Castle of Love I have come across uses this motif, underlining the particular significance which is attached to this figure.

It seems clear to me that the rearrangement of the action in front of the Luttrell Psalter's castle is specifically designed to highlight the figure of the

---

[134] *The Middle English Translations of Robert Grosseteste's* Chateau d'Amour, ed. Sajavaara, pp. 96–7.

[135] Cornelius, *The Figurative Castle*, pp. 58–67.

[136] Matthew 21. 2: 'Ite in castellum quod contra vos est; et statim invenietis asinam alligatam, et pullum cum ea: solvite et adducite mihi' ('Go ye into the *village* that is over against you, and immediately you shall find an ass tied, and a colt with her: loose them and bring them to me').

[137] Owst, *Literature and the Pulpit*, pp. 79–80.

[138] While Camille does not attribute any particular significance to the gesture, he does agree that the knight is knocking on the door: Camille, *Mirror in Parchment*, p. 118.

knight, in order to reinforce the textual allusion his action encapsulates. Not only does this image relate to the text placed above it on the page of the Psalter, it also makes a connection with other Biblical texts and exegetical traditions. As the Christ of Revelation 3. 20, the knight transforms the Castle of Love into the Castle of the Soul or the Castle of Mankind, to which Christ begs to be admitted to save souls. And as the lover of Canticles 5. 2, he knocks to be admitted to his beloved, transforming the fortress again, into the Castle of the Church. This latter text works particularly well with the trappings of the pageant Castle of Love presented in the Luttrell Psalter, paralleling the medieval reading of the Canticles as a secular love-metaphor with a deeper spiritual significance.

Once again, the mnemonic apparatus of this Castle of Love, while it has not to my knowledge been noted before, has an established devotional context. Illuminated psalters served very much as visual analogues to the popular devotional narratives responding to the demands of the Fourth Lateran Council.[139] In the fourteenth century particularly, the increasing emphasis on private devotional contemplation made luxury illustrated texts such as psalters particularly suited to the task of stimulating devotional contemplation in affluent, lay circles.[140] The mnemonic scheme of the Luttrell Psalter is not worked out in great detail in this case and there is no evidence that the artist had come across formal advice on techniques such as the architectural mnemonic, which Aelred and Grosseteste probably knew.[141] However, in this context the castle is still used as a framework for organizing a number of precepts and texts. As an architectural and allegorical form, it coexists in the worlds of chivalry and the religion, simultaneously referring to both. This example shows once again that defensive imagery has an important role to play in the medieval understanding of Christianity, directly inspired by Biblical texts. The castle forms an important part of this imagery but also plays a significant role in the organization and communication of these ideas, through its accepted use as an architectural mnemonic which can trigger the recognition of spiritual meanings.

The mnemonic function unites all the important spiritual castle texts in this chapter, and has been central to my arguments demonstrating the castle's

---

[139] S. Lewis, *Reading Images: Narrative Discourse and Reception in the Thirteenth-century Illuminated Apocalypse* (Cambridge, 1995), pp. 265, 272–3.

[140] S. Ringbom, 'Devotional Images and Imaginative Devotions: Notes on the Place of Art in Late Medieval Private Piety', *Gazette des Beaux Arts* 73 (1969), 159–70 (p. 164).

[141] It is worth noting that Geoffrey Luttrell, for whom the Psalter was produced, was lord of Irnham in Lincolnshire, and that certain illuminations have been compared to images in Lincoln Cathedral: C. Grossinger, 'Misericords', in *Age of Chivalry: Art in Plantagenet England, 1200–1400*, ed. J. Alexander and P. Binski (London, 1987), pp. 122–4 (p. 123). This may suggest a specific local knowledge of Grosseteste's *Château d'Amour*, which had been translated into Middle English by this time. It is therefore possible that the Psalter image refers directly to this tradition, but this would be hard to establish.

integration into the mainstream architectural allegories and devotional strategies of the Middle Ages. Mnemonic qualities have been noted by others in some of the texts I have discussed, but the strong link between mnemonic strategies and castle architecture has not previously been accorded special notice or comment, to my knowledge. However, I do not think it overstates the case to suggest that castle architecture came to be seen as quintessentially mnemonic in the medieval period. This can be demonstrated succinctly by the proliferation of castle-themed texts, towards the end of the medieval period, which used an architectural framework as an organizing feature and little more, such as *The Castel of Helthe* (1541), *The Castel of Memorie* (1562), *The Castell of Christians and Fortresse of the Faithfull* (1577) and *The Castell of Courtesie* (1582).[142] In all these texts, the castle appears in the title and usually in the prefatory matter, introducing the topic in an allegorical manner. However, castle imagery has no importance in the main subject matter of any of these texts, and is used only as a vessel in which to collect a series of observations on a given subject. This usage only makes sense in the context of a previous tradition of highly elaborate castle allegories where the mnemonic function of the architecture was paramount – including those I have discussed here. The sixteenth-century texts complete the cycle, demonstrating the universal recognition of the castle's ideological function by taking it for granted.

While the mnemonic function of the castle has by now been clearly demonstrated, it has often been less clear how such ideas relate to the castles built and occupied by medieval patrons. Implied links to castles and fortified ecclesiastical structures, both in Britain and in the Holy Land, have been discussed in this chapter, suggesting that buildings themselves, as well as their literary, artistic or mental representations, could be the site and subject of devotional contemplation in medieval practice. However, now a firm devotional framework has been established for the castle, and a set of Biblical texts and tenets of medieval theology attached to it, I hope it will be easier for others to map these ideas onto the design of medieval castles. The final example for this chapter seeks to show how this might be attempted. Once again, the discussion starts with a theological text using architectural allegory, but its imagery is both defensive and bodily in a particularly direct, almost visceral way.

---

[142] Thomas Elyot, *The Castel of Helthe, Corrected and Translated by the First Author Thereof* (London, 1541); Gulielmus Gratarolus, transl. Willyam Fulwod, *The Castell of Memorie: wherein is contayned the restoring, augmenting, and conserving of the Memorye and Remembraunce, with the safest remedies, and best preceptes thereunto in any wise apperteyning* (London, 1562); Thomas Woolton, *The Castell of Christians and Fortresse of the Faithfull, besseged and defended now almost six thousand yeares* (London, 1577); James Yates, Servingman, *The Castell of Courtesie, whereunto is adioyned The Hold of Humilitie, with the Chariot of Chastitie thereunto annexed* (London, 1582).

It recommends contemplation of castles by and for a group of religious who often made this connection literal, by taking up residence in the lordly fortresses of the day.

Part 7 of the thirteenth-century anchoress's guide, *Ancrene Wisse*, describes the siege of a castle. A lady is besieged by her enemies in an *eorþene* (earthen) castle,[143] while Christ, as a male admirer, offers to send her aid. The castle is not given a specific interpretation in the explanation of this tale, but it is clear that this image participates in the tradition of the spiritual castle I have been discussing throughout this chapter, with the gendered imagery of the female figure besieged in her fortress. Castles also occur as important images at other points throughout the text of *Ancrene Wisse*. In Part 1 the anchoress is told that the battlements of her castle are her cell's windows, and that she must not raise her eyes above them for fear of being shot at by her attacker, the devil. In Part 4 the anchoress is asked to compare herself to a high tower, surrounded by a deep ditch of sin, and attacked by the devil;[144] later in this book she is also invited to pour out hot tears against the devil's attack, and this is compared to a castle pouring out scalding water to guard its walls.[145] The relationship between the anchoress and the symbolic and real architecture of her anchor-hold is expressed even more clearly in Part 6, where Christ's birth and death are also described in terms of bodily and architectural enclosure:

> Marie wombe 7 þis þruh were his ancre huses. I nowðer nes he worltlich mon ah as ut of þe world forte schawin ancren þat ha ne schulen wið þe world na þing habben imeane. 3e þu ondswerest me. ah he wende ut of ba. 3e went tu alswa of baþine ancre huses. as he dude wiþ ute bruche. 7 leaf ham ba ihale. þat schal beon hwen þe gast ent ut on ende wiþ uten bruche 7 wem of his twa huses. þat an is þe licome. þet oþer os þe uttre hus. þat is as þe uttre wah abute þe castel.[146]

> (Mary's womb and this tomb were his anchor-houses. In neither was he a worldly man, but, as it were, out of the world, to show anchoresses that they must not have anything to say in common with the world. Yes, you answer me, but he went out of both. Yes, you will go likewise out of both your anchor-houses, as he did without breakage and left them both intact – that will be when the spirit goes out at the end without breakage or blemish from its two houses. The one is the body, the other is the outer house, which is like the outer wall around the castle.)[147]

Here the relationship between the anchoress and her cell is likened to the castle and the wall round it, and the physical impermeability which both

[143] *The English Text of Ancrene Riwle: Ancrene Wisse*, ed. J. R. R. Tolkien, Early English Text Society, original series 249 (1962), p. 198.
[144] Ibid., p. 117.
[145] Ibid., pp. 125–6.
[146] Ibid., p. 193.
[147] *Ancrene Wisse: Guide for Anchoresses*, ed. H. White (London, 1993), p. 173.

should, ideally, maintain.[148] The castle is an architectural expression of a physical and spiritual relationship which the anchoress must seek to remember.[149] This passage seems to refer to Biblical texts in its mention of the Virgin's intact womb, which recalls the text of Ezekiel 44. 2, as well as that of Luke 10. 38, both of which I have already discussed as important texts in architectural exegesis and castle allegories. However, like Aelred's use of the castle image in his sermon on the Assumption of the Virgin, the mnemonic image also makes use of a physical relationship with architectural space, as well as a spiritual one. Known examples of medieval religious women attached to castle anchor-holds include Idonea de Boclaund in the Tower of London, Emma de Skepeye at Dover Castle, and an unnamed female recluse who lived by the castle at Pontefract.[150] These women enacted the spiritual relationship between body and castle suggested in *Ancrene Wisse* in a very literal way, making castles the physical and mental focus of their devotional contemplation.

The fifteenth-century seal of Colchester discussed in Chapter 1 demonstrated that Luke 10. 38 could be applied to concrete architecture in a very public context. It transformed Colchester Castle into a type of the castle of Bethany through St Helena and her son, the Emperor Constantine, standing in for the Virgin Mary and Christ. In a similar way, these medieval anchorites enacted the symbolism of the castle of Bethany in identifiable castle buildings. Their bodily relationship with the defences created a living type of the castle of the Virgin, assailed by the world and the vices but impermeable to them. Their devotional exercises likewise recreated the contemplative life of the other Mary, balancing the Martha-like, active lives of the castles' other, more worldly, inhabitants. The castle, and its secular, military role within medieval life, were thus transformed into a physical locus of spiritual devotion and enclosure, as well as representing these precepts on a symbolic level.

The celebrated medieval scholar Kantorowicz famously suggested that every king approaching a city gate in the Middle Ages was transformed, through the typological symbolism of the age, into Christ entering the city of Jerusalem.[151] The symbolic power of this perception comes from the

---

[148] See Wogan-Browne, 'Chaste Bodies: Frames and Experiences', p. 27. See also J. Price, ' "Inner" and "Outer": Conceptualising the Body in *Ancrene Wisse* and Aelred's *De Institutione Inclusarum*', in *Medieval English Religious and Ethical Literature: Essays in Honour of G. H. Russell*, ed. G. Kratzmann and J. Simpson (Cambridge, 1986), pp. 192–208 (p. 192).

[149] The castle described, with its inner element and outer wall, sounds very like that of St Anselm, who is in fact quoted at another point during the text.

[150] R. M. Clay, *The Hermits and Anchorites of England* (London, 1914), p. 78.

[151] E. H. Kantorowicz, 'The "King's Advent" and the enigmatic panels in the doors of Santa Sabina', *Art Bulletin* 26 (1944), 207–31 (p. 210); see also E. H. Kantorowicz, *Laudes Regiae: A Study in Liturgical Acclamations and Medieval Ruler Worship* (Berkeley, 1958), pp. 71–2, 145–6.

juxtaposition of contemporary and ancient: a Biblical original and a medieval echo, bound together by a common understanding of the reference. This chapter, if nothing else, has demonstrated a similar shared understanding of the Biblical resonances of medieval castles, and has put forward several motifs that could be understood similarly to Kantorowicz's. Every knight seeking hospitality at a castle can be seen in the symbolic guise of Jesus entering the castle of Bethany, while every woman caught up in a castle siege became the Virgin, or closeted in anchoritic contemplation in a castle became Mary, Martha's sister. Much more work remains to be done to tease out the detailed workings of this symbolism, especially, perhaps, in its application to castle architecture and its design and planning. However, an ideological background for castle architecture, anchored, like that of ecclesiastical building, firmly in specific, well-known Biblical texts and promulgated through extensive exegesis, has now been established.

CHAPTER FOUR

The Imperial Castle

In June 1283 work began on Caernarfon Castle, part of Edward I's massive castle-building campaign designed to consolidate the English position in Wales by fortifying newly acquired territory.[1] The castle at Caernarfon alone cost over £20,000, a huge amount of money in contemporary terms, and took nearly fifty years to complete.[2] It was built at the mouth of the River Seiont, site of the ancient Welsh centre of Gwynedd; its thirteen polygonal towers and its exterior wall surface were given decorative treatment through coloured banding in the stonework, achieved by the alternation of dark and light stone courses (see Plates XIII and XIV). The castle was built on and around an older work, probably of Norman origin; also in the year of the new castle's foundation a body was found on the site and re-buried in the nearby church.[3]

In one of the most celebrated pieces of research in castle studies, Arnold Taylor transformed these facts into legends. Through medieval Welsh chronicles he found that the Roman site of Segontium, on the hill above Caernarfon, was connected in legends to Constantine the Great.[4] Taylor was also aware that Nennius, the author of the ninth-century work known as *Historia Brittonum*, had referred to a tomb at Segontium inscribed with Constantine's name, providing further evidence of imperial connections.[5] Taylor concluded that the incorporation of the Norman motte into the new castle was a material expression of continuity with the area's past, acknowledging the powerful symbolism of the ruins.[6] He also found documentary evidence to show that Edward I believed the body which had been discovered was that of the

---

[1] A. Taylor, 'Caernarvon', in H. M. Colvin, A. Taylor and R. A. Brown, *A History of the King's Works*, 6 vols. (London, 1963), I, 369–95 (p. 371).

[2] Ibid., p. 394.

[3] Ibid., pp. 369, 370, n. 1.

[4] Ibid., p. 369, n. 5.

[5] Ibid., p. 370, n. 2. Nennius thought this tomb belonged to the son of Constantine the Great, also called Constantine: 'Quintus Constantinus, Constantini magni filius, fuit, et ibi moritur, et sepulchrum illius monstratur iuxta urbem quae vocatur Cair Segeint, ut litterae, quae sunt in lapide tumuli, ostendunt' ('The fifth [to come to Britain] was Constantine, son of Constantine the Great, and there he died. His tomb is to be seen by the city called Caer Se[ge]int, as the letters on its stonework show'): Nennius, *British History and Welsh Annals*, ed. and transl. J. Morris (London, 1980), pp. 65, 25.

[6] Taylor, 'Caernarvon', pp. 369–70.

Roman emperor Magnus Maximus, the father of Constantine the Great. For Taylor this, again, was evidence of the strong symbolic connections invoked by Edward to strengthen his relationship with the illustrious ancient rulers of the place.[7] These resonances were confirmed for Taylor by the medieval Welsh text *Breuddwyd Maxen* (*The Dream of Maxen*), part of the cycle of the *mabinogi*, or *Mabinogion*, as the collection of works is usually called.[8] Magnus Maximus appears in this text as the emperor Maxen (or Macsen), who is associated with the beautiful castle of Aber Sein, situated at Arfon in Wales.[9] According to this legend the emperor marries Elen, the daughter of this castle's lord, and by this act the fortress at Arfon becomes the chief stronghold of the Island of Britain.[10] Elen is identified with St Helena, who, in medieval legend, found the True Cross and was the mother of Constantine the Great.[11]

From this accumulation of textual references and associations, Taylor was able to argue that Edward I built Caernarfon in order to make legend into reality. Caernarfon is, by this argument, a physical representation of the castle described in *Breuddwyd Maxen*, situated at the mouth of the River Seiont and recreating, Taylor argued, the huge multi-coloured towers mentioned in the text.[12] Edward's purpose in doing this, Taylor thought, was to appropriate to himself the illustrious history the Welsh associated with local legend: to make himself a ruler of Wales in accordance with its own mythography. However, Taylor also saw the polygonal towers and polychrome stonework of Caernarfon as another, complementary reference to Constantine. He detected in these features a deliberate evocation of Constantinople, the city most famously associated with the emperor whose name it bears, and under him, the capital of the Roman empire.[13] Taylor's visual comparison between

---

[7] 'Apud Kaernarvan, corpus Maximi principis, patris imperatoris nobilis Constantini, erat inventum, et rege iubente in ecclesia honorifice collocatum' ('At Caernarfon, the body of prince Maximus, father of the noble emperor Constantine, was found, and was placed honourably in the church, to the joy of the king'). Matthew of Westminster, *Flores Historiarum*, ed. H. R. Luard, Rolls Series 95, 3 vols. (1890, repr. 1965), III, 59.

[8] *Breuddwyd Maxen*, ed. I. Williams (Bangor, 1908); 'The Dream of Macsen Wledig', in *The Mabinogion*, transl. G. Jones and T. Jones (London, 1949, repr. 1950), pp. 79–88.

[9] *Breuddwyd Maxen*, ed. Williams, pp. 7, 8; 'The Dream of Macsen Wledig', transl. Jones and Jones, pp. 80, 83.

[10] 'The Dream of Macsen Wledig', transl. Jones and Jones, p. 85.

[11] Jacobus de Voragine: *The Golden Legend, Readings on the Saints*, ed. W. G. Ryan, 2 vols. (Princeton, 1993, repr. 1995), I, 278; accounts of Helena's origins are various, but often suggest that she is the daughter of a British king: de Voragine: *The Golden Legend*, I, 281. See also E. D. Hunt, *Holy Land and Pilgrimage in the Later Roman empire, AD 312–460* (Oxford, 1982), pp. 28–9; J. F. Matthews, 'Macsen, Maximus, and Constantine', *Welsh History Review* 11 (1982–3), 431–48 (pp. 439, 441–6 and *passim*).

[12] Taylor, 'Caernarvon', p. 370.

[13] In what follows I will retain Taylor's description of the city by its earlier name of Constantinople as this expresses the connection with its founder, the emperor Constantine the Great, most succinctly.

Caernarfon Castle and the outer, Theodosian land wall at Constantinople is striking. From the angle he chooses, the straight stretches of wall between the polygonal towers and the banded polychromy at Caernarfon show more than a passing resemblance to Constantinople's walls.[14] The statues of imperial eagles on the battlements at Caernarfon, still visible on the Eagle Tower (at the left hand end of the castle in Plate XIII, detail in Plate XIV), were for Taylor further visual invocations of imperial imagery.[15] He saw all these imperial resonances as part of Edward's effort to transform himself into a new Constantine. The castle and town at Caernarfon were set up as another Constantinople: the Welsh capital of the king's new empire.

Taylor's exposition of symbolic and aesthetic meaning at Caernarfon Castle was groundbreaking, and has captivated medievalists of all fields ever since. It has been repeated for the benefit of successive generations as a unique example of these qualities in castle architecture.[16] However, in more recent years scholars have begun to look for similar approaches to other castles.[17] The preceding chapters of this book show that many of the themes identified in Taylor's analysis of Caernarfon can be traced in the design and depiction of other medieval castles. Colchester Castle, for example, boasts a rival link with Constantine and Helena (see Chapter 1, pp. 39–42). The Tower of London, too, carries imperial connotations through its Trojan foundation legend, and also demonstrates the idea of one city being understood as a deliberate recreation of another city, with the castle as an essential feature of this reconstruction (see Chapter 2, pp. 54–5). In these cases, material remains are consistently understood as a point of contact with the legendary past, whether in the plinth of the temple of Claudius used as the foundation for Colchester Castle, the Roman tiles incorporated into its walls, or in the Roman city walls of Colchester and London (Chapters 1 and 2 respectively). Taylor's analysis of Caernarfon Castle has, therefore, lost its singularity. Indeed, as I have suggested, many of the phenomena he notes have close parallels in other medieval castles. While this bolsters many of Taylor's argument, closer

---

[14] This appears in A. Taylor, *The Welsh Castles of Edward I* (London, 1986), p. 2; *History of the King's Works* I, ed. Brown, Colvin and Taylor, pl. 15.

[15] Taylor, 'Caernarvon', p. 371, n. 1.

[16] For example, P. Binksi, *Westminster Abbey and the Plantagenets: Kingship and the Representation of Power, 1200–1400* (New Haven, 1995), pp. 105, 139–40; M. Prestwich, *Edward I* (London, 1988), pp. 120, 211–14; P. Draper, 'The Architectural Setting of Gothic Art', in *Age of Chivalry: Art and Society in Late Medieval England*, ed. N. Saul (Brockhampton, 1995), pp. 60–75 (pp. 60, 62); R. K. Morris, 'The Architecture of Arthurian Enthusiasm: Castle Symbolism in the Reigns of Edward I and his Successors', in *Armies, Chivalry and Warfare in Medieval Britain*, ed. M. Strickland, Proceedings of the 1995 Harlaxton Symposium (1998), pp. 63–81 (p. 65).

[17] See, for example, T. A. Heslop, 'Orford Castle, Nostalgia and Sophisticated Living', *Architectural History* 34 (1991), 36–58; Morris, 'The Architecture of Arthurian Enthusiasm'.

inspection shows up certain elements of his work which are now ripe for reassessment.

For example, the strength of the Taylor's visual comparison between Caernarfon and Constantinople is undermined when it is considered that only a tiny minority of medieval visitors to Caernarfon, or perhaps none at all, would have seen the walls of Constantinople.[18] The vast majority of observers cannot have appreciated any connection between the Welsh castle and the imperial city, so an elaborately created visual allusion would have had no resonance. It seems unlikely that the extra expense and effort of polychrome banding would have been worthwhile for such an uncertain result. Taylor's other justification of the polychrome effect is also unsound. The huge, multicoloured towers described in *Breuddwyd Maxen*, a central tenet of Taylor's argument for the local significance of Caernarfon's appearance, do not in fact belong to the castle described at Aber Sein at all. They are part of the description of another fortress, stated in the text as being located on the coast of mainland Europe, before the voyage to Britain,[19] while the fortress at Arfon is described quite plainly in comparison.[20] Taylor must have confused the references. Again, this negates the links Taylor set up between the appearance of the castle and its significance for medieval observers. Although these criticisms need to be aired, this chapter in fact sets out to confirm Taylor's emphasis on imperial imagery in medieval castle design and specifically at Caernarfon. It draws, however, on other evidence of important contemporary links between the imperial history of the area and the new castle, which Taylor did not include in his study. These alternative sources confirm some of Taylor's assumptions about the castle's imperial connotations, but at the same time shift the emphasis of the imperial symbolism away from Constantinople, to sources closer at hand.

Some of Edward I's other projects help to contextualize the political symbolism of Caernarfon Castle. The king's use of legendary history in support of his military and political ambitions is well documented. Several of these examples are particularly pertinent to the campaign of Welsh conquest and

---

[18] Taylor can come up with only one figure associated with the court of Edward I who might have visited Constantinople: Taylor, 'Caernarvon', n. 4, pp. 370–1. Moreover, Taylor himself admits that the famous medieval description of the walls of Constantinople by Villehardouin could not have spread knowledge of the appearance of the walls as it mentions neither polychromy nor polygonal towers, the features essential to Taylor's comparison of the two structures: Taylor, 'Caernarvon', p. 370, n. 4; see Geoffroy de Villehardouin, *La Conquête de Constantinople,* ed. E. Faral, Les Classiques de l'Histoire de France au Moyen Age 18–19, 2nd edn (1961), II, 32–5 for the brief and scanty description of the walls of Constantinople.

[19] This castle is described in both Macsen's dream sequence and in the journey of his emmissaries as lying at the mouth of a river near the coast, but before the sea journey to Britain: 'The Dream of Macsen Wledig', transl. Jones and Jones, pp. 79, 83.

[20] *Breuddwyd Maxen*, ed. Williams, pp. 7, 8; 'The Dream of Macsen Wledig', transl. Jones and Jones, pp. 80, 83.

assimilation. Surviving evidence from a letter of 1301, from Edward I to Pope Boniface, defends the claim of the English monarchy to overlordship of Scotland, using legendary precedents.[21] This letter asserts that the English people are descended from the eldest son of Brutus, the Trojan founder of Britain. As Wales and Scotland were governed by the younger sons of Brutus, holding these lands only in service to their elder brother, the letter argues, the English have superior rights over Wales and Scotland.[22] Wales and Scotland are paradoxically both exalted and subjugated by this precedent, as, no doubt, was Edward's intention. They are acclaimed as nations with a venerable past, participants from the first in the foundation history of Britain, included in the arrangements made by the nation's progenitor. At the same time they are declared junior partners, submitted to the rule of their more important neighbour, not to be trusted to their own resources. Such imagery raises the value of Edward's British military acquisitions, while also asserting his natural right to them.

While the letter to Pope Boniface was aimed mainly at supporting Edward's claims to Scotland, Wales was the particular target of his political showmanship shortly after its conquest, at a point when work on Caernarfon Castle was already underway. This time attention was aimed at appropriating Welsh legendary history for political ends. In 1285 Edward presented to Westminster Abbey a treasured Welsh relic believed to be a fragment of the True Cross.[23] The discovery of the True Cross is connected to Wales through the figure of St Helena – the Elen of *Breuddwyd Maxen* – whose Welsh ancestry is introduced by the *Dingestow Brut*, a thirteenth-century Welsh version of Geoffrey of Monmouth's legendary history of Britain, the *Historia regum*

---

21 Prestwich, *Edward I*, p. 121.

22 'Sire Brut e ses enfanz sa tere deviseit,/ A Loquerin Engletere, qe lors fu Bretaigne;/ Escoce à Albanak, qe dit fu Albanie;/ A Kamber dona Gales pur sa porcion,/ Qe dit fu Kambria, du Kamber prist-il noun./ A ses enfaunz pusneés dona son tenement/ De Guales e d'Escoce heritablement,/ Solunc la lei de Troie, à tenir en feé/ Pur homage e service de lour frere eyné' ('Sir Brut to his children bequeathed his land,/ To Locrine England, which was then Britain;/ Scotland to Albanac, which was called Albany;/ To Camber he gave Wales for his portion,/ Which was called Cambria, from Camber it took its name./ To his younger children he gave his lordship/ Of Wales and Scotland by inheritance,/ According to the law of Troy, to hold in fee/ By homage and service of their elder brother): '*Rescriptio regis Edwardi, ad dominum Bonefacium papam transmissa*', in *The Chronicle of Pierre de Langtoft*, ed. T. Wright, Rolls Series 47, 2 vols. (1869, repr. 1964), II, 404–5.

23 'Rex Edwardus . . . portionem Dominicae Crucis non modicam, ornatam auro et argento et lapidibus preciosis, quam de Wallia secum tulit, apud Westmonasterium cum solempni processione et concentu advexit' ('The King Edward conveyed to Westminster with solemn procession and song . . . a largish piece of the Cross of the Lord, decorated with gold and silver and precious stones, which he had brought with him from Wales'). Matthew of Westminster, *Flores Historiarum*, III, 62–3. This relic had been presented to him the year before by the Welsh themselves: Prestwich, *Edward I*, pp. 203–4.

Britannie. Helena is also the wife of Maxen and the mother of Constantine in this account[24] and it seems more than likely that a version of this text must have been the source for *Breuddwyd Maxen*.[25]

Recent research has confirmed the great importance of these particular legends for Welsh historiography and national identity, underlining Edward I's acuity in manipulating local legends to his political ends. Macsen Wledig, or Magnus Maximus, holds a position of supreme importance in Welsh national history from its earliest days.[26] He is seen as the last of the Roman emperors to rule in Britain, and, with the addition of a British family and important descendants in medieval accounts,[27] he came to be identified as 'the first ruler of an independent Britain, from whom all legitimate power flowed',[28] 'the founder of the Celtic kingdoms of the west, and so ultimately of the Welsh nation'.[29] This role has been compared to the one King Arthur later acquired,[30] and also indirectly to that of Brutus, legendary founder of Britain.[31] The latter comparison is a good one for my present purposes, since the Maximus legend shares with the Brutus myth the aim of making the British measure up to the Romans.[32] I discussed in Chapter 2 how this strategy was used in relation to the mythography of Brutus (see pp. 53–6). For a monarch who, as I have shown, knew how to use the Brutus myth, an invocation of Maximus and his local connections might well be expected at Caernarfon, the culminating conquest of the Welsh campaign. Here the legend could be used to appropriate the legitimacy attached to Maximus for the new English rule.[33] From this evidence it would seem that Maximus Magnus, rather than his son Constantine, is the most likely focus of the imperial imagery at Caernarfon.

[24] B. F. Roberts, 'Geoffrey of Monmouth, *Historia regum Britanniae* and *Brut y Brehinedd*', in *The Arthur of the Welsh: The Arthurian Legend in Medieval Welsh Literature*, ed. R. Bromwich, A. O. H. Jarman and B. F. Roberts (Cardiff, 1991), pp. 97–116 (p. 112).

[25] Ibid., p. 111 and *passim*.

[26] Dumville identifies Maximus's importance in the work of Gildas, the seventh-century Welsh historian: D. N. Dumville, 'Sub-Roman Britain: History and Legend', *History* 62 (1977), 173–92 (p. 180).

[27] Matthews, 'Macsen, Maximus, and Constantine', p. 445 and *passim*.

[28] Dumville, 'Sub-Roman Britain: History and Legend', p. 180.

[29] Matthews, 'Macsen, Maximus, and Constantine', p. 432.

[30] Dumville, 'Sub-Roman Britain: History and Legend', p. 181.

[31] D. N. Dumville, 'The Historical Value of the *Historia Britonnum*', *Arthurian Literature* 6 (1986), 1–26 (p. 20).

[32] Macsen's role in this respect is widely discussed: see, for example, Dumville, 'Sub-Roman Britain: History and Legend'; Dumville, 'The Historical Value of the *Historia Britonnum*'; A. Gransden, *Historical Writing in England c.550 to c.1307* (London, 1974), p. 10; Matthews, 'Macsen, Maximus, and Constantine'; Roberts, 'Geoffrey of Monmouth'.

[33] See J. Grenville, 'The Rows of Chester: Some Thoughts on the Results of Recent Research', *World Archaeology* 21 (1990), 446–60 (p. 457).

It is also probable that material evidence of the Roman occupation of Wales, perhaps specifically at Segontium Roman fort, was at least partly responsible for area's association with the Maximus legend, in a much wider sense than that suggested by Taylor. Standing Roman architecture, Roman roads and smaller finds such as coins have all been listed, in addition to the inscriptional evidence which Taylor cites, as causes of an enduring medieval fascination with Wales's Roman connections.[34] It therefore seems likely that imperial architecture in Britain, rather than far away at Constantinople, was the inspiration for Edward's invocation of Magnus Maximus. Several of these possibilities are explored in two articles published by R. S. Loomis a few years before Taylor's article.[35] If Taylor had come across them, he would have discovered a complex series of Arthurian and imperial links to the Caernarfon area, which would have strengthened his arguments considerably. However, they would also have directed him clearly towards the material remains of Roman culture, and specifically the Roman fort of Segontium on the hill above the new castle, as the primary focus of the area's legendary associations.

Loomis dwells at some length on the description of Constantine's tomb at 'Caer Segeint' by the ninth-century Welsh historian, Nennius, mentioned briefly by Taylor. Nennius follows his reference to this monument with the observation that Constantine sowed seeds of gold, silver and bronze on the pavement of Caer Segeint.[36] Loomis explains this as a cryptic reference to the many Roman coins found around the sites of Segontium and Caernarfon over the years, including several with inscriptions referring to Helena, the wife of Constantius; also to her son, Constantine the Great, and his son Constantine II.[37] Loomis also suggests that a Roman inscription in the area may have misled Nennius (or his source) into identifying the supposed tomb of Constantine.[38] Coins have continued to be discovered here up to the twentieth century, so it seems reasonable to suppose that similar finds may have prompted medieval observers to connect these sites directly with the rulers depicted on the coins.[39] These artefacts create a strong material context

---

[34] See for example Gransden, *Historical Writing in England c.550 to c.1307*, p. 11; Matthews, 'Macsen, Maximus, and Constantine', pp. 437–8; N. J. G. Pounds, '*The Medieval Castle in England and Wales: A Social and Political History* (Cambridge, 1990, repr. 1994), p. 174.

[35] R. S. Loomis, 'From Segontium to Sinadon – The Legends of a *Cité Gaste*', *Speculum* 22 (1947), 520–33; R. S. Loomis, 'Edward I, Arthurian Enthusiast', *Speculum* 28 (1953), 114–27.

[36] Nennius, *British History and Welsh Annals*, pp. 65, 25: 'Et ipse seminavit tria semina, id est auri, argenti aerisque, in pavimento supradictae civitatis, ut nullus pauper in ea habitaret unquam' ('He sowed three seeds, of gold, of silver, and of bronze, on the pavement of that city, that no man should ever live there poor').

[37] Loomis, 'From Segontium to Sinadon', p. 521.

[38] Ibid., p. 522.

[39] Loomis's argument is backed up by several other scholars: G. C. Boon, *Segontium Roman Fort, Caernarvonshire* (London, 1963), pp. 18–19; Matthews, 'Macsen,

for the legendary connections of the area. Indeed, Loomis suggests that a similar combination of inscription and assumption lay behind Edward I's identification of a body, found nearby, as that of Magnus Maximus, many years later.[40]

For Loomis the text *Breuddwyd Maxen* fits into precisely this context, demonstrating the real difference of his arguments from Taylor's. Loomis equates the text's 'Kaer Aber Sein'[41] ('the fortress at the mouth of the Seiont') with Segontium, the Roman fort referred to by Nennius as 'Caer Segeint'.[42] The author of *Breuddwyd Maxen*, Loomis suggests, is describing the Roman fort before its decay, in its glorious past when it was frequented by the great British founder figure, Magnus Maximus. Taylor does not seem to have understood the text in this light at all, or to have made the connection between *Breuddwyd Maxen* and Segontium Roman fort. No doubt guided by the use of the word 'castle' to describe the fortress in the English translation of the text he was using, he made a connection with the medieval castle built at Caernarfon by Edward I, but not with the remains of the Roman fortress of Segontium nearby. For Taylor, *Breuddwyd Maxen* describes a fantastic, fictional castle rather than a Roman fort and for him it was this fictional castle that Edward set out to make into a reality. In fact the Welsh word *caer* has a wide range of meanings, strikingly similar to those I attributed in Chapter 1 to the English word *castle* in its medieval usage. The *Dictionary of the Welsh Language* cites uses of the word dating from 1200, and lists its meanings as: 'fort, fortress, enclosed stronghold, castle, citadel, fortified town or city'.[43] Once again, it seems, a linguistic misunderstanding has directed the course of castle studies. While this casts doubt on the exclusive relationship set up by Taylor between the 'castle' of *Breuddwyd Maxen* and Edward's castle at Caernarfon, it opens up the possibility of a three-way relationship between the *kaer* described in medieval texts such as *Breuddwyd Maxen*, the Roman fortress on the hill and the medieval castle further down towards the river.

For Loomis, this relationship expressed the decay of civilizations and the passing of empire. He assumed from the first that the fortress described in *Breuddwyd Maxen* related to the Roman remains of Segontium.[44] He cited documentary evidence for the re-use of ashlar stone from Segontium in the building of Caernarfon Castle, seeing this as a robbing and depletion of the imperial power attached to the ancient site, marking the beginning of its

---

Maximus, and Constantine', p. 447; Gransden, *Historical Writing in England c.550 to c.1307*, p. 11.
[40] Loomis, 'From Segontium to Sinadon', pp. 521–2.
[41] *Breuddwyd Maxen*, ed. Williams, p. 8.
[42] Nennius, *British History and Welsh Annals*, p. 65.
[43] *Geiriadur Prifysgol Cymru: A Dictionary of the Welsh Language*, ed. R. J. Thomas (Cardiff, 1950–67).
[44] Loomis, 'From Segontium to Sinadon', pp. 524–7 and *passim*.

loss as a locus of potent historical associations.[45] Edward's use of material from Segontium may, though, be interpreted in a more positive way, which fits better with other evidence of his ready manipulation of powerful legendary associations. The removal of stones from the Roman fortress for use in the new castle may suggest a transfer of powerful associations, rather than their loss. This might be seen as a similar process to Edward's transfer of the powerful Welsh relic of the True Cross to Westminster. There is no suggestion that this relic lost its power through changing hands and locations; indeed, the whole point of such an exercise must have been to enhance the status of its new owner through its continued potency. A similar interpretation can be applied to the transfer of stones from Segontium to Caernarfon.

I have already suggested that the castle could often be seen in the Middle Ages as an architectural form belonging to the Roman past, and that certain medieval castles could also be projected back to give them a (spurious) ancient history. The Roman remains incorporated into the Norman castle at Colchester, for example, acted as a confirmation of the supposedly ancient origins of the castle, and linked it to legendary figures with strong imperial connections, also invoked at Caernarfon/Segontium. In this context it seems likely that Edward I, in building his new castle out of the remains of the ruined Roman fort nearby, saw himself as renewing and rebuilding the Roman fortress, using some of its original materials as an expression of material continuity between the two sites. Caernarfon Castle can thus be seen both as a renewal of the ancient Roman fort itself and as a reconstruction of the same fortress as it is imagined in its heyday, in *Breuddwyd Maxen*.

Although Loomis did not make this connection, his arguments also point towards a rationale for the distinctive appearance and symbolism of Caernarfon Castle, which would be perfectly accessible to ordinary medieval observers. Taylor remarks that 'there were . . . no English precedents' for the polychrome banding of the stonework at Caernarfon.[46] In the exact form of its banding it is true that Caernarfon is unique. However, structures of banded polychrome stonework were standing in this country long before Edward's castle, and can still be seen in many sites. The characteristic form of Roman masonry has a banded, polychrome appearance from the use of a rubble core, bound by cement and strengthened by the use of courses of tiles which span the width of the wall and so hold its mixed structure together. The tile courses are repeated at regular intervals to strengthen the wall, and tile and rubble

---

[45] Ibid., pp. 530–1. This is confirmed in more recent archaeological evidence: 'Edwardian silver pennies from the site show that the ruins were being quarried for their dressed stone at the time of the building of Caernarfon Castle and the medieval borough', Boon, *Segontium Roman Fort*, p. 4.

[46] Taylor, 'Caernarvon', p. 370.

layers form a banded structure, the red tiles contrasting against the greyish cement and rubble (see Plates VII and XVII).[47]

Admittedly, this technique is very different from that employed at Caernarfon, where two different colours of ashlar stone were used to create the banded effect (see Plates XIII and XIV). However, the similarity of the castle's appearance to this kind of Roman building was demonstrated by Taylor. The Theodosian walls of Constantinople are of Roman construction, using this technique, with tile courses between masonry layers.[48] The resemblance is certainly assisted at Caernarfon by the choice of red sandstone for the thinner bands of masonry. When freshly cut, these must have showed up very clearly against the paler sandstone on either side of them, and might well have been reminiscent of huge tile courses. Caernarfon's resemblance to the Theodosian walls of Constantinople is not, therefore, indicative of an exclusive symbolic relationship between the two. It seems to me that this similarity is incidental to the much wider visual symbolism intended at Caernarfon Castle, which was meant to remind its medieval viewers of the many Roman remains they could see all over Britain. More specifically, the general resemblance to Roman construction techniques at the castle may have referred to the local Roman fort of Segontium, while re-used stone from the fort cemented this relationship in material terms.

Stated in this bald way, this suggestion lacks detailed substantiation. However, the background for this kind of architectural symbolism and material re-use is complex, relating not just to the isolated examples of Caernarfon Castle and Segontium Roman fort. I have found enough evidence outside these examples to suggest that polychrome effects had an important role to play in the creation of imperial imagery in medieval castles and other architectural contexts. I have also identified a number of other sources, both textual and material, which demonstrate a medieval understanding that the motif of polychromy was linked to ideas of empire. In these cases there is often a strong emphasis on the material remains of Roman occupation as accompaniments to such imagery. Both these findings fit closely with the arguments presented in previous chapters that castles were regarded in the Middle Ages as representing an ancient form of architecture, projected back, as it were, into the ancient past.

The main section of this chapter examines in more detail the general and specific precedents for symbolic re-use of materials and structural polychromy in medieval castle building. Attention is focused on a few examples of these practices in castle architecture before Edward I's Caernarfon Castle,

---

[47] M. Greenhalgh, *The Survival of Roman Antiquities in the Middle Ages* (London, 1989) p. 143; J. C. Higgitt, 'The Roman Background to Mediaeval England', *Journal of the British Archaeological Association* 36 (1973), 1–15 (p. 4).

[48] A. M. Schneider, 'The City-Walls of Istanbul', transl. R. G. Austin, *Antiquity* 11 (1937), 461–8 (p. 465).

and returns finally to Caernarfon, to discuss its participation in both local and national schemes of medieval architectural symbolism.

Taylor certainly had good reasons for focusing on the figure of Constantine in his exposition of Caernarfon's symbolism, despite what I have said against these arguments. Constantine crystallizes many of the important issues surrounding the ideas of *Romanitas* and *translatio imperii* for the Middle Ages.[49] He was the first of the Roman emperors to convert to Christianity, but in 327 or 328 he also transferred the centre of his empire from Rome to a new eastern capital, which he re-named Constantinople.[50] The legendary and divinely sanctioned[51] association of the Roman empire with its original location in Rome, the Eternal City, traditional seat of Emperors and apostolic centre of Christianity,[52] made this an immensely significant move. Preceding chapters have already discussed the idea that one city could be thought of as a reproduction or renewal of another, and the transfer to Constantinople was the ultimate expression of this idea for the Middle Ages.[53] Constantine's move also embodied the idea of *translatio imperii* – encompassing both topographical and material shifts and renewals, as well as the theological concept of the transfer of divine imperial mandate – and so helped to define a concept that was crucial for the Middle Ages.

The succession of power from one empire to another through the ages of the world, often referred to as *translatio imperii*, was a concept originating in Biblical exegesis of Ecclesiasticus 10. 8. This Biblical text describes the four empires that are to succeed each other until the Day of Judgement.[54] Interpretations varied, but for the Middle Ages there was general agreement that, after the empires of Babylon, the Medo-Persians and the Graeco-Macedonians, the Roman empire was the fourth and final empire. As long as the Roman empire lasted, it was believed, the end of the world would not be due.[55] Whether it was envisaged as a religious or a political mandate, Rome's

---

[49] B. Brenk, 'Spolia from Constantine to Charlemagne: Aesthetics versus Ideology', in *Studies in Art and Archaeology in Honor of Ernst Kitzinger*, ed. W. Tronzo and I. Lavin, Dumbarton Oaks Papers 41 (1987), pp. 103–9 (pp. 104–5).

[50] R. Krautheimer, *Three Christian Capitals: Topography and Politics* (Berkeley, 1983), p. 45.

[51] A. Pagden, *Lords of All the World: Ideologies of Empire in Spain, Britain and France c.1500–1800* (New Haven, 1995), pp. 26–7.

[52] Ibid., pp. 17–18. See also Chapter 2, where I discuss exemplary cities, including Rome.

[53] W. Hammer, 'The Concept of the New or Second Rome in the Middle Ages', *Speculum* 19 (1944), 50–62 (pp. 51–6) and *passim*; Krautheimer, *Three Christian Capitals*, p. 45.

[54] Ecclesiasticus 10. 8: 'Regnum a gente in gentem transfertur' ('A kingdom is translated from one people to another').

[55] E. R. Curtius, *European Literature and the Latin Middle Ages*, transl. W. R. Trask (New York, 1953), pp. 28–9; E. Edson, *Mapping Time and Space: How Medieval Mapmakers Viewed their World* (London, 1997), pp. 99–100; R. Folz, *The Concept of Empire in*

place in this scheme was further confirmed for medieval scholars by the prediction of the city's ascendancy made to Aeneas in Virgil's *Aeneid*.[56] This text was especially important to the later Middle Ages, as it discussed Trojan participation in the Roman empire, through Aeneas, the legendary Trojan refugee and founder of Rome. Both Trojan and Roman foundation legends therefore had an important imperial significance for those medieval nations who could claim them, and were an integral part of the concept of *translatio imperii*.[57]

Constantine the Great and his eponymous city long represented the most important material and symbolic transfer of imperial might. The emphasis in this *translatio imperii* was on architecture. On his conquest of Rome, Constantine's great building projects followed the precedents of the Classical era in their scale and style: the Arch of Constantine, the Lateran Church and St Peter's.[58] However, all of these projects also involved the re-use of materials from the existing monumental architecture of the city.[59] Constantine made very literal translations, and in some cases transportations, of Classical Roman motifs and materials to form a recycled imperial iconography both in the ancient and the new capitals of the empire. Beat Brenk, among others, presents compelling arguments as to the symbolic importance of this re-use:

> Such a transference of building materials was by no means inexpensive, let alone practical, since the different heights of the columns (for example in the Lateran) had to be adjusted and levelled. In other words, it is far more difficult to work with *spolia* than with newly made, homogeneous buildings materials . . . I do not see at all how it could have been possible to save money by using *spolia*. Someone capable of erecting such numerous great buildings as Constantine had vast funds available to him. There cannot

Western Europe from the Fifth to the Fourteenth Century, transl. S. A. Ogilvie (London, 1969), pp. 45–6, 100.

[56] 'Tu regere imperio populos, Romane, memento/ (hae tibi erunt artes), pacique imponere morem,/ parcere subiectis et debellare superbos' ('You, Roman, be sure to rule the world (be these your arts), to crown peace with justice, to spare the vanquished and to crush the proud'): Virgil, 'Aeneid', in *Eclogues, Georgics, Aeneid I–VI*, ed. and transl. H. R. Fairclough, revised G. P. Goold, Loeb Classical Library 63 (1999), Book 6, lines 851–3, pp. 592–3. See Hammer, 'The Concept of the New or Second Rome', p. 50.

[57] I have already stressed the prominence of legendary founders in medieval presentation of important castles in Chapter 2. Both Roman and Trojan foundation legends play an important part in the present chapter, and draw on the same basic concept of the British desire to stand up to, or surpass, the precedent of Rome, articulated in texts such as the *Historia Britonnum* and *Historia regum Britannie*, as I discussed earlier. However, here I am interested in the articulation of imperial imagery, rather than in the construction of civic harmony or discord, or the creation of exemplary cities or castles, through such imagery.

[58] Krautheimer, *Three Christian Capitals*, pp. 15–23, 26.

[59] Brenk, 'Spolia from Constantine to Charlemagne', pp. 103–4.

have been a lack of artists, either, since the actual Triumph of Constantine was carved by contemporary sculptors.[60]

The large-scale re-use of old material from the monuments of the previous emperors Trajan, Hadrian and Marcus Aurelius cannot, then, be interpreted purely as a prudent device employed to save time or money. It was a symbolic act that transferred the legitimacy of the old order to Constantine himself in material terms, and through Constantine's actions it became inextricably linked to claims of *translatio imperii*.[61]

Constantine's achievements shaped the idea and practice of empire to such an extent that, as the Holy Roman Empire passed from one dynasty to another down to the eleventh century, successive emperors made a point of transferring the seat of empire to a new location. Constantinople, Aachen, Trier, Milan, Rheims, Tournai and Pavia are all referred to as new Romes at various points, as each took on the role of imperial capital.[62] Within this constant *translatio imperii*, the importance of material transfer and architectural salvage was maintained down to the later Middle Ages.[63] The emperors Theodoric and Theodosius both went as far as shipping materials from Rome all the way to Constantinople to maintain the perceived continuity of empire.[64] Charlemagne in turn arranged for the transportation of materials from Theodoric's palace at Ravenna for the palace in his new capital at Aachen.[65] In all these cases it can readily be appreciated that moving materials these considerable distances cannot have been the most efficient option. Symbolic re-use, motivated by the concept of *translatio imperii* seems the most likely explanation.

The re-use of Roman materials continued throughout the Middle Ages on different scales.[66] However, despite the compelling arguments that material re-use at a grand, imperial level was an expression of *translatio imperii*, it is

---

[60] Ibid., pp. 104, 106.

[61] Ibid., pp. 104–5.

[62] T. Zotz, 'Carolingian Tradition and Ottonian-Salanian Innovation: Comparative Observation on Palatine Policy in the Empire', in *Kings and Kingship in Medieval Europe*, ed. A. J. Duggan (London, 1993), pp. 69–100; Hammer, 'The Concept of the New or Second Rome'.

[63] R. G. Calkins, *Medieval Architecture in Western Europe from A.D. 300 to 1500* (New York, 1998), p. 66 and *passim*; Zotz, 'Carolingian Tradition', pp. 69–70, 77–9, 88–9, 98.

[64] Brenk, 'Spolia from Constantine to Charlemagne', pp. 107–8; Krautheimer, *Three Christian Capitals*, p. 49.

[65] Brenk, 'Spolia from Constantine to Charlemagne', p. 108. Charlemagne's official coronation as Roman emperor occurred there at Christmas 800: K. J. Conant, *Carolingian and Romanesque Architecture 800 to 1200* (Harmondsworth, 1959, repr. 1978), pp. 31–2.

[66] See Greenhalgh, *The Survival of Roman Antiquities in the Middle Ages*; D. Stocker, 'Rubbish Recycled: A Study of the Re-use of Stone in Lincolnshire', in *Stone: Quarrying and Building in England, AD 43–1525*, ed. D. Parsons (Chichester, 1990), pp. 83–101; T. Eaton, *Plundering the Past: Roman Stonework in Medieval Britain* (Stroud, 2000).

much harder to make such arguments convincing for more humble recycling. This lesser scale of activity not surprisingly accounts for the vast majority of medieval re-uses of Roman materials, and can often be explained by economic necessity.[67] This need not rule out additional symbolic motives for these cases, but they can often be harder to detect. A case in point is furnished by the defensive walls built round a large number of towns in what was then Gaul, probably in the late third or the early fourth century.[68] The re-use in these walls of large quantities of material from earlier Roman monuments has led to two different views about the possible symbolic or economic motivations of the builders. Greenhalgh summarizes the arguments neatly:

> The first . . . states that the walls were erected in Gaul to cope with the invasions of the third century: the inhabitants of the towns therefore had to use material to hand (largely the tombstones of their ancestors) with a pressing need . . . The second argument is that such walls (although clearly necessary and incorporating only a fraction of the city), were too carefully constructed – indeed, in some cases too consciously beautified . . . to be a response to any one pressing threat.[69]

Greenhalgh presents both arguments here as part of his wider point that a choice between these two alternatives is not always necessary. His study is full of documented examples of the re-use of Roman materials in pressing economic and sometimes defensive need, which were nevertheless interpreted as symbolic by contemporary commentators. It is this argument, that symbolic motives can lie alongside more material needs, which I wish to apply to the examples of re-use in the later Middle Ages. For this purpose, the construction of these Gallic defensive walls, as well as their historiography,

---

[67] David Stocker sets up a tripartite model of re-use, in which he distinguishes between casual, functional and iconic reasons for re-use. He classifies casual re-use as that carried out haphazardly for ease and economy; functional re-use involves the recycling of structural members for the purpose for which they were originally made, but is also for economic reasons. Iconic re-use he detects only where images or inscriptions are re-used and displayed prominently: Stocker, 'Rubbish Recycled'. However, Tim Eaton argues, very sensibly, that this model relies only on the materials re-used and does not allow for interpretation of particular circumstances of re-use as possibly carrying meaning in themselves: Eaton, *Plundering the Past*, p. 135 and *passim*. I have therefore sought a different model for the discussion of re-use. I am most grateful to Tim Eaton for allowing me to see a draft of his work before it was published.

[68] R. M. Butler, 'The Roman Walls of Le Mans', *The Journal of Roman Studies* 48 (1958), 33–9.

[69] Greenhalgh, *The Survival of Roman Antiquities in the Middle Ages*, p. 42; see also M. Todd, *The Walls of Rome* (London, 1978), p. 78; T. F. C. Blagg, 'The Re-use of Monumental Masonry in Late Roman Defensive Walls', in *Roman Urban Defences in the West*, ed. J. Maloney and B. Hobley, Council for British Archaeology Research Report 51 (1983), pp. 130–5.

provides some interesting insights. They are built using the characteristic Roman construction method of cemented rubble, with layers of tiles at regular intervals as levelling and bonding courses.[70] However, in certain circumstances this method can itself become a decorative as much as a structural device.[71] In the walls of Le Mans, for example, the tile courses penetrate the core of the wall only to a depth of two tiles,[72] and so cannot carry out their full structural function of binding the wall together across its width. As they are not fully functional, these tile courses must therefore indicate some wish to achieve the appearance of levelling courses. Although they might not be considered particularly decorative, these tile bands do play an aesthetic and symbolic function, helping to create the appearance of a typically Roman style of masonry.

There are, then, two ideas of re-use or *translatio* encapsulated in the walls of Le Mans. One is expressed in the materials re-used in the construction of the walls, of Roman provenance. The other is articulated by the arrangement of these salvaged materials to resemble a characteristically Roman style of architecture. While the rationale for recycling may be expediency, the aesthetic element reveals a more complex motivation. It may be that even the decorative mimicry seen at Le Mans performs a practical purpose. Perhaps it is meant to eke out an inadequate supply of tiles, to create the impression that the walls are strongly bonded in the reliable Roman fashion. Without documentary evidence it is hard to tell how such banding schemes were valued in a particular time or place. However, this example does demonstrate that issues of re-use need not be purely symbolic or entirely practical. Elements of both these motives may be combined in one building project.

A comparable mixture of motives can be found in the attitude of the first castle-builders in Britain towards the re-use of Roman materials. When the Normans arrived in England in 1066 they did not have to look far for evidence of the architecture of the ancient Roman empire, and they did not neglect it when they found it. All over the country the Normans built their castles in the shelter of the Roman walls which were still standing in many places. I have already discussed in Chapter 2 the Norman propensity for siting castles within existing urban defences. It has been reckoned that, of the

---

[70] Greenhalgh, *The Survival of Roman Antiquities in the Middle Ages*, p. 143; Higgitt, 'The Roman Background to Mediaeval England', p. 4.

[71] Greenhalgh, *The Survival of Roman Antiquities in the Middle Ages*, p. 44; Todd, *The Walls of Rome*, p. 69.

[72] Butler, 'The Roman Walls of Le Mans', p. 34. Webster stresses the necessity of the full course of tiles for any structural advantage: 'The most important function of these tile-lacing courses was to bind the wall together, . . . the tile courses being to the full thickness of the wall and holding the whole together laterally'; G. Webster, 'Tiles as a Structural Component in Buildings' in *Roman Brick and Tile: Studies in Manufacture, Distribution and Use in the Western Empire*, ed. A. McWhirr, British Archaeological Reports International Series 68 (1979), pp. 285–93 (p. 291).

thirty-seven royal castles established before 1100, twenty were built within town defences, and twelve of these were in towns of Roman origins.[73] This tally does not even include London, arguably the most important of the new Norman castles, and also situated in the corner of the Roman town walls.[74] Yet more castles were associated with Roman remains of other kinds. At Pevensey the corner of the Roman fort was turned into a castle during the Conquest of 1066, and this model was followed at Portchester (around 1120), Brough (around 1100) and Bowes (1170s onwards), where Norman keeps were all built inside the substantial remains of Roman forts.[75] Other castles such as Dover (1066 onwards) were sited on or close to Roman remains of different kinds.[76]

In many of these cases it is apparent that there were pressing practical reasons for choosing these sites. Those Roman towns in which new castles were built were all populous at the time of the Conquest.[77] I noted in Chapter 2 that the conquerors probably targeted urban centres with their castle building as a means of imposing royal and administrative control on the populace (see p. 49). The remains of the Roman road network also facilitated transport to these sites, and were utilized by the Normans for this purpose.[78] Political expedients probably also contributed to re-use. At Pevensey and London the standing Roman defensive walls would have saved valuable time for the new invaders, who were hastily throwing up defences to consolidate their positions. Colchester seems to have been built around 1074–6[79] in response to a Danish raid on the east coast,[80] so the large existing foundation plinth must have made the construction job considerably quicker and easier. Raw materials for building, available from the ruinous Roman buildings all around the town, must also have been important here. Re-cycled Roman materials were used extensively in the castle,[81] where large amounts of Roman tile can be clearly seen to this day (see Plates IV and V).[82]

---

[73] Pounds, *The Medieval Castle in England and Wales*, p. 57.

[74] S. Thurley, E. Impey and P. Hammond, *The Tower of London* (London, 1996), pp. 45–6; *A History of the King's Works*, ed. Colvin, Taylor and Brown, II, 707.

[75] B. Cunliffe, *Excavations at Portchester Castle*, Society of Antiquaries of London Research Committee Report 34 (1977), p. 74; D. F. Renn, *Norman Castles in Britain* (London, 1973), p. 120; J. Charlton, *Brough Castle* (London, 1986, repr. 1992), p. 1.

[76] R. A. Brown, *Dover Castle, Kent* (London, 1985, repr. 1995), pp. 3–4; G. Port, *Scarborough Castle* (London, 1989, repr. 1998), pp. 13–14; and Renn, *Norman Castles in Britain*, p. 307. I discuss the example of Dover in more detail later in this chapter.

[77] Pounds, *The Medieval Castle in England and Wales*, p. 57.

[78] Ibid., pp. 57–8.

[79] P. J. Drury, 'Aspects of the Origins and Development of Colchester Castle', *The Archaeological Journal* 139 (1983), 302–419 (p. 302).

[80] Pounds, *The Medieval Castle in England and Wales*, p. 21.

[81] Drury, 'Aspects of the Origins and Development of Colchester Castle', p. 319.

[82] M. R. Hull, *Roman Colchester*, Society of Antiquaries of London Research Committee Report 20 (1958), p. 30.

The practical motives for the choice of Roman sites, and for the re-use of Roman materials there, are not in doubt. There is also some evidence to suggest that the symbolism of this siting and re-use was not lost on the Norman castle builders. I have already noted several sites where early castles were built in close proximity to Roman remains of different kinds. When looked at in more detail, some of these juxtapositions reveal a close understanding by the Norman builders of Roman materials, construction methods and even architectural forms. This evidence can be read in the manner of the Le Mans walls, as an attempt to imitate or emulate Roman architecture, as well as to repair and re-cycle its remains.

The characteristically Roman technique of building out of rubble banded with tile was not only a continental practice. Many prominent Roman remains in Britain, including ones with which medieval castles are associated, display this technique. The Roman city wall of London (Plate VII) and the Roman *pharos* or lighthouse at Dover (Plate XVII) are good examples. However, this technique, or variations on it, sometimes involving re-use of Roman materials, can also be found in medieval castle architecture and occurs consistently in those castles near to extant Roman remains. It does not seem unreasonable in these cases to look for conscious displays of *Romanitas* and *translatio imperii*.

At Chepstow Castle, a Norman foundation, Roman tiles salvaged probably from the nearby Roman town of Caerwent are incorporated into the Great Tower (1067–75).[83] It is possible that some of the cut stone used in the construction of the tower may also be from Caerwent or other Roman sites,[84] but the tiles are treated rather differently from the rest of the stonework. They run around the building at lintel height in a single course several tiles thick, and their striking appearance is heightened by the way they lift over the arched and decorated tympanum of the main door, echoing its shape (see Plate XII). This use seems to be a deliberately decorative. At the same time, a connection is maintained with the Roman method of tile banding, as commentators have remarked.[85] While the tile course decorates the building as a whole, it also serves to distinguish the tiles themselves, displaying them in a prominent position and grouping them together to make maximum impact. This treatment marks out the tiles as a special, or even a precious material, comparable to the beautifully carved stone of the tympanum they surmount, chosen to grace the most prestigious building of the castle. It might be assumed that tiles are not in themselves particularly decorative or precious, but they must have been perceived as being so, to be used in this way on a prestigious

---

[83] J. Knight, *Chepstow Castle and Port Wall*, revised edn (Cardiff, 1991), p. 37.

[84] Knight, *Chepstow Castle and Port Wall*, p. 38; Eaton endorses the likelihood of Caerwent as a site for stone re-used at Chepstow, but he also provides calculations to show that sites as far afield as Lydney Park or Caerleon could also be candidates: Eaton, *Plundering the Past*, pp. 39, 54–5.

[85] Knight, *Chepstow Castle and Port Wall*, p. 38.

building. It seems likely, therefore, that Chepstow's Norman builders appreciated the Roman associations of the tiles, and endeavoured to use them in a such a way as to show off the tiles, and perhaps to reflect in some degree the tile courses used in Roman architecture.[86]

Colchester Castle (Plates IV and V) is undoubtedly the most prominent example of a Norman castle in England constructed using Roman remains. There are many practical reasons that may have made this the most sensible course, as I have already indicated. However, the Norman builders of the castle also imitated the Roman rubble and tile technique on a grand scale, if rather untidily. As the whole castle keep is constructed using this method, the technique certainly carries a practical function, and so is very different from the obviously aesthetic use of tiles at Chepstow. It would be easy to dismiss the idea that the banding at Colchester carries any symbolic or aesthetic meaning, because the end result does not look neat or well-planned. In many places on the castle, however, the tiles seem to be arranged carefully, in spite of the lack of uniformity of the whole and the haste with which the building seems to have been put up. Plate V, for example, shows several clearly visible horizontal lines of tiles, set at regular intervals. This certainly looks like a deliberate effect,[87] and shows obvious similarities with the Roman remains in the immediate vicinity of the castle.[88]

However, while these examples of re-use of Roman materials, techniques and aesthetics in Norman castles are suggestive, they do not provide proof of a Norman intention to emulate Roman architectural forms for aesthetic

---

[86] Eaton supports this idea, citing my arguments about the Chepstow tiles in his book: Eaton, *Plundering the Past*, p. 137.

[87] Derek Renn noticed not only the patterning in the tile courses of Colchester Castle keep, but also a regularity in the use of the many different materials of which the building is made. He found that, from above the plinth, a band of small limestone blocks is followed by one of tiles, then one of cemented rubble, another of tiles, another of rubble, then tiles and limestone again, and so on: D. F. Renn, 'The Decoration of Guildford Castle Keep', *Surrey Archaeological Collections* 55 (1958), 4–6; Higgit agrees: 'The Roman Background to Medieval England', p. 4.

[88] The apsidal projections in the plan of Colchester Castle keep and the White Tower at London have been identified as a reference to Roman architectural styles, particularly because, in the case of Colchester, this feature was thought to arise from the plan of the Roman temple underlying the Norman structure. However, archaeologists have recently raised objections to this stratigraphic interpretation. It has also emerged that Norman keeps in France before the Conquest show similar apsidal projections, lessening the mystique of early English examples. A similar form is also achieved at Pevensey by the incorporation of a Roman bastion into the main building, so it may be that some Roman associations do attach to this form. However, until clearer archaeological evidence becomes available for Colchester and the Tower, it seems best to leave this debate for the present. See R. A. Brown, 'The White Tower of London', in *The Middle Ages*, ed. B. Ford, The Cambridge Guide to the Arts in Britain 2 (1988), pp. 254–63 (p. 255); G. Parnell, *English Heritage Book of the Tower of London* (London, 1993), pp. 19–20.

reasons. In order to ascertain whether such proof exists, it is necessary to look for associations of *Romanitas* and *translatio imperii* in other forms of Norman culture.

I suggested in Chapter 1 that castle words were used in the period after the Conquest in a fairly flexible way. They could indicate defensive enclosures ranging from Roman forts to Anglo-Saxon fortresses and towns, as well as the defences built by the invading Normans. Furthermore, the Latin word *castellum*, used in Classical and Biblical texts, would not have been distinguished from any other medieval use of Latin and vernacular castle words. The combination of these two factors seems to have led medieval commentators to the conclusion that castles very similar to their own existed in Classical contexts, and medieval observers may well have interpreted the remains of Roman forts in just this way. It seems to me that the decision to build Norman castles within such structures might not, then, be seen as an adaptation of the remains to a new purpose, but rather as a restoration to an ancient form and function they were believed to have had in the past. It may, indeed, be that the reverence for Roman tiles at Chepstow and the attempt at Colchester (though an unsophisticated one) to reproduce the appearance of Roman architecture on a Roman foundation, should all be interpreted in this light.

Other elements of Norman practice at the Conquest demonstrate clearly a desire to emulate certain aspects of Roman culture in the establishment of Norman rule in Britain. The system of aristocratic hierarchies and titles the Normans employed was drawn from that used in the Roman empire.[89] A similar derivation applies to the military insignia used by the Normans,[90] including their seals, which were in some cases antique Roman intaglios, specially imported for the purpose.[91] These examples all show the perception and cultivation of continuity between Roman and Norman cultures. The last instance also illustrates the appreciation and re-use of Roman materials, and the high status uses to which re-used objects were put. More explicit emulation of Roman culture can be found in the literature of the early Norman rule in Britain.

The *Gesta Guillelmi* was written by William of Poitiers about twenty years after the Conquest.[92] William was for many years chaplain to the Conqueror[93] and wrote to justify his patron's claim to the English throne. Events are

---

[89] D. Crouch, *The Image of Aristocracy in Britain, 1000–1300* (London, 1992), pp. 28–9, 43.
[90] Ibid., pp. 180–2, 199.
[91] Ibid., p. 244.
[92] William of Poitiers, *The Gesta Guillelmi of William of Poitiers*, ed. and transl. R. C. H. Davis and M. Chibnall (Oxford, 1998), p. xxi. See also Gransden, *Historical Writing in England c.550 to c.1307*, pp. 99–102.
[93] William of Poitiers, *The Gesta Guillelmi*, pp. xv–xvi.

described in such a way as to prove the Norman claim to England, stressing Duke William's right of inheritance from Edward the Confessor and presenting the Normans' victory in battle as a sign of favour from God. It might thus be said that William of Poitiers reflects the official propaganda of the Norman regime.[94] William's emphases are thus rather different from those employed in the early twelfth century by Geoffrey of Monmouth: Geoffrey fulfilled a somewhat similar justificatory brief, as I have suggested, but from a native British standpoint (see Chapter 2, pp. 54–5). William nevertheless articulates Norman claims to cultural and literary as well as religious authority in terms of the imperial past, just as Geoffrey did in later years. Like his learned contemporaries, William was well versed in Classical literature and his work is full of allusions to works by Caesar, Virgil, Sallust, Cicero, Juvenal, Tacitus, Statius, Suetonius and Plutarch, Vegetius and Lucan.[95] These references claim the weight of Classical authority by their very presence in the *Gesta Guillelmi*. But William of Poitiers also manipulates this material to bolster the Conqueror's achievements. Duke William is not only associated with Classical heroes and emperors in this text, but he also betters them. The description of the Battle of Hastings provides a good example. Here the Conqueror is eulogized in Classical mode:

> Argivorum rex Agamemnon habens in auxilio multos duces atque reges, unicam urbem Priami dolo vix evertit obsidionis anno decimo . . . Item Roma sic adulta opibus, ut orbi terrarum vellet praesidere, urbes aliquot devicit singulas pluribus annis. Subegit autem urbes Anglorum cunctas dux Guillelmus copiis Normanniae uno die ab hora tertia in vesperum, non multo extrinsecus adiutorio. Si tuerentur eas moenia Troiana, brevi talis viri manus et consilium excinderint Pergama.

> (Agamemnon, king of the Argives, with the help of many leaders and kings, barely succeeded in reducing Priam's single city after a ten-year siege . . . Likewise Rome, after growing so great in wealth that it wished to rule over the whole world, conquered a few cities one by one, over many years. But Duke William with the forces of Normandy subjugated all the cities of the English in a single day, between the third hour and the evening, without much outside help. Even if the walls of Troy had defended its citadel, the strong arm and counsel of such a man would soon have destroyed it.)[96]

Here the Conqueror is praised as speedier in siege warfare than Agamemnon himself and quicker at conquering nations than the Roman empire. William of Poitiers has chosen these comparisons carefully. He aligns the Normans consistently with the victorious sides, but also uses this opportunity to celebrate previous successful campaigns against the British. His references recall

---

94   Ibid., p. xxvi.
95   Ibid., pp. xviii, xix, xxi–xxiii.
96   William of Poitiers, *The Gesta Guillelmi*, Book 2, paragraph 26, pp. 142–3.

the Roman conquest of Britain and the Greek victory against the Trojans, pre-empting British claims to superior status through their supposed Trojan ancestry.

However, the Trojan foundation legend was soon to be appropriated by the Normans themselves. The political capital of foundation and descent is exploited by other Norman sources at around this point, and here again the Norman claim is set up in opposition to British claims. Reynolds records that early in the eleventh century Dudo of St Quentin derived the Normans' ancestors, the *Daci* or *Dani*, from the *Danai* or Dacians (the Greek side in the Trojan war) giving them a rival status to the British and once again placing them on opposing sides.[97] However, by a further twist, Dudo assimilated the ancestry of the Greeks and Trojans, thereby also assimilating Norman and British legendary genealogies. Orderic Vitalis supported this genealogy in the twelfth century, confirming the eclipse of his own British nation's foundation legend.[98] Classical allusions are thus employed to support the Norman cause in every possible way, simultaneously acknowledging and bettering the claims made by the British, and so subsuming these claims to the greater Norman power.

Importantly, these symbolic, political and mythographic strategies could be expressed in architectural terms, as when William of Poitiers invokes the walls and citadel of Troy as a measure of the greatness of the Conqueror's victory (in the passage quoted above). I have already noted the Conqueror's innovative architectural expression of his righteous victory in building Battle Abbey (see Chapter 3, p. 89). The idea that the Conquest was god-willed was one of the major justifications of Norman rule expressed in the *Gesta Guillelmi*. However, the Normans' use of surviving Roman structures, materials and sites, and the re-creation of Roman building techniques, can be seen as another, complementary attempt at justification. Material *translatio* is an architectural analogue to Norman Classical allusions, likening the structural achievements of the Normans to the architecture of the great empire which had preceded them in conquering England. It is clear, then, that the Normans used Classical allusions with cultural and political acuity and strove to reproduce them in more than one medium as an expression of their aspirations. It seems likely that this Classical symbolism extended to architectural expression. As I will argue shortly, the new Norman castles quickly became the focus of such imagery. However, the evidence which is perhaps most helpful in shedding light on the imperial symbolisms achievable in medieval castle architecture starts after the Norman castle-building campaigns in England.

---

[97] S. Reynolds, 'Medieval *Origines gentium* and the Community of the Realm', *History* 68 (1983), 375–90 (p. 376).

[98] Ibid., p. 386. Although Orderic spent his adult life at the Norman monastery of St Evroul, he was born and brought up in Shrewsbury: M. Chibnall, *The World of Orderic Vitalis* (Oxford, 1984), pp. 3–4.

This does not help to fill in the gaps as far as the intentions behind earlier buildings go, but it does confirm the kinds of association I have been suggesting, both ideological and material.

Dover was an early Norman castle with very tangible Roman affinities, through the standing Roman remains on the site. Dover was crucial in the Norman invasion, and was fortified as one of the earliest actions of the Conquest campaign.[99] The most impressive stage of the castle's expansion came around a century later, when Henry II built the great square keep in the inner bailey, starting in 1182 (Plate XV).[100] It is massive and square, like the much earlier White Tower at the Tower of London or Colchester Castle keep (see Plates VI and IV). Nevertheless, Dover displays some particularly novel features in English castle design, such as its innovative system of flushing latrines and running water.[101] Records in the Pipe Rolls also show that the keep was part of a very ambitious building campaign at Dover: probably the most expensive architectural undertaking of Henry II's reign.[102]

My particular interest lies in the treatment of the outer surfaces of this prestigious building. The whole keep is neatly finished in ashlar. On three sides of the building, starting at the bottom and ending about halfway up, massive bands of differently coloured masonry can be discerned (see Plate XV).[103] These are made of alternating sections of light Caen stone and dark Kentish ragstone. The banding pattern on Dover Castle keep does not continue around the whole building, but the part that was completed is nonetheless impressive, and is notably concentrated on the façade of the building which greets the visitor first entering the inner bailey from the King's Gateway.[104] The huge bands created at Dover hardly resemble the kinds of structural polychromy I have been discussing in relation to Roman remains and re-used materials. There are no tiles involved, and the polychrome effect does not appear to have any structural rationale. The stones making up the bands are of two different types, in terms of size as well as colour (see Plate XVI). The

---

[99] R. A. Brown, 'An Historian's Approach to the Origins of the Castle in England', *Archaeological Journal* 126 (1969), 131–48 (pp. 144–5). I have discussed Brown's analysis of this Dover evidence in Chapter 1 (pp. 19–20), but have no quarrel with his archaeological evidence for the Norman fortifications on the site.

[100] J. Goodall, 'The Key of England', *Country Life* (18 March 1999), 45–7 (p. 45).

[101] J. Goodall, 'In the Power House of Kent', *Country Life* (25 March 1999), 110–13 (p. 110).

[102] Goodall, 'The Key of England', *Country Life*, p. 45.

[103] Ibid., p. 46.

[104] It is interesting to note that this pattern stops about halfway up the building (see Plate XV). This seems to coincide with a break in the construction of the keep which occurred between 1185 and 1188. After the resumption of the work, the bands were discontinued for some reason. It should, however, be noted that the existing bands on the keep are visually striking, and those on the northwest face of the building would be seen to particular advantage by anyone entering the inner bailey. I am most grateful to John Goodall, who has discussed his analysis of these details with me.

Kentish ragstone is used in small pieces, the Caen in larger, as befits the properties of the two different stones.[105] The bands in which they are laid are of uniform width, without the thin bands which occur when tile-lacing is used or evoked. The bands at Dover are also far too big to resemble rubble-and-tile work closely. However, as I have already mentioned, Dover castle comes complete with its own set of Roman remains, and these certainly do display the characteristically banded masonry (see Plate XVII). In what became the outer bailey of the castle, a Roman *pharos* (a lighthouse or signal station) is situated. The banded construction of the *pharos* is quite clear from my photograph, which also shows how tile and stone are alternated in thin bands of colour round the arches of the window apertures. These decorative details are particularly emphatic. Is it possible that the banded design of Henry II's great keep at Dover is linked in any way to the banded masonry of the Roman remains at Dover or elsewhere?

It is clear that, at the time of the new building work at Dover Castle, there was an awareness of Roman activity in that area. Wace's *Roman de Brut*, presented in 1155 to Henry's queen, Eleanor of Aquitaine,[106] discusses Caesar's British campaign in some detail.[107] In the struggle for control of Dover described in this text, Caesar encamps in the town to await the decisive battle of the Roman invasion.[108] Wace also specifies some architectural products of Roman power, such as the town of Exeter in England, but also a tower in Boulogne and various towns and castles ('chastels e citez') throughout Europe.[109] This last reference confirms an observation I have already identified in other contexts: the idea that Roman fortifications could be described interchangeably with castles, or even identified with them. In the literary production of Henry II's court, then, the Dover area, and castles in general, could have strong connections with imperial Rome.

Other literary productions of Henry's court circle confirm this fascination with ancient, imperial architecture. However, they provide a somewhat different slant on the kind of decorative finishes employed at Dover. The *Roman*

---

[105] Caen is a high quality, expensive stone, often used for the finer elements of a building such as window surrounds; ragstone is cheaper, is often used in less regular sizes and shapes, and does not take as fine a finish as Caen. These two stone types were used in a more typical relationship at the White Tower at London, where the walls are composed of ragstone with Caen dressings. See T. W. Tatton-Brown, 'Building Stone in Canterbury c.1070–1525', in *Stone: Quarrying and Building in England*, ed. Parsons, pp. 70–82 (p. 72); T. W. Tatton-Brown, 'Medieval Building Stone at the Tower of London', *London Archaeologist* 6.13 (1991), 361–6; B. Worssam and T. Tatton-Brown, 'Kentish Rag and Other Kent Building Stones', *Archaeologia Cantiana* 112 (1993), 93–125 (pp. 93–4).

[106] Wace, *Wace's Roman de Brut: A History of the British*, ed. and transl. J. Weiss (Exeter, 1999), p. xiii.

[107] Ibid., pp. 100–122.

[108] Ibid., p. 116.

[109] Ibid., pp. 122, line 4826; 106, lines 4204–5; 98, lines 3853–4.

de Troie was another of the volumes dedicated to Queen Eleanor, sometime between 1160 and 1170, by Benoit de Sainte-Maure.[110] I have already discussed this text within the context of Trojan foundation legends and the ideal depiction of the city of Troy in its relationship with its citadel-tower. Like later Middle English treatments of the same topic, Benoit mentions that the walls and tower-citadel of Troy are made of fine marble of many different colours, which he describes vividly.[111] Similar details can be found in other romances of this type and period, such as the *Roman d'Eneas*.[112] However, Benoit's description is most strikingly applied to a tower-keep which, I argued in Chapter 2, should be imagined as very similar to the keeps belonging to medieval castles like the Tower of London or, indeed, Dover itself. The description of structural polychromy on a castle keep is very striking in a poem probably written by an official poet of the English court at the time,[113] and provides a context of prestigious historical associations for polychrome effects.

While Dover keep does not boast bright colours and precious marbles for its polychrome design, its materials are significantly finer in their finish and general appearance than the rubble-and-tile construction seen in structures like the Dover *pharos*, or for that matter, Colchester Castle keep. As both Dover keep and the *Roman de Troie* are contemporary products of the same royal patronage, it does not seem unlikely that a motif from one might be transferred to the other. Apart from this generic reference to the exotic architecture of the *romans d'Antiquité*,[114] the form of the polychromy deployed at Dover does seem to have a complementary relationship to the banded Roman architecture seen at Dover and elsewhere. The motif on Dover keep is banding: not any of the other possible polychrome designs, such as chequers, which might be suggested by descriptions such as that of the multi-coloured marbles in the *Roman de Troie*. The keep therefore seems to invite comparison with the much earlier Roman tower, but outdoes it in the richness and scale of its materials. These differences between the medieval and Roman stonework do not necessarily rule out a deliberate reference in the later building to the earlier one. They

---

[110] Ibid., p. xiii.

[111] 'De marbre fin e de liois/ Jaunes e verz, indes e blois . . ./ De Marbre blanc, inde, safrin,/ Jaune, vermeil, pers e porprin': Benoit de Sainte-Maure, *Le Roman de Troie par Benoit de Sainte-Maure*, ed. L. Constans, 6 vols. (Paris, 1968), I, lines 3011–12, 3063–4. See discussion, Chapter 2, pp. 59–60.

[112] *Eneas: A Twelfth-Century Romance*, transl. J. A. Yunck (New York, 1974), lines 407–70, p. 64.

[113] Wace, *Wace's Roman de Brut*, p. xiii.

[114] For discussion of the *Romans d'Antiquité* as a group, see G. R. de Lage 'Les "Romans Antiques" dans l'histoire ancienne jusqu' à César', *Le Moyen Age* 63 (1957), 267–309; G. R. de Lage, 'Les Romans Antiques et la représentation de l'Antiquité', *Moyen Age* 67 (1961), 247–91; E. M. Jeffreys, 'The Comnenian Background to the *Romans d'Antiquité*', *Byzantion* 50 (1980), 455–86.

articulate a discrepancy similar to the one between the archaeological and literary models of imperial architecture available to the medieval world: the Roman remains with their rubble and tile bands are physically impressive but utilitarian, while imagined castles of Trojan princes glisten with multicoloured precious stones but cannot be attained in material reality.

Henry II himself understood this split attitude toward imperial heritage, articulated as a division between Roman and Trojan precedents. Henry claimed the English throne through his descent on his grandfather's side from the Conqueror. I discussed earlier in this chapter the somewhat roundabout way in which the Normans managed to justify their descent from the Trojans at around the time of the Conquest, in what seems to have been a concerted effort to match British claims to Trojan descent. The poems of Benoit and Wace, the most notable literary output associated with the court of Henry II, were further attempts to consolidate the Normans' claims to Trojan ancestry.[115] However, Henry had a subsidiary claim to imperial dignity through his mother Matilda, daughter of Henry I and wife of the Holy Roman Emperor Henry V. It seems that Henry II of England chose the nickname 'Fitzempress' to emphasize the alternative imperial connections he carried in his own right.[116] Henry therefore embodied a dual inheritance of imperial origins. The architectural symbolism deployed at Dover fits this agenda neatly. The finely executed, bold polychrome banding is reminiscent of the ancient splendours of Troy, re-created by descendants of Trojans in England. The imperial force of Rome is also witnessed in the castle's outer bailey by the Roman tower. This is alluded to in the banded design of the new keep as an extra bolster to the imperial posturing of the Plantagenet dynasty.

Similar architectural iconography can be detected in a building campaign at England's most important castle, the Tower of London, some sixty years later. Around 1240, Henry III was building new defences at the Tower. The remains of a water gate from this date have recently been discovered in the western portion of the Tower moat.[117] This seems to fit with documentary references in the *Chronica majora* of Matthew Paris, which describe the collapse of a gateway and walls at the Tower in the years 1240 and 1241.[118] Paris's entry for 1240 states that 'the masonry structure of a certain renowned gate, which the king had constructed most sumptuously with great labour, was struck as if by an earthquake, and fell down along with its forebuildings and

---

[115] These arguments apply whether these poems were commissioned by Queen Eleanor or Henry himself. Jeffreys, 'The Comnenian Background to the *Romans d'Antiquité*', pp. 458–60.

[116] Ibid., pp. 459–60.

[117] E. Impey, 'The Western Entrance to the Tower of London, 1240–1241', *Transactions of the Middlesex Archaeological Society* 48 (1998), 58–75.

[118] Impey, 'The Western Entrance to the Tower of London', pp. 59, 65, 66–7; Matthew Paris, *Matthaei Parisiensis, Monachi Sancti Albani, Chronica Majora*, ed. H. R. Luard, Rolls Series 57, 7 vols. (1872–83), IV, 80, 94.

outworks'.[119] The intriguing description of the appearance of the buildings as 'sumptuoso' (most sumptuous) and constructed 'nimis labore' (with great labour) can also possibly be explained by the archaeological remains in the moat. Finds suggest that the gate was faced with courses of differently coloured masonry, of greeny-grey Purbeck marble and creamy Reigate stone.[120] This lavish use of materials does seem to fit with the phrases Matthew Paris uses. Not only was the structure polychrome, but one of the stones used for the banding was Purbeck, a kind of limestone which can take a polish and so has been prized for centuries as a kind of English marble.[121] Both these qualities are reminiscent of the marble polychromy in poems such as the *Roman de Troie*. As Chapter 2 demonstrated, Trojan associations at the Tower would have been highly appropriate in a medieval context. The Tower of London, and probably the White Tower especially, were attributed to Brutus, the legendary Trojan founder of Britain (see Chapter 2). However, as with Dover, it is clear that medieval writers knew that much Roman activity had also taken place in and around London.

Geoffrey of Monmouth was the first author to identify Brutus's capital city, Troia Nova, as London. I detailed in Chapter 2 the way he made this connection through references to place names in accounts of the British campaigns of Julius Caesar, which suggested that Caesar had fought a tribe called the Trinovantes on the north bank of the Thames (see pp. 54–5). Geoffrey's identification of the Trinovantes with the town of New Troy, or Trinovantum, would have made it more likely that subsequent readers of Caesar and Orosius would locate this part of his campaign in London. Archaeological evidence was also available to confirm Roman activity in London. Just one example is the banded Roman city wall, against which the Normans built the Tower of London, and which can still be seen standing in places to this day (see Plate VII).[122] The banded polychrome watergate at the Tower may have referred to this Roman wall in its surface decoration, while surpassing its humble materials. This effect, though short-lived, must have been even more impressive than the banded design at Dover because of the use of Purbeck marble. This comes closer than ever to the vision of ancient Trojan splendour conjured up by Benoit de Sainte-Maure, but marble carried imperial and,

---

[119] 'Structura lapidea cujusdam nobilis portae, quam sumptuoso nimis labore rex construxerat, quasi quodam terrae motu concussa, cum suis antemuralibus et propugnaculis . . . corruit.' Matthew Paris, *Matthaeu Parisiensis, Monachi Sancti Albani, Chronica Majora*, 4, p. 80; discussed in Impey, 'The Western Entrance to the Tower of London', pp. 65–6.

[120] Impey, 'The Western Entrance to the Tower of London', p. 69.

[121] See R. Leach, *An Investigation into the Use of Purbeck Marble in Medieval England*, 2nd edn (Hartlepool, 1975); J. Blair, 'Purbeck Marble', in *English Medieval Industries: Craftsmen, Techniques, Products*, ed. J. Blair and N. Ramsay (London, 1991), pp. 41–56.

[122] See D. Perring, *Roman London* (London, 1991), pp. 90–1; G. Milne, *English Heritage Book of Roman London: Urban Archaeology in the Nation's Capital* (London, 1995), pp. 120–2.

specifically, Roman connotations in its own right at this period too. Henry III's reign is in fact remarkable for other deployments of marble polychrome artefacts with imperial connotations.

In 1268 the Cosmati pavement was completed in the sanctuary of Westminster Abbey, a site of immense importance in the coronation ceremony of the English monarchs.[123] The pavement is made up of hundreds of pieces of cut stone of different colours and types, many of them precious marbles specially imported from Rome for use in the pavement by the abbot of Westminster.[124] Interpretations of the specific symbolisms of this pavement are too complex to rehearse here, but commentators agree on the immense ideological significance of the journey made by the stones from Rome, and the importance of marble as a symbolic material.[125] The inscription added to the pavement on the death of Henry III, and the epitaph of the abbot of Westminster (who acted as courier for the stones) both place emphasis on the source and nature of the materials.[126] The pavement was a thirteenth-century enactment of *translatio imperii*, focused on the characteristically imperial substance, marble, and its polychrome effects. Both the action and the stone type fit with accounts of the material transfers made by ancient emperors, which I have already discussed.

The use of Purbeck marble for the matrix of the Cosmati pavement at Westminster, surrounding the imported marbles and stones,[127] is particularly interesting in view of the probable use of Purbeck banding on the Tower gate. Italian Cosmati works use white marble matrices to offset the coloured components.[128] Surviving pieces of alabaster in the Westminster pavement show that white marble was available for the project,[129] but Purbeck was nevertheless the preferred matrix material both for the sanctuary pavement and for all the related Cosmati work carried out at Westminster, including the shrine of Edward the Confessor and Edward II's own tomb.[130] This deliberate choice marks Purbeck out as a precious substance in its own right, showing that it must have been considered a fit background for the more colourful and rare continental marbles. However, it also denotes the ready availability of Purbeck in

---

[123] P. Binski, 'The Cosmati at Westminster and the English Court Style', *Art Bulletin* 72 (1990), 6–34 (p. 31); R. Foster, *Patterns of Thought: The Hidden Meaning of the Great Pavement of Westminster Abbey* (London, 1991), p. 2.

[124] Binski, 'The Cosmati at Westminster', p. 8; Foster, *Patterns of Thought*, pp. 2, 14 and *passim*.

[125] Binski, 'The Cosmati at Westminster', pp. 8, 10, 12–13; Foster, *Patterns of Thought*, pp. 3, 93, 164 and *passim*.

[126] Binski, 'The Cosmati at Westminster', pp. 10, 13; Foster, *Patterns of Thought*, pp. 3, 93–4.

[127] Binski, 'The Cosmati at Westminster', pp. 9–10; Foster, *Patterns of Thought*, p. 34.

[128] Binski, 'The Cosmati at Westminster', p. 9.

[129] Ibid., p. 10; Foster, *Patterns of Thought*, p. 39.

[130] Binski, 'The Cosmati at Westminster', pp. 9–10.

large quantities at this period.[131] This helps to explain how a material with precious connotations could be used in large-scale architectural projects like the Tower gate. Although it would never be possible to employ precious, imported marbles in the lavish architectural displays described in romances, Purbeck was more economically viable, was considered a marble, and carried connotations of empire. However, there were times when even Purbeck was beyond the means of the king. Documentary references preserve the fact that Edward had a faux marble effect applied to pillars and arches in the hall at Guildford castle and posts in his chamber at Ludgershall.[132] The use of Purbeck on the façade of the Tower gate therefore marks out the structure as one of great symbolic significance. This lavish use of materials certainly deserves the description 'sumptuoso' applied by Matthew Paris. More specifically, it conveys the imperial pretensions Henry wished to attach to his architectural achievements.

The association between imperial imagery and English royal architecture was not confined to Henry III's commissions. Edward I seems to have continued his father's programme of Cosmati monuments at Westminster, commissioning Henry III's Cosmati-work tomb,[133] and possibly even personally selecting and importing the marble for the project. The materials probably came from France rather than Rome,[134] but the design of the tomb relates strongly to Italian models, which Edward may have seen while travelling through Italy at the time he learned of his father's death.[135] The relationship between this and Edward I's other major polychrome project has not gone unnoted. Paul Binski makes an explicit link between the imperial ideology expressed in the tomb of Henry III and the distinctive design of Caernarfon Castle. He suggests that the common use of polychromy in both projects bears witness to 'a royal visual culture that demonstrates its awarenesss . . . of the typology and significance of materials'.[136] Binski follows Taylor's account of the symbolism of Edward I's Caernarfon,[137] but the symbolic strategies employed in the castle and the tomb are even closer, if my revisions to Caernarfon's interpretation are accepted.

I noted earlier in this chapter that material from the nearby Roman site of Segontium was used in the construction of Edward I's castle at Caernarfon. This can be read as a material transfer with imperial significance: as a *translatio imperii*, in fact. It echoes the material transfers carried out by Edward and his father Henry III, when they imported marble stones for their respective Cosmati projects at Westminster Abbey. This material symbolism at both

131 Blair, 'Purbeck Marble', p. 74.
132 L. F. Salzman, *Building in England to 1540: A Documentary History* (Oxford, 1952), p. 159.
133 Binski, 'The Cosmati at Westminster', pp. 19–22.
134 Ibid., pp. 19–20.
135 Ibid., pp. 22–3.
136 Ibid., p. 32.
137 Binski, *Westminster Abbey and the Plantagenets*, pp. 105, 139–40.

Westminster and Caernarfon is twofold. The materials in both cases invoke Roman architecture in their aesthetic appearance and arrangement. At the same time, they also show a continuing awareness of the imperial symbolism of material transfer. As I have suggested, these dual aspects of imperial symbolism are consistently seen in the use of polychromy in English castle architecture. In the early Norman castles of Colchester and Chepstow, Roman materials are re-used in ways that suggest a respect for Roman architecture and materials. From this period castles were also understood to relate to Roman defensive architecture, due to linguistic connections between the two. In later examples of polychrome banding at Dover and the Tower of London, standing Roman structures nearby ensure a visual comparison between medieval and Roman banding patterns, but the medieval work is differentiated in appearance and material from the Roman remains, suggesting the recreation of a more exalted imperial past. This is also expressed through literary composition in legends concerning Rome, as I will show shortly, and Troy, the culture that was believed to have preceded and given birth to Rome as well as Britain.[138]

At Caernarfon Castle, these symbolic strategies merge. The banding motif employed at Caernarfon articulates this approach perfectly. It retains the characteristically Roman aesthetic of narrow bands of red between wide bands of masonry, but enlarges this to a huge scale, using beautifully cut stone. The polychrome banding thus imitates the Roman aesthetic, while surpassing its materials and scale. Material *translatio* also transfers potent imperial symbolisms from the Roman fort of Segontium to the new centre of imperial control in the castle. Re-use is not only a prudent deployment of local resources here, but a *translatio imperii*. It imitates the transfer of imperial materials and resonances practised by Constantine and subsequent Holy Roman Emperors: like theirs, it signifies the geographical and symbolic relocation of imperial power and asserts the legitimate succession of the new regime. However, the castle at Caernarfon expresses Welsh traditions of the Roman mandate for power mainly through the figure of Magnus Maximus, rather than through Constantine, his son.

This explanation places the polychrome banding at Caernarfon within the context of British architecture for the first time. The motif is one which, I have shown, had been used before on certain important English castles, but was consistently deployed in relation to Roman architecture and its characteristic tile-banded masonry. This indigenous context solves the problems created by Taylor's comparison of Caernarfon with Constantinople. I pointed out earlier that such a reference would be wasted on the vast majority of medieval visitors to Caernarfon, who would have had no idea of the appearance of Constantinople's walls. A link with Constantinople is present in the design of Caernarfon, through the resemblance to banded Roman architecture in general. However, links with other English castles, and with Roman architecture

---

[138] See Chapter 2, pp. 53–4.

extant in medieval Britain, would surely have been of more immediate relevance in conveying imperial associations to medieval observers.

The evidence I have provided for the symbolism of polychromy in castle architecture relies mainly on association, as I have found no explicit statements of intent to create imperial imagery from those responsible for commissioning or building English medieval castles. However, the reactions of medieval observers do demonstrate particularly strong imperial associations for polychrome castles. Various polychrome castles are, for example, ascribed to ancient, imperial builders in further instances of the projection of castles back into the ancient past. This is a rather different situation from the one which has proved so interesting at Caernarfon. There the evidence for legendary associations is exceptionally rich for around the time at which the castle was being built. It therefore seems very likely that specific imperial associations were built in to the castle from the start. This was the feature that made Taylor's interpretation so compelling, as it allowed an insight into the cultural forces which the castle's medieval designers were attempting to express. However, evidence does not to my knowledge exist to demonstrate the way in which observers regarded such imagery at the time. In the other cases, this situation is reversed. Evidence for the attribution of a legendary founder exists, but it is recorded some considerable time after the castle's medieval foundation, and often after the addition of imperial polychrome banding. While there is thus a gap between the architectural creation of imperial imagery and its reception, I hope to show that some relationship of cause and effect can be established between the two. This is not necessarily a neat relationship. In some cases, as for example with the Trojan foundation myth at the Tower of London, rumours of imperial connections may have arisen very gradually, drawing on only the most general architectural cues. In other cases, as at Caernarfon, the legend may well have been the primary force, dictating the imperial imagery of the castle architecture. However, the conjunction between legend and polychrome banding does seem to hold good.

I will not repeat in detail the evidence for the imperial foundation legends I have already mentioned in other chapters: Brutus's foundation of the Tower of London (Chapter 2, pp. 57–8) and Cole's foundation of Colchester Castle (Chapter 1, p. 41). I have also discussed both of these castles in this chapter in terms of their symbolic polychrome banding and significant proximity to Roman remains. However, the dating of these various developments is worth repeating here. The first recorded connection between Colchester Castle and Cole comes from 1372,[139] while the castle itself, built on and with Roman remains, dates from around 1074–6. The Tower of London, or more specifically its most important element, the White Tower, was built in the 1070s.

---

[139] G. Rosser, 'Myth, Image and Social Process in the English Medieval Town', *Urban History* 23.1 (1996), 5–25 (p. 10).

The first reference I have found to its supposed foundation by Brutus comes from Gervase of Tilbury, writing around 1214 to 1218.[140] The polychrome banding of Henry III's gate at the Tower probably dates from 1240. A subsequent legendary development also credited Julius Caesar with the foundation of the Tower; this surfaces in Nicholas Trevet's Anglo-Norman *Cronicles*, written probably between 1328 and 1335.[141] In the same source, Julius Caesar also emerges as Dover's legendary founder; Dover Castle, as with the Tower, was originally a product of the Conquest campaign, and the polychrome keep dates from 1182.

In the majority of these cases, the imperial legend seems to lag some way behind the imperial phase of the castle architecture. However, it is possible that the late date of several of these legends may be due to loss in the documentary record, rather than late origin. For example, the link between the city of Colchester and Cole was made by Geoffrey of Monmouth around 1138. So, too, was the link between London and Brutus. The subsequent attribution of the castle to the founder of the city is not a big step, and could probably have happened at any intermediate stage before the emergence of these castle foundation legends into the extant written record. Oral traditions may also have been involved, leaving no dateable traces. This leaves the relationship between architecture and legend tantalisingly uncertain. However, there are hints of the kinds of processes that might have been at work. Written accounts concerning Dover Castle are particularly suggestive.

As I have mentioned, the Dominican Nicolas Trevet provides the first documented reference to Dover's Caesarian foundation, in his Anglo-Norman chronicle written for the edification and entertainment of Edward I's daughter Mary.[142] From this dedication, it can be imagined that Britain's legendary history is an important part of this work, inserted chronologically into the Biblical history that represents the bulk of the account.[143] Trevet attributes several castles to Caesar quite casually and without further explanation, including them in a long list:

> Julius Cesar . . . en monstrance de la Conqueste faite sur la terre du Brutaine, q'ore est dit Engleterre, edifa le chastel de Dovre et de Canterburi et de Roncestre et de Loundres[144]

---

[140] Gervase of Tilbury, *Otia Imperialia: Recreation for an Emperor*, ed. S. E. Banks and J. W. Binns, Oxford Medieval Texts Series (2002), pp. 398–400, Book 2, section 17; discussed in Chapter 2, pp. 57–60.

[141] *A Manual of the Writings in Middle English 1050–1500*, ed. A. E. Hartung, 10 vols. (New Haven, 1967–98), VIII, 2667.

[142] Gransden, *Historical Writing in England c.550–1307*, p. 504.

[143] Ibid.; Nicolas Trevet, 'The Anglo-Norman Chronicle of Nicolas Trivet', ed. A. Rutherford (unpublished Ph.D. dissertation, University of London, 1932), pp. 14, 52.

[144] Trevet, 'The Anglo-Norman Chronicle', p. 110.

(Julius Caesar . . . in demonstration of the Conquest made of the realm of Britain, as England was called, built the castle of Dover and of Canterbury and of Rochester and of London)

This is not the place to examine in detail into the legend of Caesar's successful conquest of Britain and the foundation myths arising from it, as this has already been done very thoroughly[145] (it is perhaps worth noting in passing that both Rochester and Canterbury castles are in close contact with Roman remains).[146] However, Trevet's work was well-researched, and his own additions and alterations to his source material are limited.[147] It seems likely, therefore, that he gained this information from some source that has not survived.

A monastic chronicle surviving in a much later manuscript provides a suggestion of the kind of process by which Trevet might have arrived at his Caesarian attributions. The document in question is bound in with a miscellaneous collection of texts in the British Library manuscript Cotton Vespasian B.XI, and covers folios 72–9. For cataloguing purposes it is entitled *Cronicon Sancti Martini de Dover*, referring to the monastery of St Martin to which the text refers.[148] The text documents the history of Dover Castle, as well as St Martin's monastery, in some detail, beginning with Brutus's arrival in Britain and ending with the reign of Henry II. Julius Caesar also plays his part, and is connected specifically with building activities at Dover: the text records that Caesar built a tower as a treasury, in the place where the castle of Dover was later built. It even specifies that the same tower still stands next to the church in the castle. This is an unmistakable reference to the Roman *pharos* or signal-station at Dover Castle, whose banded appearance I have already discussed:

Iulius Caesar fecit unam turrim in loco ubi nunc est castrum Doverr' ad reponendum illuc thesaurum suum. Quae quidem Turris nunc stat ibidem in Castro Doverr' iuxta ecclesiam

(Julius Caesar built a tower in the place where the Castle of Dover now is, to place his treasury in. This very same tower now stands in Dover Castle next to the Church)[149]

---

[145] See H. Nearing, 'Caesar's Sword', *Modern Language Notes* 63 (1948), 403–5; H. Nearing, 'Julius Caesar and the Tower of London', *Modern Language Notes* 63 (1948), 228–33; H. Nearing, 'Local Caesar Traditions in Britain', *Speculum* 24 (1949), 218–27; H. Nearing, 'The Legend of Julius Caesar's Britsh Conquest', *Publications of the Modern Languages Association* 64 (1949), 889–929. I also discuss this legend in more detail in A. Wheatley, 'The Tower of London in Myth and Legend', in *The White Tower*, ed. E. Impey (forthcoming).

[146] Pounds, *The Medieval Castle in England and Wales*, p. 1; Eaton, *Plundering the Past*, p. 29.

[147] Trevet, 'The Anglo-Norman Chronicle of Nicolas Trivet', Introduction, pp. 19–23 and *passim*.

[148] See T. Hardy, *Descriptive Catalogue of Materials Relating to the History of Great Britain and Ireland*, Rolls Series 26, 3 vols. (1865, repr. 1964), II, 263.

[149] London, British Library MS Cotton Vespasian B.IX, fol. 72.

This text is preserved in a fifteenth-century document.[150] It is therefore well after texts such as Trevet's *Cronicles* and the alliterative poem *The Parlement of the Thre Ages* (1370), which refer to the whole of Dover Castle as Caesar's work.[151] However, it does seem to preserve an intermediate phase in the development of Dover's imperial foundation legend, before the medieval castle was explicitly involved. It seems reasonably likely that such a reference existed long before syntheses such as Trevet's; it may have been preserved in local legend and written down later, or survive only in later accounts. This will probably remain a speculation. It is therefore difficult to determine whether this legend existed in some form before Dover keep was decorated with polychrome banding. However, it is easy enough to imagine how, once the Roman *pharos* was identified as Julius Caesar's work, the impressive banded tower in the castle proper might have been attributed to Caesar by association, and so, eventually, the whole castle.

This example does not provide any easy answers to the complex interactions of architectural and narrative symbolism. However, it does hint at the powerful effect Roman remains could have on the medieval structures nearby, spreading polychromy and gradually transforming entire sites with their imperial connotations. It seems to me highly likely that the polychrome banding deployed on English castles was intended to perpetuate these associations in the minds of medieval observers, as well as causing fresh Roman associations in its own right.

I argued in more detail in my first chapter for an enduring medieval belief that the castle was a form of architecture that had been used by the Romans. I have shown in this chapter how important imperial imagery was in the articulation of English political power and royal and national identity in medieval Britain. I have also provided ample evidence that medieval castles could evoke, or be confused with, the fortresses of antiquity. Within this context, Caernarfon Castle cannot be seen as a unique example of an imperial castle. I have identified several other castles, from the Conquest onwards, which deployed visual signals and legendary material in very similar ways to those identified at Caernarfon, but imperial imagery is not necessarily restricted to those I have identified. The castles I have discussed were all royal, built with great expenditure of resources and discussed extensively in

---

[150] Another reference to this tradition, of a similar date, in the *Historia regum Angliae* of John Rous is mentioned in Nearing, 'Local Caesar Traditions in Britain', p. 220.

[151] *A Manual of the Writings in Middle English*, ed. Hartung, V, 1501. 'Thane Sir Sezere hymselven, that Julyus was hatten,/ Alle Inglande he aughte at his awnn will,/ When the Bruyte in his booke Bretayne it callede./ The trewe toure of London in his tyme he makede,/ And craftely the condithe he compaste thereaftire,/ And then he droghe hym to Dovire and duellyde there a while,/ And closede ther a castelle with cornells full heghe': 'The Parlement of the Thre Ages', in *Wynnere and Wastoure and The Parlement of the Thre Ages*, ed. W. Ginsberg (Kalmazoo, 1992), lines 405–11, p. 55.

the documentary record. With such important precedents, it is more than likely that examples of imperial association, possibly even of banded polychromy, remain at other sites still to be identified. Renn's list of Norman polychromy, appended to his article on Guildford Castle, offers one starting-place for further investigation.[152]

Castles were a supremely appropriate architectural form with which to express ideas of *translatio imperii*, as they represented to the Middle Ages, I have argued, continuity with Roman empire-building and defensive architecture. The polychrome banding and symbolic re-use I have identified are outward displays of this imperial identity. However, the linguistic evidence I have cited shows that imperial associations are inherent in the very architectural form and idea of the castle. Even without polychromy, therefore, medieval castles carry imperial connotations. As I mentioned earlier, the plain stone castle of Pevensey is surrounded by Roman defences. It is associated with these ancient remains through location, but also takes on a similar form, with its rounded bastions and straight stretches of wall. The polychrome banding and meaningful re-use I have identified in several castles gives expression to this kind of general resemblance. However, for each instance of bright imperial polychromy, dozens of less obvious imperial resonances should be expected. In medieval accounts Julius Caesar founded castles throughout Europe,[153] and the castles of other Roman emperors litter the pages of the *Gesta Romanorum*.[154] Castles also feature on a regular basis in medieval translations of Vegetius.[155] Castles with Roman and more generally imperial associations have been available to historians for generations. It is only surprising that this textual tradition has not been applied to the architectural evidence before.

---

[152] Renn, 'The Decoration of Guildford Castle Keep', p. 6.

[153] See Nearing, 'Caesar's Sword'; Nearing, 'Julius Caesar and the Tower of London'; Nearing, 'Local Caesar Traditions in Britain'; Nearing, 'The Legend of Julius Caesar's Britsh Conquest'.

[154] *A Middle English Version of the* Gesta Romanorum *edited from Gloucester Cathedral MS 22*, ed. K. I. Sandred (Uppsala, 1971); discussed in Chapter 1, p. 38.

[155] *The Earliest English Translation of Vegetius' De re militari*, ed. G. Lester (Heidelberg, 1988).

Conclusion

The aim of this book has been to establish the medieval castle as a meaningful architecture, involved in a sophisticated series of ideological relationships with its cultural context. I have set out to trace the architectural iconography of the castle through references in visual and textual sources, and to retrace this iconography back to the physical architecture of the medieval buildings themselves. The conclusions presented here summarize those reached in each chapter of this book, but also point to wider implications and further possibilities for research.

Linguistic analysis shows that many modern definitions of the medieval castle do not match the understanding of the word and concept in medieval use. The castle was not perceived in medieval England as an essentially feudal, private form of architecture imported by the Normans, as historians so often see it now. The word *castle* seems to have indicated a defensive enclosure of a much more general kind, applicable to urban fortifications, small houses and ecclesiastical foundations as well as the private defences with which the word is exclusively associated in modern use. The castle also had important historical connotations for medieval readers, via the Latin word *castellum* which appears in Biblical and Classical writings. The principles of historical linguistics suggest that a medieval reader would have understood this word in accordance with the general medieval meaning of castle words. It follows that castles of the medieval type were believed to have existed in important ancient contexts long before the introduction of the form to Britain around the Norman Conquest.

This linguistic reappraisal of the medieval castle has far-reaching implications which can be traced in depictions of castles in medieval art and literature and in the architecture of medieval castle buildings themselves. Through civic imagery on seals and in city descriptions and foundation legends, and in the spatial arrangement of city and castle defences, the urban castle became an important component in the imagery of the city. It was appropriated to represent both the harmony of the ideal city and the social and political tensions of everyday urban experience. These qualities could be expressed in visual and textual depictions, but they could also be built into the fabric of cities in the harmony of their spatial layout, or taken away from cities when these boundaries and hierarchies were disrupted by conflict. These findings challenge conventional analyses of the urban castle as a predominantly oppressive force, demonstrating instead its dual role in articulating social harmonies as well as tensions. This reflected a historical understanding of the urban castle as an ancient form of architecture, appearing in Classical sources and legendary histories.

Spiritual imagery of the castle was likewise based on a very literal understanding of the word *castellum* in Biblical texts and contexts. Specific texts, such as Luke 10. 38, were central to the medieval understanding of both castle architecture and Biblical systems of architectural symbolism. These texts were the basis of an iconography for castles, similar to that applied to medieval ecclesiastical architecture, built up of different spiritual texts and references, but also expressing a spiritual idea in the building as a whole. Bodily allegories of the Virgin were an important part of this imagery and architectural mnemonics also became an integral part of castle ideology. At a physical level, such ideas can be found reflected in medieval building projects in the Holy Land at sites associated with Biblical castle texts, in fusions of ecclesiastical and defensive architecture, such as the deployment of defensive motifs on church buildings, and in castle buildings. The castle, in both its ideal and real forms, could thus be understood as a trigger to devotional thought. This evidence confirms the integration of certain Biblical sites and buildings into the mainstream understanding of the medieval castles, contrary to most current definitions.

Classical texts also encouraged medieval readers to believe that the castle was an ancient architectural form, for similar reasons. From the Conquest onwards castles were associated with the material evidence of the Roman culture in Britain. Imperial connotations were also emphasized in legends that credited important imperial figures with the foundation of famous castles actually built in the medieval period. This was reflected in the design of the castles themselves, in polychrome banding reminiscent of the banded masonry characteristic of the Roman architecture which was abundantly visible in medieval Britain. Re-use of Roman materials, too, underlined the affinities between the two architectures, reflecting the ancient imperial custom of expressing *translatio imperii* through material transfer. The medieval castle was thus understood as a reflection of imperial ideas, but it was also a symbolic reconstruction and reclamation of what seems to have been considered a characteristically Roman architectural form.

These different strands of meaning have been treated in separate chapters in this study, but it should nevertheless be clear, even from a brief summary, that there are intimate connections between them. The idea of the castle as an ancient form of architecture with important historical resonances is shared between Biblical and Classical contexts. The civic and communal affinities of the castle form also reflect both these concerns, through the imagery of ideal cities and their citadels, both Classical and Biblical. This study has shown that these ideas all operate at a linguistic level, but also at more explicitly intellectual levels, featuring for example in descriptions of castle architecture and in the design of that architecture itself. The castle thus works as an architectural referent for complex and interlinked ideas of civic harmony, devotional piety and imperial power, both in general and very specific ways.

In the first chapter I used the fifteenth-century civic seal of Colchester to demonstrate the intimate ways in which all these ideas could be linked in medieval imagery pertaining to one particular castle. Colchester has reappeared in each chapter, confirming this introductory argument, but it is not unique in this. Other castles have also recurred in several places, showing that it is not unusual for one castle to bring together a complex series of linked connotations. Caernarfon exemplifies planned unity between town and castle in its spatial arrangement, for example, while its decorative treatment, material structure and siting also invoke strong imperial connotations. The Tower of London mirrors both these themes, but also carries spiritual connotations expressed through civic imagery, emphasizing its exemplary status and invoking ideas of ancient architecture. The presence in the late Middle Ages of an anchorite at the Tower also underlines its devotional connotations. Dover, too, was a spiritual castle housing an anchorite, but also participates in the imperial imagery shared by the Tower and other castles. Colchester, then, is by no means the only castle with links to multiple ideological themes and resonances. The linguistic evidence presented at the beginning of this book suggests that all three themes – of community, spirituality and empire – are implicit in the most basic medieval understanding of the castle.

There is therefore plenty of scope for future research into the idea of the castle in medieval England. It would certainly be worth investigating the themes I have identified in relation to contexts that deploy less explicit imagery. The castles that have been the main focus of this discussion were all important royal establishments and consequently attracted extravagant building programmes. They also generated relatively extensive local mythography and a certain amount of visual and textual representation. It is this network of references in different media that has made it possible for me to analyse these sites through an interdisciplinary approach to the idea of the castle. However, lesser castles may well have supported very similar iconographies on a smaller scale, represented in less obvious ways in their design and medieval reception. Visual and textual descriptions, too, may employ these themes through less obvious imagery, implied in verbal or visual echoes and nuances rather than stated unambiguously in the sources.

A possible source for other manifestations of castle imagery might be sought in the castles associated with the Arthurian legends, for example. The spiritual implications of these romances are clear, especially in the various grail legends[1] in which castles in Britain and the Holy Land play an

---

[1] See for example K. Pratt, 'The Cistercians and the *Queste del Saint Graal*', *Reading Medieval Studies* 21 (1995), 69–96; L. N. de Loose, 'A Story of Interpretations: The *Queste del Saint Graal* as Metaliterature', in *The Grail: A Casebook*, ed. D. B. Mahoney (New York, 2000), pp. 237–59.

important part.[2] The historical connotations of the castle are also played out in Arthurian legends, which are dated to a distant period shortly after the time of Christ, when the pagan Roman empire was still a force to be contended with in British circles.[3] Specific medieval castles are back-dated to the Arthurian period just as they are to other early periods of British history. The castles of Carlisle, Winchester, Guildford, Tintagel, Arundel, Dover and the Tower of London, to mention only a few, feature in various Arthurian legends.[4] Arthurian castles also carry interesting implications for urban defences – for example, in the conception of Camelot, which is both a city and a castle. Such connotations are, I suggest, to be expected, and once identified these could perhaps be traced further to those actual medieval castles implicated in these legends.

There are thus many ways in which the methodology and findings of this study could be applied to further research. I have obviously been subject to certain restrictions of time, space and resources, which have confined my own researches to a small range of examples. However, this book presents evidence for a whole new range of ideological elements in the medieval understanding of the castle. If this evidence is accepted, many aspects of the modern critical approach to medieval castles will need to be re-assessed and modified. Not least, the modern definition of the medieval castle will need to be broadened, to bring modern investigations into line with the practical and ideological conceptions of the castle which were current in the medieval world.

[2] *The Grail Castle and its Mysteries*, ed. L. Olschki and E. Vinaver and transl. J. A. Scott (Manchester, 1966); M. Whitaker, 'Castles, Courts and Courtesy', in her *Arthur's Kingdom of Adventure: The World of Malory's Morte Darthur* (Cambridge, 1984), pp. 31–51 (33–4).

[3] See for example L. Johnson, 'King Arthur at the Crossroads to Rome', in *Noble and Joyous Histories: English Romances 1375–1650*, ed. E. ni Cuilleanáin and J. D. Pheifer (Dublin, 1993), pp. 87–111; F. Riddy, 'Contextualizing the *Morte Darthur*: Empire and Civil War', in *A Companion to Malory*, ed. E. Archibald and A. S. G. Edwards. Arthurian Studies 37 (1996), pp. 55–73.

[4] See, for example, Thomas Malory, *The Works of Sir Thomas Malory*, ed. E. Vinaver, 2nd edn, 3 vols. (Oxford, 1967), II, 1164; II, 1065; I, 9; II, 635; III, 1250; III, 1164. I have explored some of the Arthurian legends featuring Carlisle Castle in 'King Arthur lives in merry Carleile', *Carlisle and Cumbria: Roman and Medieval Architecture, Art and Archaeology*, British Archaeological Asssociation Conference Transactions 27, forthcoming.

BIBLIOGRAPHY

Primary sources

Ailred of Rievaulx. *'Sermo XVII: In Assumptione beatae Mariae'*. *Patrologiae Latinae Cursus Completus*. Ed. J. P. Migne. Paris, 1844–64. 195, cols. 303–4.

Ancrene Wisse: Guide for Anchoresses. Transl. H. White. London, 1993.

The Anglo-Saxon Chronicle. Ed. and transl. M. J. Swanton. London, 1996.

The Anglo-Saxon Chronicle: A Collaborative Edition 6. MS D: A Semi-diplomatic Edition. Ed. G. P. Cubbin. Cambridge, 1996.

Anselm of Canterbury. *'Homilia IX'*. *Patrologiae Latinae Cursus Completus*. Ed. J. P. Migne. Paris, 1844–64. 158, cols. 644–9.

Benoit de Sainte-Maure. *Le Roman de Troie par Benoit de Sainte-Maure*. 6 vols. Ed. L. Constans. Paris, 1904, repr. 1968.

Biblia Sacra Vulgatae Editionis. 1959.

Breuddwyd Maxen. Ed. I. Williams. Bangor, 1908.

Caxton, William. *Caxton's* Eneydos, *1490, Englished from the French* Livre des Eneydes, *1483*. Ed. W. T. Cutley and F. J. Furnivall. Early English Text Society, extra series 57. 1890, repr. 1962.

Chaucer, Geoffrey. *The Riverside Chaucer*. Ed. L. D. Benson. 3rd edn. Oxford, 1987, repr. 1992.

'Concordia Facta inter Regem Ricardum II et Civitatem Londonie'. Ed. and transl. C. Smith. Unpublished Ph.D. dissertation. Princeton University, 1972.

Cursor Mundi. Ed. R. Morris. Early English Text Society, original series 57, 59, 62, 66. 1874–7, repr. 1961.

Daniel, Walter. *Walter Daniel's Life of Aelred, Abbot of Rievaulx*. Ed. F. M. Powicke. London, 1950.

The Earliest English Translation of Vegetius' De re militari. Ed. G. Lester. Heidelberg, 1988.

Elyot, Thomas. *The Castel of Helthe, Corrected and Translated by the First Author Thereof*. London, 1541.

Eneas: A Twelfth-Century Romance. Transl. J. A. Yunck. New York, 1974.

The English Text of Ancrene Riwle: Ancrene Wisse. Ed. J. R. R. Tolkien. Early English Text Society, original series 249. 1962.

FitzStephen, William. *'Descriptio nobilissimae civitatis Londoniae'*. *Materials for the History of Thomas Becket, Archbishop of Canterbury*. Ed. J. C. Robertson. Rolls Series 67. 6 vols. 1877, repr. 1965. III, 2–8.

Geoffrey of Monmouth. *The* Historia regum Britannie *of Geoffrey of Monmouth, 1. Bern, Burgerbibliothek, MS. 568*. Ed. N. Wright. 1985, repr. 1996.

Geoffrey of Monmouth. *The* Historia regum Britannie *of Geoffrey of Monmouth, 2. The First Variant Version: A Critical Edition*. Ed. N. Wright. 1988.

Gervase of Tilbury. *Otia Imperialia: Recreation for an Emperor*. Ed. S. E. Banks and J. W. Binns. Oxford Medieval Texts Series. Oxford, 2002.

The 'Gest Hystoriale' of the Destruction of Troy: An Alliterative Romance translated from Guido de Colonna's 'Hystoria Troiana'. Ed. G. A. Panton. Early English Text Society, original series 39, 56. 1869 and 1874, repr. 1969.

Gower, John. *The Complete Works of John Gower.* Ed. G. C. Macaulay. 4 vols. Oxford, 1902.

Gower, John. *The Major Latin Works of John Gower.* Transl. E. W. Stockton. Seattle, 1962.

Gratarolus, Guilielmus. *The Castell of Memorie: wherein is contayned the restoring, augmenting, and conserving of the Memorye and Remembraunce, with the safest remedies, and best preceptes thereunto in any wise apperteyning.* Transl. Willyam Fulwod. London, 1562.

Grosseteste, Robert. *Le Château d'Amour de Robert Grosseteste, Eveque de Lincoln.* Ed. J. Murray. Paris, 1918.

Henry of Huntingdon. *Henrici Archidiaconi Huntendunensis: Historia Anglorum.* Ed. T. Arnold. Rolls Series 74. 1879.

The Holy Bible Translated from the Latin Vulgate: The Old Testament first published by the English College at Douay and the New Testament first published by the English College at Rheims. London, 1899.

Joseph of Exeter. *The Iliad of Dares Phrygius.* Transl. G. Roberts. Capetown, 1970.

Joseph of Exeter. *Joseph Iscanus: Werke und Briefe.* Ed. L. Gompf. Leiden, 1970.

Laȝamon. *Brut or Hystoria Brutonum.* Ed. W. R. J. Barron and S. C. Weinberg. Harlow, 1995.

The Mabinogion. Ed. and transl. G. Jones and T. Jones. London, 1949, repr. 1950.

Malory, Thomas. *The Works of Sir Thomas Malory.* Ed. E. Vinaver. 2nd edn. 3 vols. Oxford, 1967.

Materials for the History of Thomas Becket, Archbishop of Canterbury. Ed. J. C. Robertson. Rolls Series 67. 6 vols. 1877, repr. 1965.

Matthew of Westminster. *Flores Historiarum.* Ed. H. R. Luard. Rolls Series 95. 3 vols. 1890, repr. 1965.

Medieval English Lyrics: A Critical Anthology. Ed. R. T. Davies. London, 1966, repr. 1971.

The Middle English Translations of Robert Grosseteste's Château d'Amour. Ed. K. Sajavaara. Mémoires de la Société Néophilologique de Helsinki 32. 1967.

A Middle English Version of the Gesta Romanorum edited from Gloucester Cathedral MS 22. Ed. K. I. Sandred. Uppsala, 1971.

The Middle Portion of the Life of Christ. Ed. C. Horstmann. Münster, 1873.

Nennius. *British History and Welsh Annals.* Ed. and transl. J. Morris. London, 1980.

Nevill, William. *The Castell of Pleasure by William Nevill: The Text of the First Issue with Variant Readings from the Reprint of 1518.* Ed. R. D. Cornelius. Early English Text Society, original series 179. 1930, repr. 1971.

Old English Homilies and Homiletic Treatises of the Twelfth and Thirteenth Centuries. Ed. R. Morris. Early English Text Society, original series 34. 1867–73.

Orderic Vitalis. *The Ecclesiastical History of Orderic Vitalis.* Ed. M. Chibnall. 6 vols. Oxford, 1990.

Paris, Matthew. *Matthaeu Parisiensis, Monachi Sancti Albani, Chronica Majora.* Ed. H. R. Luard. Rolls Series 57. 7 vols. 1872–83.

Patrologiae Latinae Cursus Completus. Ed. J. P. Migne. 221 vols. Paris, 1844–64.

The Poems of the Pearl Manuscript: Pearl, Cleanness, Patience, Sir Gawain and the Green Knight. Ed. M. Andrew and R. Waldron. Exeter, 1987, repr. 1994.

'Rescriptio regis Edwardi, ad dominum Bonefacium papam transmissa'. *The Chronicle of Pierre de Langtoft*. Ed. T. Wright. Rolls Series 47. 2 vols. 1869, repr. 1964. II, 404–5.

Sawles Warde: An Early English Homily Edited from the Bodley, Royal and Cotton MSS. Ed. R. M. Wilson. Leeds School of English Language Texts and Monographs 3. 1938.

The Seege or Batayle of Troye. Ed. M. E. Barnicle. Early English Text Society, original series 172. 1927, repr. 1971.

The Southern Passion. Ed. B. D. Brown. Early English Text Society, original series 169. 1927.

Trevet, Nicolas. 'The Anglo-Norman Chronicle of Nicolas Trivet'. Ed. A. Rutherford. Unpublished Ph.D. dissertation. University of London, 1932.

Vegetius. *Flavi Vegeti Renati Epitoma Rei Militaris*. Ed. C. Lang. Leipzig, 1885.

Villehardouin, Geoffroy de. *Villehardouin: La Conquête de Constantinople*. Ed. E. Faral. Les Classiques de l'Histoire de France au Moyen Age 18–19. 2nd edn. 1961.

Virgil. 'Aeneid'. *Eclogues, Georgics, Aeneid I–VI*. Ed. and transl. H. R. Fairclough, revised G. P. Goold. Loeb Classical Library 63. 1999.

Voragine, Jacobus de. *The Golden Legend, Readings on the Saints*. Ed. and transl. W. G. Ryan. 2 vols. Princeton, 1993. repr. 1995.

Wace. *Wace's Roman de Brut: A History of the British*. Ed. and transl. J. Weiss. Exeter, 1999.

Walsingham, Thomas. *Historia Anglicana*. Ed. H. T. Riley. Rolls Series 28. 2 vols. 1863.

William of Malmesbury. *William of Malmesbury: Historia Novella, The Contemporary History*. Ed. E. King and transl. K. R. Potter. Oxford, 1998.

William of Poitiers. *Gesta Guillelmi: The Deeds of William*. Ed. and transl. R. C. H. Davis and M. Chibnall. Oxford, 1998.

(?) William of Shoreham. 'A Song to Mary'. *Medieval English Lyrics: A Critical Anthology*. Ed. R. T. Davies. London, 1966, repr. 1971. Pp. 103–5.

Woolton, Thomas. *The Castell of Christians and Fortresse of the Faithfull, beseged and defended now almost six thousand yeares*. London, 1577.

Wyclif, John. *Select English Works of John Wyclif*. Ed. T. Arnold. 3 vols. Oxford, 1869.

Wyclif, John. 'Sermon LXIV'. *Select English Works of John Wyclif*. Ed. Arnold. I, 197–201.

Wynnere and Wastoure and The Parlement of the Thre Ages. Ed. W. Ginsberg. Kalamazoo, 1992.

Yates, James, Servingman. *The Castell of Courtesie, whereunto is adoiyned The Hold of Humilitie, with the Chariot of Chastitie thereunto annexed*. London, 1582.

Secondary sources

Ackerman, R. W. ' "Pared out of Paper": *Gawain* 802 and *Purity* 1408'. *Journal of English and Germanic Philology* 56 (1957), pp. 410–17.

Aird, W. M. 'An Absent Friend: The Career of Bishop William of St Calais'. *Anglo-Norman Durham 1093–1193*. Ed. D. Rollason, M. Harvey and M. Prestwich. Woodbridge, 1994. Pp. 283–97.

Alexander, J., and Binski, P., ed. *Age of Chivalry: Art in Plantagenet England, 1200–1400*. London, 1987.

Amos, A. C., di Paulo Healey, A., Holland, J., McDougall, D., McDougall, I., Porter, N., and Thompson, P., ed. *Dictionary of Old English*. Toronto, 1988– .

Archibald, E. and Edwards, A. S. G., ed. *A Companion to Malory*. Arthurian Studies 37 (1996).

Armitage, E. S. *The Early Norman Castles of the British Isles*. London, 1912.

Astley, H. J. D. 'Mediaeval Colchester – Town, Castle and Abbey – from MSS. in the British Museum'. *Transactions of the Essex Archaeological Association* 8 (1903), pp. 117–35.

Attreed, L. 'The Politics of Welcome: Ceremonies and Constitutional Development in Later Medieval English Towns'. *City and Spectacle in Medieval Europe*. Ed. B. A. Hanawalt and K. L. Reyerson. Minneapolis, 1994. Pp. 208–31.

Ayton, A., and Price, J. E., ed. *The Medieval Military Revolution*. London, 1995.

Bachrach, B. S. 'The Cost of Castle Building: The Case of the Tower at Langeais, 992–994'. *The Medieval Castle: Romance and Reality*. Ed. K. Reyerson and F. Powe. Dubuque, 1984. Pp. 47–62.

Baker, D. 'Aelred of Rievaulx and Walter Espec'. *Haskins Society Journal* 1 (1989), pp. 91–8.

Barber, M., ed. *The Military Orders: Fighting for the Faith and Caring for the Sick*. Aldershot, 1994.

Barlow, F. *The Feudal Kingdom of England, 1042–1216*. London, 1974.

Bedos-Rezak, B. 'Towns and Seals: Representation and Signification in Medieval France'. *Bulletin of the John Rylands Library* 72.3 (1990), pp. 35–48.

Benson, C. D. *The History of Troy in Middle English Literature: Guido delle Colonne's 'Historia Destructionis Troiae' in Medieval England*. Woodbridge, 1980.

Beresford, M. *New Towns of the Middle Ages: Town Plantation in England, Wales and Gascony*. London, 1967.

Binski, P. 'The Cosmati at Westminster and the English Court Style'. *Art Bulletin* 72 (1990), pp. 6–34.

Binksi, P. *Westminster Abbey and the Plantagenets: Kingship and the Representation of Power, 1200–1400*. New Haven, 1995.

Binns, J. W., and Banks, S. E. *Gervase of Tilbury and the Encyclopaedic Tradition: Information Retrieval from the Middle Ages to Today*. Leicester, 1999.

Birch, W. de G. *Catalogue of Seals in the Department of Manuscripts in the British Museum*. 6 vols. London, 1892.

Blagg, T. F. C. 'The Re-use of Monumental Masonry in Late Roman Defensive Walls'. *Roman Urban Defences in the West*. Ed. J. Maloney and B. Hobley. Council for British Archaeology Research Report 51. 1983. Pp. 130–5.

Blair, J. 'Purbeck Marble'. *English Medieval Industries: Craftsmen, Techniques, Products*. Ed. J. Blair and N. Ramsay. London and Rio Grande, 1991. Pp. 41–56.

Blair, J., and Pyrah, C., ed. *Church Archaeology: Directions for the Future*. Council for British Archaeology Research Report 104. 1996.

Blair, J., and Ramsay, N., ed. *English Medieval Industries: Craftsmen, Techniques, Products*. London, 1991.

Bloom, J. H. *English Seals*. London, 1906.

Boas, A. J. *Crusader Archaeology: The Material Culture of the Latin East*. London, 1999.

Boffey, J., and King, P., ed. *London and Europe in the Later Middle Ages.* London, 1995.

Bonde, S. 'Castle and Church Building at the Time of the Norman Conquest'. *The Medieval Castle: Romance and Reality.* Ed. K. Reyerson and F. Powe. Dubuque, 1984. Pp. 79–96.

Bonde, S. *Fortress Churches of Languedoc: Architecture, Religion and Conflict in the High Middle Ages.* Cambridge, 1994.

Boon, G. C. *Segontium Roman Fort, Caernarvonshire.* London, 1963.

Brenk, B. 'Spolia from Constantine to Charlemagne: Aesthetics versus Ideology'. *Studies in Art and Archaeology in Honor of Ernst Kitzinger.* Ed. W. Tronzo and I. Lavin. Dumbarton Oaks Papers 41. 1987. Pp. 103–9.

Brewer, D. S., and Gibson, J., ed. *A Companion to the Gawain-poet.* Cambridge, 1997.

Brimacombe, P. *A Tale of Two Cathedrals: Old Sarum, New Salisbury.* London, 1997.

Bromwich, R., Jarman, A. O. H., and Roberts, B. F., ed. *The Arthur of the Welsh: The Arthurian Legend in Medieval Welsh Literature.* Cardiff, 1991.

Brooke, C. N. L., with Keir, G. *London 800–1216: The Shaping of a City.* London, 1975.

Brown, P. 'The Prison of Theseus and the Castle of Jalousie'. *The Chaucer Review* 26 (1991), pp. 147–72.

Brown, R. A. *English Medieval Castles.* London, 1954.

Brown, R. A. 'An Historian's Approach to the Origins of the Castle in England'. *The Archaeological Journal* 126 (1969), pp. 131–48.

Brown, R. A. *Dover Castle, Kent.* London, 1985, repr. 1995.

Brown, R. A. 'The White Tower of London'. *The Middle Ages.* Ed. B. Ford. The Cambridge Guide to the Arts in Britain 2. 1988. Pp. 254–63.

Brown, R. A., Prestwich, M., and Coulson, C. *Castles: A History and Guide.* Poole, 1980.

Burrow, J. A., and Turville-Petre, T. *A Book of Middle English.* Oxford, 1992.

Butler, R. M. 'The Roman Walls of Le Mans'. *The Journal of Roman Studies* 48 (1958), pp. 33–9.

Caine, C. 'Our Cities: Sketched 500 Years Ago'. *Journal of the British Archaeological Association* 4 (1898), pp. 319–21.

Calkins, R. G. *Medieval Architecture in Western Europe from A.D. 300 to 1500.* New York, 1998.

Callus, D. A., ed. *Robert Grosseteste, Scholar and Bishop: Essays in Commemoration of the Seventh Centenary of his Death.* Oxford, 1955, repr. 1969.

Camille, M. *The Medieval Art of Love: Objects and Subjects of Desire.* London, 1998.

Camille, M. *Mirror in Parchment: The Luttrell Psalter and the Making of Medieval England.* London, 1998.

Cantor, L. *The English Medieval Landscape.* London, 1982.

Carruthers, M. J. *The Book of Memory: A Study of Memory in Medieval Culture.* Cambridge, 1990.

Carruthers, M. *The Craft of Thought: Meditation, Rhetoric, and the Making of Images, 400–1200.* Cambridge Studies in Medieval Literature 34. 1998.

Charlton, J. *Brough Castle.* London, 1986, repr. 1992.

Cherry, J. 'Imago Castelli: The Depiction of Castles on Medieval Seals'. *Château Gaillard* 15 (1990), pp. 83–90.

Chibnall, M. *The World of Orderic Vitalis.* Oxford, 1984.

Chibnall, M. 'Orderic Vitalis on Castles'. *Studies in Medieval History Presented to R. Allen Brown*. Ed. C. Harper-Bill, C. J. Holdsworth and J. Nelson. Woodbridge, 1989. Pp. 43–56.

Chorpenning, J. 'The Literary and Theological Method of the *Castillo Interior*'. *Journal of Hispanic Philology* 3 (1979), pp. 121–33.

Chorpenning, J. 'The Monastery, Paradise, and the Castle: Literary Images and Spiritual Development in St Teresa of Ávila'. *Bulletin of Hispanic Studies* 62 (1985), pp. 245–57.

Clark, G. T. *Mediaeval Military Architecture in England*. London, 1884.

Clark, J. 'Trinovantum – the Evolution of a Legend'. *Journal of Medieval History* 7 (1981), pp. 135–51.

Clark, P., and Slack, P., ed. *Crisis and Order in English Towns, 1500–1700*. London, 1972.

Clay, R. M. *The Hermits and Anchorites of England*. London, 1914.

Cocke, T., and Kidson, P. *Salisbury Cathedral: Perspectives on the Architectural History*. London, 1993.

Coldstream, N. 'The Kingdom of Heaven: Its Architectural Setting'. *Age of Chivalry: Art in Plantagenet England, 1200–1400*. Ed. J. Alexander and P. Binski. London, 1987. Pp. 92–7.

Coldstream, N. *Medieval Architecture*. Oxford, 2002.

Colvin, H. M., Taylor, A. J., and Brown, R. A., ed. *A History of the King's Works*. 6 vols. London, 1963.

Conant, K. J. *Carolingian and Romanesque Architecture 800 to 1200*. Harmondsworth, 1959, repr. 1978.

Coppack, G. *Helmsley Castle*. London, 1997. 2nd edn.

Cornelius, R. D. *The Figurative Castle: A Study in the Mediaeval Allegory of the Edifice with Especial Reference to Religious Writings: A Dissertation*. Bryn Mawr, 1930.

Coulson, C. 'Structural Symbolism in Medieval Castle Architecture'. *Journal of the British Archaeological Association* 132 (1979), pp. 73–90.

Coulson, C. 'Hierarchism in Conventual Crenellation'. *Medieval Archaeology* 26 (1982), pp. 69–100.

Coulson, C. 'Bodiam Castle: Truth and Tradition'. *Fortress* 10 (August 1991), pp. 13–15.

Coulson, C. 'Some Analysis of the Castle of Bodiam, East Sussex', *Medieval Knighthood* 4 (1992), pp. 51–107.

Coulson, C. 'Battlements and Bourgeoisie: Municipal Status and the Apparatus of Urban Defence'. *Medieval Knighthood* 5 (1995), pp. 119–75.

Coulson, C. 'The State of Research: Cultural Realities and Reappraisals in English Castle-Study'. *Journal of Medieval History* 22 (1996), pp. 171–208.

Coulson, C. *Castles in Medieval Society: Fortresses in England, France, and Ireland in the Central Middle Ages*. Oxford, 2003.

Crick, J. C. *The* Historia regum Britannie *of Geoffrey of Monmouth 4. Dissemination and Reception in the Later Middle Ages*. 1991.

Crouch, D. *The Image of Aristocracy in Britain, 1000–1300*. London, 1992.

Cunliffe, B. *Excavations at Portchester Castle*. Society of Antiquaries of London Research Committee Report 34. 1977.

Curtius, E. R., transl. Trask, W. R. *European Literature and the Latin Middle Ages*. New York, 1953.

Davison, B. K. 'The Origins of the Castle in England: The Institute's Research Project'. *The Archaeological Journal* 124 (1967), pp. 202–11.

de Lage, G. R. 'Les "Romans Antiques" dans l'Histoire Ancienne jusqu' à César'. *Le Moyen Age* 63 (1957), pp. 267–309.

de Lage, G. R. 'Les Romans Antiques et la representation de l'Antiquité'. *Moyen Age* 67 (1961), pp. 247–91.

de Loose, L. N. 'A Story of Interpretations: The *Queste del Saint Graal* as Metaliterature'. *The Grail: A Casebook*. Ed. D. B. Mahoney. New York, 2000. Pp. 237–59.

Dean, M. A. 'Early Fortified Houses: Defenses and Castle Imagery between 1275 and 1350 with Evidence from the Southeast Midlands'. *The Medieval Castle: Romance and Reality*. Ed. K. Reyerson and F. Powe. Dubuque, 1984. Pp. 147–74.

Detsicas, A., ed. *Collectanea Historica: Essays in Memory of Stuart Rigold*. Maidstone, 1981.

Dixon, P. 'The Donjon of Knaresborough: The Castle as Theatre'. *Château Gaillard* 14 (1988), pp. 121–40.

Dixon, P., and Lott, B. 'The Courtyard and the Tower: Contexts and Symbols in the Development of the Late Medieval Great House'. *Journal of the British Archaeological Association* 146 (1993), pp. 93–101.

Dixon, P., and Marshall, P. 'The Great Keep at Hedingham Castle: A Reassessment'. *Fortress* 18 (August 1993), pp. 16–23.

Dixon, P., and Marshall, P. 'The Great Tower in the Twelfth Century: The Case of Norham Castle'. *The Archaeological Journal* 150 (1993), pp. 410–32.

Drage, C. 'Urban Castles'. *Urban Archaeology in Britain*. Ed. J. Schofield and R. Leech. Council for British Archaeology Research Report 61 (1987), pp. 117–32.

Draper, P. 'The Architectural Setting of Gothic Art'. *Age of Chivalry: Art and Society in Late Medieval England*. Ed. N. Saul. Brockhampton, 1995. Pp. 60–75.

Drury, P. J. 'Aspects of the Origins and Development of Colchester Castle'. *The Archaeological Journal* 139 (1983), pp. 302–419.

Duggan, A. J., ed. *Kings and Kingship in Medieval Europe*. London, 1993.

Dumville, D. N. 'Sub-Roman Britain: History and Legend'. *History* 62 (1977), pp. 173–92.

Dumville, D. N. 'The Historical Value of the *Historia Britonnum*'. *Arthurian Literature* 6 (1986), pp. 1–26.

Dutton, M. L. 'The Conversion and Vocation of Aelred of Rievaulx: A Historical Hypothesis'. *England in the Twelfth Century*. Ed. D. Williams. Proceedings of the 1988 Harlaxton Symposium. 1990. Pp. 31–49.

Eales, R. 'Royal Power and Castles in Norman England'. *The Ideals and Practice of Medieval Knighthood* 3 (1990), pp. 49–78.

Eaton, T. *Plundering the Past: Roman Stonework in Medieval Britain*. Stroud, 2000.

Edson, E. *Mapping Time and Space: How Medieval Mapmakers Viewed their World*. London, 1997.

English, B. 'Towns, Mottes and Ringworks of the Conquest'. *The Medieval Military Revolution*. Ed. A. Ayton and J. E. Price. London, 1995. pp. 45–61.

Everson, P. 'Bodiam Castle, East Sussex: Castle and its Designed Landscape'. *Château Gaillard* 17 (1994), pp. 79–84.

Everson, P. Appendix 1. *Lincoln Castle*. Ed. P. Lindley. Society for Lincolnshire History and Archaeology Occasional Monographs 11. Forthcoming.

Fairclough, G. 'Meaningful Constructions: Spatial and Functional Analysis of Medieval Buildings'. *Antiquity* 66 (1992), pp. 348–66.

Faulkner, P. A. 'Domestic Planning from the Twelfth to the Fourteenth Century'. *The Archaeological Journal* 115 (1958), pp. 150–84.

Faulkner, P. A. 'Castle Planning in the Fourteenth Century'. *The Archaeological Journal* 120 (1963), pp. 215–35.

Federico, S. 'A Fourteenth-century Erotics of Politics: London as a Feminine New Troy'. *Studies in the Age of Chaucer* 19 (1997), pp. 121–55.

Fellows, J. 'Sir Bevis of Hamtoun in Popular Tradition'. *Proceedings of the Hampshire Archaeological and Natural History Society* 42 (1986), pp. 139–45.

Fergusson, P., and Harrison, S. *Rievaulx Abbey: Community, Architecture, Memory.* New Haven, 1999.

Fernie, E. 'The Ground Plan of Norwich Cathedral and the Square Root of Two'. *Journal of the British Archaeological Association* 129 (1976), pp. 77–86.

Fernie, E. 'Anglo-Saxon Lengths: The Northern System, the Perch and the Foot'. *The Archaeological Journal* 142 (1985), pp. 246 54.

Fernie, E. 'Contrasts in Methodology and Interpretation of Medieval Ecclesiastical Architecture'. *The Archaeological Journal* 145 (1988), pp. 344–64.

Fernie, E. 'Archaeology and Iconography: Recent Developments in the Study of English Medieval Architecture'. *Architectural History* 32 (1989), pp. 18–29.

Field, P. J. C. 'Nennius and his History'. *Studia Celtica* 30 (1996), pp. 159–65.

Flint, V. J. 'The *Historia regum Britanniae* of Geoffrey of Monmouth: Parody and its Purpose. A Suggestion'. *Speculum* 54 (1979), pp. 447–68.

Folz, R., transl. Ogilvie, S. A. *The Concept of Empire in Western Europe from the Fifth to the Fourteenth Century.* London, 1969.

Ford, B., ed. *The Middle Ages.* The Cambridge Guide to the Arts in Britain 2. 1988.

Foster, R. *Patterns of Thought: The Hidden Meaning of the Great Pavement of Westminster Abbey.* London, 1991.

Frankl, P. *The Gothic: Literary Sources and Interpretations through Eight Centuries.* Princeton, 1960.

Frugoni, C. *A Distant City: Images of Urban Experience in the Medieval World.* Princeton, 1991.

Fulton, H. 'The Feminised Town in Medieval Chivalric Literature'. Forthcoming.

Fulton, H. *Representations of Urban Culture in Medieval Literature.* Forthcoming.

Fulton, H. 'The Medieval Town as Allegory'. *Representations of Urban Culture in Medieval Literature.* Forthcoming.

Gaines, B. 'Malory's Castles in Text and Illustration'. *The Medieval Castle: Romance and Reality.* Ed. K. Reyerson and F. Powe. Dubuque, 1984. Pp. 215–28.

Gem, R. 'Towards an Iconography of Anglo-Saxon Architecture'. *Journal of the Warburg and Courtauld Institutes* 46 (1983), pp. 1–18.

Gem, R. 'Lincoln Minster: Ecclesia Pulchra, Ecclesia Fortis'. *Medieval Art and Architecture at Lincoln Cathedral.* Ed. T. A. Heslop and V. A. Sekules. British Archaeological Association Conference Transactions 8. 1986. Pp. 9–28.

Gilchrist, R. *Gender and Material Culture: The Archaeology of Religious Women.* London, 1994.

Gilchrist, R. 'Medieval Bodies in the Material World: Gender, Stigma and the Body'. *Framing Medieval Bodies.* Ed. S. Kay and M. Rubin. Manchester, 1994. Pp. 43–61.

Gilchrist, R. 'Norwich Cathedral: A Biography of the North Transept'. *Journal of the British Archaeological Association* 151 (1998), pp. 107–36.

Gilchrist, R. 'The Contested Garden: Gender, Space and Metaphor in the Medieval English Castle'. *Gender and Archaeology: Contesting the Past.* London, 1999. Pp. 109–45.

Gilchrist, R. *Gender and Archaeology: Contesting the Past.* London, 1999.

Gillingham, J. 'The Context and Purposes of Geoffrey of Monmouth's *History of the Kings of Britain'. Anglo-Norman Studies* 13 (1990), pp. 99–118.

Glanville, P. *London in Maps.* London, 1972.

Glare, P. G. W., ed. *Oxford Latin Dictionary.* Oxford, 1982.

Goodall, J. 'The Key of England'. *Country Life* (18 March 1999), pp. 45–7.

Goodall, J. 'In the Power House of Kent'. *Country Life* (25 March 1999), pp. 110–13.

Gransden, A. *Historical Writing in England c.550 to c.1307.* London, 1974.

Green, J. A. *The Aristocracy of Norman England.* Cambridge, 1997.

Greenhalgh, M. *The Survival of Roman Antiquities in the Middle Ages.* London, 1989.

Grenville, J. 'The Rows of Chester: Some Thoughts on the Results of Recent Research'. *World Archaeology* 21 (1990), pp. 446–60.

Grossinger, C. 'Misericords'. *Age of Chivalry: Art in Plantagenet England, 1200–1400.* Ed. J. Alexander and P. Binski. London, 1987. Pp. 122–4.

Hallam, E. M. 'Monasteries as"War Memorials": Battle Abbey and La Victoire'. *The Church and War.* Ed. W. J. Shiels. Studies in Church History 20. 1983. Pp. 47–57.

Hallissy, M. 'Writing a Building: Chaucer's Knowledge of the Construction Industry and the Language of the *Knight's Tale'. Chaucer Review* 32 (1997–8), pp. 239–59.

Hammer, W. 'The Concept of the New or Second Rome in the Middle Ages'. *Speculum* 19 (1944), pp. 50–62.

Hanawalt, B. A., and Reyerson, K. L., ed. *City and Spectacle in Medieval Europe.* Minneapolis, 1994.

Hardy, T. *Descriptive Catalogue of Materials Relating to the History of Great Britain and Ireland.* Roll Series 26. 3 vols. 1865, repr. 1964.

Harper-Bill, C., Holdsworth, C. J., and Nelson, J., ed. *Studies in Medieval History Presented to R. Allen Brown.* Woodbridge, 1989.

Hartung, A. E., ed. *A Manual of the Writings in Middle English 1050–1500.* 10 vols. New Haven, 1967–98.

Harvey, P. D. A. *Mappa Mundi: The Hereford World Map.* London, 1996.

Harvey, P. D. A., and McGuinness, A. *A Guide to British Medieval Seals.* London, 1996.

Hebron, M. *The Medieval Siege: Theme and Image in Middle English Romance.* Oxford, 1997.

Heslop, T. A. 'Orford Castle, Nostalgia and Sophisticated Living'. *Architectural History* 34 (1991), pp. 36–58.

Heslop, T. A. *Norwich Castle Keep: Romanesque Architecture and Social Context.* Norwich, 1994.

Heslop, T. A., and Sekules, V. A., ed. *Medieval Art and Architecture at Lincoln Cathedral.* British Archaeological Association Conference Transactions 8. 1986.

Higgitt, J. C. 'The Roman Background to Mediaeval England'. *Journal of the British Archaeological Association* 36 (1973), pp. 1–15.

Hindle, B. P. *Medieval Town Plans.* Princes Risborough, 1990.

Hull, M. R. *Roman Colchester.* Society of Antiquaries of London Research Committee Report 20. 1958.

Hunt, E. D. 'Constantine and the Holy Land (ii) Helena – History and Legend'. *Holy Land and Pilgrimage in the Later Roman Empire, AD 312–460*. Oxford, 1982. Pp. 28–49.

Hunt, E. D. *Holy Land and Pilgrimage in the Later Roman Empire, AD 312–460*. Oxford, 1982.

Hunt, R. W. 'The Library of Robert Grosseteste'. *Robert Grosseteste, Scholar and Bishop: Essays in Commemoration of the Seventh Centenary of his Death*. Ed. D. A. Callus. Oxford, 1955, repr. 1969. Pp. 121–45.

Hyde, J. K. 'Mediaeval Descriptions of Cities'. *Bulletin of the John Rylands Library* 48 (1965–6), pp. 308–40.

Impey, E. 'The Western Entrance to the Tower of London, 1240–1241'. *Transactions of the Middlesex Archaeological Society* 48 (1998), pp. 58–75.

Impey, E., ed. *The White Tower*. Forthcoming.

Jeffers, R. L., and Lehiste, I. *Principles and Methods for Historical Linguistics*. Cambridge, MA, 1982, repr. 1989.

Jeffreys, E. M. 'The Comnenian Background to the *Romans d'Antiquité*'. *Byzantion* 50 (1980), pp. 455–86.

Johnson, L. 'King Arthur at the Crossroads to Rome'. *Noble and Joyous Histories: English Romances 1375–1650*. Ed. E. ni Cuilleanáin and J. D. Pheifer. Dublin, 1993. Pp. 87–111.

Jones, C., ed. *Historical Linguistics: Problems and Perspectives*. London, 1993.

Kantorowicz, E. H. 'The "King's Advent" and the enigmatic panels in the doors of Santa Sabina'. *Art Bulletin* 26 (1944), pp. 207–31.

Kantorowicz, E. H. *Laudes Regiae: A Study in Liturgical Acclamations and Medieval Ruler Worship*. Berkeley, 1958.

Kastovsky, D. 'Semantics and Vocabulary'. *The Beginnings to 1066*. Ed. R. M. Hogg. The Cambridge History of the English Language 1. 1992. Pp. 290–408.

Kay, S., and Rubin, M., ed. *Framing Medieval Bodies*. Manchester, 1994.

Kennedy, H. *Crusader Castles*. Cambridge, 1994.

Kenyon, J. R. *Castles, Town Defences, and Artillery Fortifications in Britain: A Bibliography*. 3 vols. London, 1978–90.

Kenyon, J. R. *Medieval Fortifications*. London, 1990.

Kidson, P. 'Architectural History'. *A History of Lincoln Minster*. Ed. D. Owen. Cambridge, 1994. Pp. 14–46.

Kidson, P., Fernie, E. C., and Crossley, P., ed. *Medieval Architecture and its Intellectual Context: Essays in Honour of Peter Kidson*. London, 1990.

Kidson, P., Murray, P., and Thompson, P. R., ed. *A History of English Architecture*. Harmondsworth, 1965.

King, D. J. C. *Castellarium Anglicanum: An Index and Bibliography of the Castles in England, Wales and the Islands*. 2 vols. New York, 1983.

King, D. J. C., and Alcock, L. 'Ringworks of England and Wales'. *Château Gaillard* 3 (1969), pp. 90–127.

Knight, J. *Chepstow Castle and Port Wall*. Revised edn. Cardiff, 1991.

Koechlin, R. *Les ivoires gothiques français*. 3 vols. Paris, 1924.

Kratzmann, G., and Simpson, J., ed. *Medieval English Religious and Ethical Literature: Essays in Honour of G. H. Russell*. Cambridge, 1986.

Krautheimer, R. 'Introduction to an Iconography of Medieval Architecture'. *Studies in Early Christian, Medieval and Renaissance Art* (1969), pp. 115–50.

Krautheimer, R. *Three Christian Capitals: Topography and Politics*. Berkeley, 1983.

Kurtz, B. E. ' "The Small Castle of the Soul": Mysticism and Metaphor in the European Middle Ages'. *Studia Mystica* 15.4 (1992), pp. 19–39.

La Corte, D. 'The Abbatial Concerns of Aelred of Rievaulx Based on his Sermons of Mary'. *Cistercian Studies Quarterly* 30 (1995), pp. 267–73.

Lass, R. *Historical Linguistics and Language Change*. Cambridge, 1997.

Latham, R. E., and Howlett, D. R., ed. *Dictionary of Medieval Latin from British Sources*. Oxford, 1975– .

Lavedan, P. *Représentation des villes dans l'art du Moyen Âge*. Paris, 1954.

Leach, R. *An Investigation into the Use of Purbeck Marble in Medieval England*. 2nd edn. Hartlepool, 1975.

Legge, M. D. *Anglo-Norman Literature and its Background*. Oxford, 1963.

Lewis, C. T., and Short, C., ed. *A Latin Dictionary*. Oxford, 1958.

Lewis, S. *The Art of Matthew Paris in the* Chronica majora. Aldershot, 1987.

Lewis, S. *Reading Images: Narrative Discourse and Reception in the Thirteenth-century Illuminated Apocalypse*. Cambridge, 1995.

Lilley, K. D. *Urban Life in the Middle Ages, 1000–1450*. Houndmills, 2002.

Lindenbaum, S. 'Ceremony and Oligarchy: The London Midsummer Watch'. *City and Spectacle in Medieval Europe*. Ed. B. A. Hanawalt and K. L. Reyerson. Minneapolis, 1994. Pp. 171–88.

Lindley, P., ed. *Lincoln Castle*. Society for Lincolnshire History and Archaeology Occasional Monographs 11. Forthcoming.

Lloyd-Kimbrel, D. 'Architectonic Allusions: Gothic Perspectives and Perimeters as an Approach to Chaucer'. *Mediaevistik* 1 (1988), pp. 115–24.

Longhurst, M. H. *Victoria and Albert Museum Department of Architecture and Sculpture Catalogue of Carvings in Ivory*. 2 vols. London, 1929.

Loomis, R. S. 'The Allegorical Siege in the Art of the Middle Ages'. *American Journal of Archaeology* 23.3 (1919), pp. 255–69.

Loomis, R. S. 'From Segontium to Sinadon – The Legends of a *Cité Gaste*'. *Speculum* 22 (1947), pp. 520–33.

Loomis, R. S. 'Edward I, Arthurian Enthusiast'. *Speculum* 28 (1953), pp. 114–27.

Mahoney, D. B., ed. *The Grail: A Casebook*. New York, 2000.

Maloney, J., and Hobley, B., ed. *Roman Urban Defences in the West*. Council for British Archaeology Research Report 51. 1983.

Mann, J. 'Allegorical Buildings in Mediaeval Literature'. *Medium Aevum* 63 (1994), pp. 191–210.

Marsden, P. 'Baynard's Castle'. *London Archaeologist* 1.14 (1972), pp. 315–16.

Matthews, J. F. 'Macsen, Maximus, and Constantine'. *Welsh History Review* 11 (1982–3), pp. 431–48.

McAleer, J. P. 'Rochester Cathedral: The North Choir Aisle and the Space between it and "Gundulf's Tower" '. *Archaeologia Cantiana* 112 (1993), pp. 127–65.

McAleer, J. P. 'The So-called Gundulf's Tower at Rochester Cathedral: A Reconsideration of its History, Date and Function'. *The Antiquaries Journal* 78 (1998), pp. 111–76.

McKenzie, A. D. 'French Medieval Castles in Gothic Manuscript Painting'. *The Medieval Castle: Romance and Reality*. Ed. K. Reyerson and F. Powe. Dubuque, 1984. Pp. 199–214.

McMahon, A. M. S. *Understanding Language Change*. Cambridge, 1994.

McNeill, T. *English Heritage Book of Castles*. London, 1992.

McNulty, J. 'The Endowment of the Chapel of St. Michael in Clitheroe Castle'. *Transactions of the Historical Society of Lancashire and Cheshire* 91 (1939), pp. 159–63.

McNulty, J. 'Clitheroe Castle and its Chapel: Their Origins'. *Transactions of the Historical Society of Lancashire and Cheshire* 93 (1942), pp. 45–53.

McWhirr, A., ed. *Roman Brick and Tile: Studies in Manufacture, Distribution and Use in the Western Empire*. British Archaeological Reports International Series 68. 1979.

Millar, E. G. *The Luttrell Psalter: Additional Manuscript 42130 in the British Museum*. London, 1932.

Milroy, J. 'On the Social Origins of Language Change'. *Historical Linguistics: Problems and Perspectives*. Ed. C. Jones. London, 1993. Pp. 215–36.

Milne, G. *English Heritage Book of Roman London: Urban Archaeology in the Nation's Capital*. London, 1995.

Morley, B. 'Aspects of Fourteenth-century Castle Design'. *Collectanea Historica: Essays in Memory of Stuart Rigold*. Ed. A. Detsicas. Maidstone, 1981. Pp. 104–13.

Morris, R. K. 'The Architecture of the Earls of Warwick in the Fourteenth Century'. *England in the Fourteenth Century*. Ed. W. M. Ormrod. Proceedings of the 1985 Harlaxton Symposium. 1986. Pp. 161–74.

Morris, R. K. 'The Architecture of Arthurian Enthusiasm: Castle Symbolism in the Reigns of Edward I and his Successors'. *Armies, Chivalry and Warfare in Medieval Britain*. Ed. M. Strickland. Proceedings of the 1995 Harlaxton Symposium. 1998. Pp. 63–81.

Morris, R. *Churches in the Landscape*. London, 1989.

Nathanson, J. *Gothic Ivories of the Thirteenth and Fourteenth Centuries*. London, 1951.

Nearing, H. 'Caesar's Sword'. *Modern Language Notes* 63 (1948), pp. 403–5.

Nearing, H. 'Julius Caesar and the Tower of London'. *Modern Language Notes* 63 (1948), pp. 228–33.

Nearing, H. 'The Legend of Julius Caesar's Britsh Conquest'. *Publications of the Modern Languages Association* 64 (1949), pp. 889–929.

Nearing, H. 'Local Caesar Traditions in Britain'. *Speculum* 24 (1949), pp. 218–27.

ni Cuilleanáin, E., and Pheifer, J. D., ed. *Noble and Joyous Histories: English Romances 1375–1650*. Dublin, 1993.

Nolan, B. *The Gothic Visionary Perspective*. Princeton, 1977.

Norton, E. C., and Park, D., ed. *Cistercian Art and Architecture in the British Isles*. Cambridge, 1986.

Olschki, L., and Vinaver, E., eds., and Scott, J. A., transl. *The Grail Castle and its Mysteries*. Manchester, 1966.

O'Neil, B. St J. *Castles: An Introduction to the Castles of England and Wales*. London, 1954.

Ormrod, W. M., ed. *England in the Fourteenth Century*. Proceedings of the 1985 Harlaxton Symposium. 1986.

Ormrod, W. M. 'In Bed with Joan of Kent: The King's Mother and the Peasants' Revolt'. *Medieval Women: Texts and Contexts in Late Medieval Britain: Essays for Felicity Riddy*. Ed. J. Wogan-Browne, R. Voaden, A. Diamond, A. Hutchinson, C. M. Meale and L. Johnson. Turnhout, 2000. Pp. 277–92.

Owen, D., ed. *A History of Lincoln Minster*. Cambridge, 1994.

Owen, D. M. *Church and Society in Medieval Lincolnshire*. Lincoln, 1971.

Owst, G. R. *Literature and the Pulpit in Medieval England*. 2nd edn. Oxford, 1961.

Pagden, A. *Lords of All the World: Ideologies of Empire in Spain, Britain and France c.1500–1800*. New Haven, 1995.

Palliser, D. M. 'The Birth of York's Civic Liberties, c.1200–1354'. *The Government of Medieval York: Essays in Commemoration of the 1396 Royal Charter*. Ed. S. Rees Jones. York, 1997. Pp. 88–107.

Parnell, G. *English Heritage Book of the Tower of London*. London, 1993.

Parsons, D., ed. *Stone: Quarrying and Building in England, AD 43–1525*. Chichester, 1990.

Pedrick, G. *Borough Seals of the Gothic Period*. London, 1904.

Perring, D. *Roman London*. London, 1991.

Phythian-Adams, C. 'Ceremony and the Citizen: The Communal Year at Coventry, 1450–1550'. *Crisis and Order in English Towns, 1500–1700*. Ed. P. Clark and P. Slack. London, 1972. Pp. 57–85.

Platt, C. *The Castle in Medieval England and Wales*. London, 1982.

Port, G. *Scarborough Castle*. London, 1989, repr. 1998.

Pounds, N. J .G. *The Medieval Castle in England and Wales: A Social and Political History*. Cambridge, 1990, repr. 1994.

Pratt, K. 'The Cistercians and the *Queste del Saint Graal*'. *Reading Medieval Studies* 21 (1995), pp. 69–96.

Prestwich, M. *Edward I*. London, 1988.

Price, J. ' "Inner" and "Outer": Conceptualising the Body in *Ancrene Wisse* and Aelred's *De Institutione Inclusarum*'. *Medieval English Religious and Ethical Literature: Essays in Honour of G. H. Russell*. Ed. G. Kratzmann and J. Simpson. Cambridge, 1986. Pp. 192–208.

Pringle, D. 'Templar Castles on the Road to Jerusalem'. *The Military Orders: Fighting for the Faith and Caring for the Sick*. Ed. M. Barber. Aldershot, 1994. Pp. 148–66.

Rees Jones, S., ed. *The Government of Medieval York: Essays in Commemoration of the 1396 Royal Charter*. York, 1997.

Renn, D. F. 'The Decoration of Guildford Castle Keep'. *Surrey Archaeological Collections* 55 (1958), pp. 4–6.

Renn, D. F. *Norman Castles in Britain*. London, 1973.

Renn, D. F. 'Burhgeat and Gonfanon: Two Sidelights from the Bayeux Tapestry'. *Anglo-Norman Studies* 16 (1994), pp. 177–98.

Reyerson, K., and Powe, F., ed. *The Medieval Castle: Romance and Reality*. Dubuque, 1984.

Reynolds, S. 'The Rulers of London in the Twelfth Century'. *History* 57 (1972), pp. 337–57.

Reynolds, S. *An Introduction to the History of Medieval Towns*. Oxford, 1977.

Reynolds, S. 'Medieval *Origines Gentium* and the Community of the Realm'. *History* 68 (1983), pp. 375–90.

Reynolds, S. *Fiefs and Vassals: The Medieval Evidence Reinterpreted*. Oxford, 1994.

Reynolds, S. *Kingdoms and Communities in Western Europe, 900–1300*. 2nd edn. Oxford, 1997.

Rickman, T. *An Attempt to Discriminate the Styles of Architecture in England from the Conquest to the Reformation*. London, 1819.

Riddy, F. 'Contextualizing the *Morte Darthur*: Empire and Civil War'. *A Companion to Malory*. Ed. E. Archibald and A. S. G. Edwards. Arthurian Studies 37 (1996), pp. 55–73.

Riley-Smith, J. *The First Crusade and the Idea of Crusading*. Cambridge, 1986.

Riley-Smith, J. *The Crusades: A Short History*. London, 1987, repr. 1992.

Riley-Smith, J. *The Atlas of the Crusades*. London, 1990.

Riley-Smith, J. *The First Crusaders, 1095–1131*. Cambridge, 1997.

Ringbom, S. 'Devotional Images and Imaginative Devotions: Notes on the Place of Art in Late Medieval Private Piety'. *Gazette des Beaux Arts* 73 (1969), pp. 159–70.

Roberts, B. F. 'Geoffrey of Monmouth, *Historia regum Britanniae* and *Brut y Brehinedd*'. *The Arthur of the Welsh: The Arthurian Legend in Medieval Welsh Literature*. Ed. R. Bromwich, A. O. H. Jarman and B. F. Roberts. Cardiff, 1991. Pp. 97–116.

Rodwell, W. *The Archaeology of the English Church: The Study of Historic Churches and Churchyards*. London, 1981.

Rodwell, W. *English Heritage Book of Church Archaeology*. London, 1989.

Rodwell, W. 'Church Archaeology in Retrospect and Prospect'. *Church Archaeology: Directions for the Future*. Ed. J. Blair and C. Pyrah. Council for British Archaeology Research Report 104. 1996. Pp. 197–202.

Rollason, D., Harvey, M., and Prestwich, M., ed. *Anglo-Norman Durham 1093–1193*. Woodbridge, 1994.

Ross, C. *The Custom of the Castle from Malory to Macbeth*. Berkeley, 1997.

Rosser, G. 'Myth, Image and Social Process in the English Medieval Town'. *Urban History* 23.1 (1996), pp. 5–25.

Round, J. H. *Geoffrey de Mandeville: A Study of the Anarchy*. London, 1892.

Round, J. H. 'Tower and Castle'. *Geoffrey de Mandeville: A Study of the Anarchy*. Pp. 328–46.

Sabine, C. J. 'Numismatic Iconography of the Tower of David and the Holy Sepulchre: An Emergency Coinage Struck during the Siege of Jerusalem, 1187'. *Numismatic Chronicle* 19.7 (1979), pp. 122–32.

Salzman, L. F. *Building in England to 1540: A Documentary History*. Oxford, 1952.

Saul, N., ed. *Age of Chivalry: Art and Society in Late Medieval England*. Brockhampton, 1995.

Scattergood, J. 'Misrepresenting the City: Genre, Intertextuality and William FitzStephen's *Description of London* (c.1173)'. *London and Europe in the Later Middle Ages*. Ed. J. Boffey and P. King. London, 1995. Pp. 1–34

Schneider, A. M., transl. Austin, R. G. 'The City-Walls of Istanbul'. *Antiquity* 11 (1937), pp. 461–8.

Schofield, J., and Leech, R., ed. *Urban Archaeology in Britain*. Council for British Archaeology Research Report 610. 1987.

Schofield, J., and Vince, A. *Medieval Towns*. London, 1994.

Sheeran, G. *Medieval Yorkshire Towns: People, Buildings, Spaces*. Edinburgh, 1998.

Shichtman, M. B., and Finke, L. A. 'Profiting from the Past: History as Symbolic Capital in the *Historia regum Britannie*'. *Arthurian Literature* 12 (1993), pp. 1–35.

Shiels, W. J. *The Church and War*. Studies in Church History 20 (1983).

Simpson, J. 'The Other Book of Troy: Guido delle Colonne's *Historia destructionis Troiae* in Fourteenth-Century England'. *Speculum* 73 (1998), pp. 397–423.

Smith, E. B. *Architectural Symbolism of Imperial Rome and the Middle Ages*. Princeton, 1956.

Southern, R. W. *Robert Grosseteste: The Growth of an English Mind in Medieval Europe.* 2nd edn. Oxford, 1992.

Stocker, D. 'Rubbish Recycled: A Study of the Re-use of Stone in Lincolnshire'. *Stone: Quarrying and Building in England, AD 43–1525.* Ed. D. Parsons. Chichester, 1990. Pp. 83–101.

Stocker, D. 'The Shadow of the General's Armchair'. *The Archaeological Journal* 149 (1992), pp. 415–20.

Stocker, D. 'The Two Early Castles of Lincoln'. *Lincoln Castle.* Ed. P. Lindley. Society for Lincolnshire History and Archaeology Occasional Monographs 11. Forthcoming.

Stocker, D., and Vince, A. 'The Early Norman Castle at Lincoln and a Re-evaluation of the Original West Tower of Lincoln Cathedral'. *Medieval Archaeology* 41 (1997), pp. 223–33.

Strang, B. M. H. *A History of Old English.* London, 1970, repr. 1974.

Strickland, M., ed. *Armies, Chivalry and Warfare in Medieval Britain.* Proceedings of the 1995 Harlaxton Symposium. 1998.

Svensson, A.-M. *Middle English Words for 'Town': A Study of Changes in a Semantic Field.* Göteborg, 1997.

Tatlock, J. S. P. *The Legendary History of Britain: Geoffrey of Monmouth's* Historia regum Britannie *and its Early Vernacular Versions.* Berkeley, 1950.

Tatton-Brown, T. W. 'Building Stone in Canterbury c.1070–1525'. *Stone: Quarrying and Building in England, AD 43–1525.* Ed. D. Parsons. Chichester, 1990. Pp. 70–82.

Tatton-Brown, T. W. 'Medieval Building Stone at the Tower of London'. *London Archaeologist* 6.13 (1991), pp. 361–6.

Tatton-Brown, T. W. ' "Gundulf's" Tower'. *Friends of Rochester Cathedral: Report for 1990/1.* Rochester, 1992. Pp. 7–12.

Taylor, A. J. 'Caernarvon'. *A History of the King's Works.* Ed. H. M. Colvin, A. J. Taylor and R. A. Brown. London, 1963. Vol. 1, pp. 369–95.

Taylor, A. J. *Studies in Castles and Castle-Building.* London, 1985.

Taylor, A. J. *The Welsh Castles of Edward I.* London, 1986.

Taylor, C., Everson, P., and Wilson-North, W. R. 'Bodiam Castle, Sussex'. *Medieval Archaeology* 5 (1961), pp. 169–75.

Thomas, R. J., ed. *Geiriadur Prifysgol Cymru: A Dictionary of the Welsh Language.* Cardiff, 1950–67.

Thompson, A. H. *Military Architecture in England during the Middle Ages.* London, 1912.

Thompson, M. W. 'Associated Monasteries and Castles in the Middle Ages: A Tentative List'. *The Archaeological Journal* 143 (1986), pp. 305–21.

Thompson, M. W. *The Decline of the Castle.* Cambridge, 1987.

Thompson, M. W. *The Rise of the Castle.* Cambridge, 1991.

Thompson, M. 'Castles'. *A Companion to the Gawain-poet.* Ed. D. S. Brewer and J. Gibson. Cambridge, 1997. pp. 119–30.

Thurley, S., Impey, E., and Hammond, P. *The Tower of London.* London, 1996.

Tittler R. *Architecture and Power: The Town Hall and the English Urban Community c.1500–1640.* Oxford, 1991.

Todd, M. *The Walls of Rome.* London, 1978.

Tronzo, W., and Lavin, I., ed. *Studies in Art and Archaeology in Honor of Ernst Kitzinger*. Dumbarton Oaks Papers 41. 1987.

Turner, D. J. 'Bodiam Castle, Sussex: True Castle or Old Soldier's Dream House?' *England in the Fourteenth Century*. Ed. W. M. Ormrod. Proceedings of the 1985 Harlaxton Symposium. 1986. Pp. 267–77.

Turville-Petre, T. 'The Author of the *Destruction of Troy'*. *Medium Aevum* 57 (1988), pp. 264–69.

van Emden, W. 'The Castle in Some Works of Medieval French Literature'. *The Medieval Castle: Romance and Reality*. Ed. K. Reyerson and F. Powe. Dubuque, 1984. Pp. 1–26.

Verbruggen, J. F. 'Note sur le sens des mots castrum, castellum, et quelques autres expressions qui désignent des fortifications' *Revue belge de philologie et d'histoire* 28.1 (1950), pp. 147–55.

Warner, G. F., and Gilson, J. P. *Catalogue of the Western MSS in the Old Royal and King's Collections in the British Museum*. 4 vols. London, 1921.

Waswo, R. 'Our Ancestors, the Trojans: Inventing Cultural Identity in the Middle Ages'. *Exemplaria* 7.2 (1995), pp. 269–90.

Webster, G. 'Tiles as a Structural Component in Buildings'. *Roman Brick and Tile: Studies in Manufacture, Distribution and Use in the Western Empire*. Ed. A. McWhirr. British Archaeological Reports International Series 68. 1979. Pp. 285–93.

Wheatley, A. 'King Arthur lives in merry Carleile'. *Carlisle and Cumbria: Roman and Medieval Architecture, Art and Archaeology*. British Archaeological Association Conference Transactions 27. Forthcoming.

Wheatley, A. 'The Tower of London in Myth and Legend'. *The White Tower*. Ed. E. Impey. Forthcoming.

Whitaker, M. A. 'Otherworld Castles in Middle English Arthurian Romance'. *The Medieval Castle: Romance and Reality*. Ed. K. Reyerson and F. Powe. Dubuque, 1984. Pp. 27–46.

Whitaker, M. 'Castles, Courts and Courtesy'. *Arthur's Kingdom of Adventure: The World of Malory's Morte Darthur*. Cambridge, 1984. Pp. 31–51.

Whittick, C. 'Dallingridge's Bay and Bodiam Castle's Millpond – Elements of a Medieval Landscape'. *Sussex Archaeological Collections* 131 (1993), pp. 119–23.

Wickham, G. *Early English Stages 1300–1660*. 3 vols. London, 1980.

Wickham, G. *A History of the Theatre*. Oxford, 1985.

Williams, A. 'A Bell-house and a Burh-geat: Lordly Residences in England before the Norman Conquest'. *Medieval Knighthood* 4 (1992), pp. 221–40.

Williams, D., ed. *England in the Twelfth Century*. Proceedings of the 1988 Harlaxton Symposium. 1990.

Williams, G. A. *Medieval London: From Commune to Capital*. London, 1963.

Wilson, C. *The Gothic Cathedral: The Architecture of the Great Church, 1130–1530*. London, 1990.

Wogan-Browne, J. 'Chaste Bodies: Frames and Experiences'. *Framing Medieval Bodies*. Ed. S. Kay and M. Rubin. Manchester, 1994. Pp. 24–42.

Wogan-Browne, J., Voaden, R., Diamond, A., Hutchinson, A., Meale, C. M., and Johnson, L., ed. *Medieval Women: Texts and Contexts in Late Medieval Britain: Essays for Felicity Riddy*. Turnhout, 2000.

Worssam, B., and Tatton-Brown, T. 'Kentish Rag and Other Kent Building Stones'. *Archaeologia Cantiana* 112 (1993), pp. 93–125.

Yates, F. A. *The Art of Memory*. London, 1966.

Zotz, T. 'Carolingian Tradition and Ottonian-Salanian Innovation: Comparative Observations on Palatine Policy in the Empire'. *Kings and Kingship in Medieval Europe*. Ed. A.J. Duggan. London, 1993. Pp. 69–100.

INDEX

YORK MEDIEVAL PRESS: PUBLICATIONS

God's Words, Women's Voices: The Discernment of Spirits in the Writing of Late-Medieval Women Visionaries, Rosalyn Voaden (1999)

Pilgrimage Explored, ed. J. Stopford (1999)

Piety, Fraternity and Power: Religious Gilds in Late Medieval Yorkshire 1389–1547, David J. F. Crouch (2000)

Courts and Regions in Medieval Europe, ed. Sarah Rees Jones, Richard Marks and A. J. Minnis (2000)

Treasure in the Medieval West, ed. Elizabeth M. Tyler (2000)

Nunneries, Learning and Spirituality in Late Medieval English Society: The Dominican Priory of Dartford, Paul Lee (2000)

Prophecy and Public Affairs in Later Medieval England, Lesley A. Coote (2000)

The Problem of Labour in Fourteenth-Century England, ed. James Bothwell, P. J. P. Goldberg and W. M. Ormrod (2000)

New Directions in later Medieval Manuscript Studies: Essays from the 1998 Harvard Conference, ed. Derek Pearsall (2000)

Cistercians, Heresy and Crusadse in Occitania, 1145–1229: Preaching in the Lord's Vineyard, Beverly Mayne Kienzle (2001)

Guilds and the Parish Community in Late Medieval East Anglia, c. 1470–1550, Ken Farnhill (2001)

The Age of Edward III, ed. J. S. Bothwell (2001)

Time in the Medieval World, ed. Chris Humphrey and W. M. Ormrod (2001)

The Cross Goes North: Processes of Conversion in Northern Europe, AD 300–1300, ed. Martin Carver (2002)

Henry IV: The Establishment of the Regime, 1399–1406, ed. Gwilym Dodd and Douglas Biggs (2003)

Youth in the Middle Ages, ed. P. J. P Goldberg and Felicity Riddy (2004)

Rites of Passage: Cultures of Transition in the Fourteenth Century, ed. Nicola F. McDonald and W. M. Ormrod (2004)

York Studies in Medieval Theology

I   *Medieval Theology and the Natural Body*, ed. Peter Biller and A. J. Minnis (1997)

II   *Handling Sin: Confession in the Middle Ages*, ed. Peter Biller and A. J. Minnis (1998)

III   *Religion and Medicine in the Middle Ages*, ed. Peter Biller and Joseph Ziegler (2001)

IV *Texts and the Repression of Medieval Heresy*, ed. Caterina Bruschi and Peter Biller (2002)

York Manuscripts Conference

Manuscripts and Readers in Fifteenth-Century England: The Literary Implications of Manuscript Study, ed. Derek Pearsall (1983) [Proceedings of the 1981 York Manuscripts Conference]

Manuscripts and Texts: Editorial Problems in Later Middle English Literature, ed. Derek Pearsall (1987) [Proceedings of the 1985 York Manuscripts Conference]

Latin and Vernacular: Studies in Late-Medieval Texts and Manuscripts, ed. A. J. Minnis (1989) [Proceedings of the 1987 York Manuscripts Conference]

Regionalism in Late-Medieval Manuscripts and Texts: Essays celebrating the publication of 'A Linguistic Atlas of Late Mediaeval English', ed. Felicity Riddy (1991) [Proceedings of the 1989 York Manuscripts Conference]

Late-Medieval Religious Texts and their Transmission: Essays in Honour of A. I. Doyle, ed. A. J. Minnis (1994) [Proceedings of the 1991 York Manuscripts Conference]

Prestige, Authority and Power in Late Medieval Manuscripts and Texts, ed. Felicity Riddy (2000) [Proceedings of the 1994 York Manuscripts Conference]

Middle English Poetry: Texts and Traditions. Essays in Honour of Derek Pearsall, ed. A. J. Minnis (2001) [Proceedings of the 1996 York Manuscripts Conference]